What readers are saying about
From Clinician to Confident CEO

"With this inspiring book, *From Clinician to Confident CEO*, Casey Truffo offers therapists needed strategies for creating a highly profitable therapy business. Using a combination of practical information, time-tested business models and joyful enthusiasm for the business of therapy, Casey shows readers how to become successful CEOs."

Lynn Grodzki, LCSW, MCC
Author of *Building Your Ideal Private Practice*, 2nd Edition

"How I wish I had had Casey Truffo's, *From Clinician to Confident CEO* earlier in my career. She unlocks all the mysteries about running a profitable therapy business stress-free. Filled with instruction, examples and step-by-step action plans, this book will likely be the one you go back to again and again through your career."

Bill O'Hanlon, author of *Do One Thing Different*

"Read it! Inhale it! Swallow it whole (or even in pieces)! In this book, Casey Truffo puts her knowledge of and appreciation for seeing a clinical practice as a "business" into a readable, practical and enlightening package that will shave years off of your learning curve! As a practitioner of both law (18 years) and mental health (43 years), this is best short cut to success I've ever seen! My one regret is that she didn't write this 43 years ago."

Steve Frankel, Ph.D., J.D

"Reading this book is like having an experienced and compassionate elder walk you down a wisdom path to success in private practice. And nobody does a better job than Casey Truffo of teaching therapists practical ways to make a living at our healing craft. She has put it all together here. A must read for anyone in private practice or contemplating starting one. Bravo, Casey!"

William Doherty, Ph.D., University of Minnesota, co-founder with Elizabeth Thomas of The Doherty Relationship Institute, author of *Take Back Your Marriage*.

"Truffo calls profit PRO-FIT - the measure of the financial fitness of your professional business. When I read those words, it made my heart sing. *From Clinician to Confident CEO* will do the same for you. You are about to discover the steps necessary to make your therapy business run easier and more profitably... you know, the exact thing that will make your heart sing."

Mike Michalowicz, Author of *Profit First*

"From Clinician to Confident CEO is the book that all therapists should read as early in their careers as possible. In this book, Casey Truffo shares the business building skills we absolutely need- but didn't learn in graduate school. If you want to build a sustainable and profitable therapy business, without burning out- read and apply this book right now. I wish I'd had this book when I first started my therapy business. It would have saved me a lot of confusion and frustration. I'm certain it will do the same for you."

Rachna Jain, PsyD, Author of *Internet Marketing for the Rest of Us: Your In Depth Guide to Profitable Popularity*

"Drawing on her vast experience as a clinician, business coach and most importantly business owner, Casey Truffo has written an outstanding book for clinicians. In *From Clinician to Confident CEO*, Casey takes the clinician on a precise journey through the crucial mindset, systems and financial policies that are essential for creating very successful practices. She points out hidden areas of growth, efficiency and profit that elude most clinicians. I highly recommend this book to any clinician who wants to take their practice not just to the next level, but beyond what they thought was even possible."

Joe Bavonese, PhD
Director, Uncommon Practices

"Casey gets the energetic heart of a therapist's practice. In her new book, she spells out exactly how to become your own visionary, giving you the precise formula for creating a practice that leapfrogs the traditional model and flourishes in the modern world. Run, don't walk, to grab your copy!"

Julie Steelman, author of *The Effortless Yes Selling System*

FROM
CLINICIAN
TO *Confident*
CEO

YOUR STEP-BY-STEP GUIDE TO
MORE EASE, MORE TIME OFF, AND MORE PROFIT

CASEY TRUFFO
MFT

FROM CLINICIAN TO CONFIDENT CEO:
Your Step-By-Step Guide to More Ease,
More Time Off, and More Profit

Published by:
Therapist Leadership Institute Press
A division of Be A Wealthy Therapist, LLC

Printed in the United States of America
ISBN: 978-0-9906688-1-7 Paperback Edition
978-0-9906688-2-4 Digital Edition

Library of Congress Control Number: 2015914253

Author Contact:
Casey Truffo
13217 Jamboree Road, Suite 111
Tustin, CA 92782
United States

(949) 309-2590
Casey@BeAWealthyTherapist.net
www.BeAWealthyTherapist.net

To my Dad, David Perriman, who taught me (long before the women's movement) that I could go as far as I wanted to go in business. Thank you for believing in me.

I love you, Dad.

CONTENTS

Introduction

Dear Clinician,

When I started Be A Wealthy Therapist, a practice-building training company in the early 2000s, private practitioners were incensed that I was advocating "being wealthy." There was a predominant (and yet unstated) cultural view that being a counselor meant one had to be poor and help the poor. The idea of wanting to have a financially successful business was thought of as shameful or greedy. My colleagues tried to talk me out of our company name: "Don't be so in their face, Casey."

I remember in an early practice-building workshop, one clinician stood up and said, "I do not choose poverty for my business or me. I am worth more than that." The others looked away from her as if embarrassed for her.

At that time, my primary teachings were:

1. Money is not bad and
2. Marketing is not bad

I spent the next decade teaching brave clinicians how to move out of their clinician role and into their marketing role and earn a decent income.

And what a decade it has been! I have had the honor and

privilege of watching private practitioners around the world grow their therapy businesses. They understand now that in order to have a financially sustainable business, they must attract new clients. They have learned simple marketing skills and consistently implement their plans. Many have full caseloads. Many more expanded their practices and added additional clinicians!

And that is leading to a new problem.

Many therapy business owners are tired and edging toward burnout. Many experts attribute this to "compassion fatigue." We spend hours upon hours in sessions with clients who are hurting. It can be heartbreaking work for even the most tough-skinned among us. But I think that is only part of why private practitioners can become burned out.

You see, it takes more than being a good clinician and good marketing person to run a successful small business. Most private practitioners haven't been taught the other skills necessary to run a business. This leads to difficulty managing everything from finances to operations to facilities and technology. In addition, since many clinicians don't even know they need to *do* those functions, they don't budget time for them. And the cycle of stress and overwork continues.

And what are we to do when our practices get full? How can we continue to increase our impact and income when we run out of available "butt in chair" hours? That adds a whole new series of financial and human resources decisions.

We must realize that we are actually the CEO of our therapy business. It is time to add some new CEO skills to your tool belt. As you learn and implement these new skills and roles, you will reduce your stress, increase your income, and have systems to help you know your numbers and make strategic business decisions. The best part is that your reward is not only a viable and sustainable business, but also less stress, more ease, more time, and more income.

I am writing this book in the hope that it will be the start of a new era for therapy business owners. My goal is for therapy business owners to understand all the roles in their business and have the skills and systems to manage their financially successful businesses with ease. I want you to wake up each day feeling confident… the confident CEO of your business.

I am also writing this book, as it is my story, too. It took me a long time to be willing to look at my therapy business finances and understand them. Seriously. One year not very long ago, I realized that after I paid all my expenses, my business netted me exactly $1,000 for the year. That meant I made about 50 cents an hour. No wonder I was exhausted and unhappy.

It also took me quite a while to do less people-pleasing in my business and start making sound decisions for the business. I had an overactive sense of responsibility and would make decisions that would hurt the business in the hopes that others would not be disappointed or inconvenienced. The impact of "worshiping responsibility at the altar" took a bit longer to conquer. Truth be told, I still occasionally slip.

I found my way out by studying sound business techniques and applying them to our unique business of therapy. And I was helped on my journey by some amazing guides and mentors. I am beyond grateful for their stewardship.

Over several months, I began implementing the business and finance skills I teach in this book in my own businesses – skills beyond marketing for new clients. As I did so, my profit rose 400% in just five months. I stood up for myself more in business situations. My confidence was higher than ever. Business was fun again! I loved working with my clients and had time for the other roles in my business, too!

I want that for you, too. Exhaustion and burnout are not okay.

Running a business at a loss is not okay. It is time to fill in the missing pieces to our business education.

In this book you will learn:

- Why having a financially sustainable practice takes more than good clinical skills and marketing

- How to develop, document, and implement policies, procedures, and systems (Running your business will be a no-brainer)

- Key metrics to track and review that show the progress of your business

- How to create your business budget and always have money saved for taxes and business expansion

- And how to think and make decisions like a CEO

My wish for you is that you always and continually love your business and love your life. You deserve to enjoy the amazing life that you make possible because you are sustained through your financially successful business. And my hope is that this book can help to fill in the missing pieces on your journey from Clinician to Confident CEO.

Love and blessings,

Casey

CHAPTER ONE

The Five Ingredients to a Happy, Healthy, and Wealthy Therapy Business

When did you decide you wanted to be in private practice? Was it because you woke up one day with what Michael Gerber calls the "entrepreneurial seizure" – where you woke up deciding that this was the last day you'd work for someone else?

Or was it more measured, where you gradually understood that you wanted to be your own boss? You wanted to be in charge of your own hours. You wanted to be able to choose your clients rather than have someone else choose them for you.

May I ask you a question?

How is it going?

When we started studying as students, we studied between 100 and 400 theories and techniques with the one single goal of helping people feel better. We went through thousands of hours of supervised practice (some would call it indentured servitude) prior to licensure. We studied for hours – alone and in groups for the licensing exam. Then one day the envelope came! We were now a licensed therapist!

Unfortunately, the excitement of those early days might be wearing off.

Maybe you're feeling confused, overwhelmed, burned out, or just plain disenchanted. If you are, you aren't alone. And it is not your fault.

You didn't learn about marketing in your graduate education program. You also didn't learn about managing your finances, customer service, quality assurance, facilities management, and technology.

Yet these are just a handful of the operations you perform daily... along with being a clinician.

The secret to being less overworked and feeling more in control is to understand the different functions of a business and to develop systems, policies, and procedures to make the day-to-day running of your business easier to manage and less time-consuming. When you have these in place, you can be the confident, relaxed CEO your business needs. I want you to end each day full of joy and excitement. I want you to feel energized as you confidently run your practice, know your numbers, and are prepared for the unexpected. You can do that when you know what to do and how to do it.

Before we get deep into the day-to-day operations that will make running your business easier, let's take a big picture view of what it takes to have a financially sustainable therapy business. This is true whether we are talking about a one-person, part-time office or whether we are talking about a center with dozens of clinicians.

The Five Ingredients to A
Happy, Healthy, Wealthy
Therapy Business

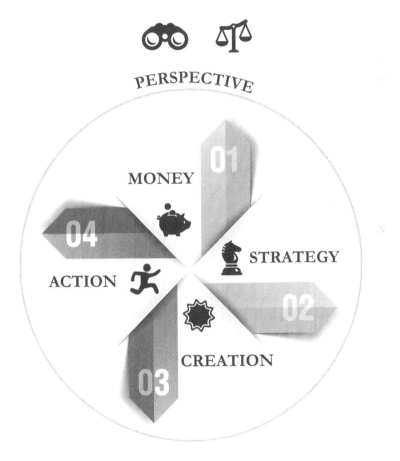

I have identified five ingredients to create a happy, healthy, and yes, wealthy therapy business. The first is what I call "Money

Wisdom." As a therapy business owner, it is critical that we manage our money. I like to say, "manage your money and you manage your destiny." Eighty percent of small businesses fail in the first five years and they do so because the owners do not understand their numbers. We want to have an awareness of our monthly income and expenses. We want to be able to project our cash flow for the rest of the year. We want to establish our business as a profitable business.

The second ingredient for a happy, healthy, and wealthy therapy business is your "Business Strategy." Why does your business exist? Yes, you want to pay for your personal expenses – your living expenses. Your business is here to support the lifestyle that you want. So go beyond the idea of just covering your expenses. Every day, you help people reach their dreams. But what about your dreams? I know you have dreams. Perhaps you want to take that trip to Tuscany. Or maybe for you it's about going to more yoga retreats. Imagine turning to your beloved and saying, "Honey, if you want to retire, I have us covered." This is the primary reason for your business. Then, ask the question, "Whom am I called to serve?" to further refine your business strategy. Perhaps you want to work with teens and their families to help them through the difficult teenage years. Or maybe you love working with women struggling to feel "good enough." For me, couples are the group we felt called to serve. Once you are clear on whom your business is called to serve, you can dive deep into their head and heart and learn the words that you can use to attract them into your office.

The third ingredient to a happy, healthy, and wealthy therapy business is creating a plan for growth. There are actually two types of growth plans for your business. The first one won't be a surprise to you. It is a client attraction growth plan. This is also called a marketing plan. You want to attract the ideal clients that you have identified in your business strategy. The second is your client service plan – what services will you offer in your therapy business? When you are first starting out, this will most likely be one-to-one sessions. After your practice is full, you may decide to service more people by adding additional clinicians to your business.

The fourth ingredient to our happy, healthy, and wealthy therapy business is a series of action steps. Traditionally, we think of action plans as related to implementing our marketing activities. But as you are going to discover, you can create action plans and systems for all operations in your therapy business. You can develop policies and procedures that will give you more ease and more feeling of control over your business and your time. It doesn't happen overnight, but if you take the time to create these systems, policies, and procedures for managing your business, I promise you one day you will wake up with an amazing feeling of comfort and confidence. How cool is that?

Our first four ingredients include money wisdom, business strategy, creation plans for growth, and action steps. These four ingredients are things that you do or create. Our fifth ingredient involves how we think about ourselves, our businesses, and our level of success. We call this fifth ingredient Perspective.

In the book *Systematic Training in the Skills of Virginia Satir*, author Sharon Loeschen quotes iconic family therapist Virginia Satir as saying, "People can't see their own backsides." How true is that? All of us grew up with a unique set of beliefs and ideas about success. What did you learn about money, wealth, and success? Were you raised by very successful entrepreneurial parents who believed in you? Do you believe in you? Some therapists have a twinge of doubt about whether they really deserve success.

And what about money? I believe most people have a "money set point." This is an amount that we feel we deserve and we feel we can earn. I've heard more than one therapist say, "Somewhere in my head, I have a belief or understanding that I cannot make more money than my parents." One client told me that she felt guilty if her business made a profit. Other therapists tell me they worry that people will think they are greedy if they want to "earn more than break-even" in their business.

I understand that family-of-origin beliefs are strong. Now is the time to bring them out into the open and test their validity. After all, this is your business; it is not your hobby. If you want to be one of the 20% of small businesses that succeed, you must make a profit. You must be okay with knowing your numbers and making money.

My recommendation is to watch for wherever you say, "I can't." Really? Has anybody else done it before? And if they did, why not you? Apply whatever techniques you use in your therapy with your clients to yourself to help reduce these limiting beliefs.

Most importantly, please don't judge yourself negatively for having limiting beliefs. They are simply a product of our human experience. Let's forgive ourselves and move on.

So how do we become the competent CEO our business needs? What do we need to learn? What do we need to do?

Let's start at the beginning.

In Summary:

The secret to being less overworked and feeling more in control is to understand the different functions of a business. Whether you run a one-person shop or a large practice, there are five key ingredients to a financially sustainable therapy business: Money Wisdom, a concrete Business Strategy, a Growth Plan, and an Action Plan to put your Business Strategy and Growth Plans into practice. The fifth ingredient, Perspective, is how you look at yourself, your belief system about success and money, and your ability to recognize and grow beyond any limiting beliefs.

Next Steps:

1. Keep reading…

CHAPTER TWO

The Five Roles of the Business Owner

One of my guilty pleasures is watching restaurant makeover shows on the Food Network channel. The story usually goes like this: a very nice man has worked as a chef in a local restaurant for many years. One day he wakes up and decides he wants to open his own restaurant. In the beginning, things are going fairly well, but pretty soon problems arise. Fewer customers are dining at the restaurant. The chef starts to raid his savings and even mortgages his home to meet the monthly bills.

At that point, Chef Robert Irvine visits the failing restaurant. He quickly helps the chef understand that as an owner, he has many roles in addition to his chef role. Robert Irvine helps the restaurant owner learn how to manage his operations, usually by identifying standards, policies, and procedures. The restaurant owner is also taught how to manage the finances for the restaurant. This includes budgeting, setting prices, paying bills, and managing his cash flow. Often they will discuss marketing and how to help get the word out about the restaurant. The chef turned restaurant owner is also encouraged to be the visionary in his business. This means looking ahead and seeing what the future for the business is.

At the end of the show, the remodeled restaurant is revealed and we see how well this restaurant is succeeding. The chef has grown from paying attention to only one role (cooking) to managing all the operations of the restaurant. The result is more money, less stress and effort required to run the day-to-day operations, and usually more time off for the owner.

Therapy business owners can learn a lot from this example. You have been trained to be a good clinician. The clinician role is actually what some call the technical role in your business – similar to the chef in a restaurant. As a clinician, you perform the "delivery of the service" function for the therapy business. And, as a good clinician, your goal is to deliver high-quality, effective psychotherapy and have good clinical outcomes. This is what helps your clients get better.

However, clinician is only one of the roles or functions in a therapy business. The other four functions include:

- Operations
- Finance
- Marketing
- Visionary

Let's take a look at all five roles and functions in more detail.

Clinical Role

Consider what you do in your role as clinician. The first time you see a new client, you welcome them into your practice. You get information about the presenting problem and the client's history. If you decide that you are a good match for this client, you explain your office policies and the rules of confidentiality. As you continue in treatment with this client, you engage with the client during regular therapy sessions, offering interventions and monitoring progress. At times, you might need to re-explain and enforce your office policies. You are always on the lookout for any risk factors, emergencies, and legal or noncompliance issues, and take appropriate action. You document the client's progress with progress notes. When needed, you reach out to connect with others involved with this client and his treatment. You manage the beginning, middle, and end phases of treatment. When the client ends treatment, you do appropriate closure with the client. As a clinician, you keep current on licensing requirements, including continuing education requirements.

This is a role you are very familiar with. Let's take a look at the other four roles in a therapy business. You may do these yourself or you may have help.

Business Operations Role

There are four areas that are covered by business operations.

Front Office: This involves the receptionist function as well as the client scheduling function. Someone must answer the phone and/or return voicemails. New client inquiries are assessed for appropriateness and clients are scheduled. New clients are given all of the information they need to find the office and attend the first session. Intake paperwork is set up for each new client.

Back Office: This involves billing clients and any third-party payers. In a cash practice, this means charging credit cards, endorsing checks, and managing actual cash. In insurance-based practices, it can involve insurance verifications for any new clients and billing for sessions. It may involve billing clients for copayments. Invoices or receipts may be sent to clients as part of this function as well. Back office support also can include tasks such as making bank deposits, and picking up and distributing mail.

<u>Facilities:</u> You want to present a clean and comfortable environment to your clients. Facilities management includes janitorial services. This means making sure that the trash is taken out on a regular basis, restrooms are cleaned and supplied, and floors vacuumed. If you offer snacks or beverages, you want to make sure that area is well-stocked and clean.

<u>Technology:</u> Therapists rely more and more on technology. Many of us have our calendars online, as well as having notes in practice management systems. We need to make sure that we have our data exported and backed up from all of these systems in the event that something bad, like a hard drive crash, happens.

Finance Role

In most therapy businesses, the finance role is the most avoided (or ignored) function. It involves collecting overdue accounts and paying the regular operating expenses. It also includes setting the fees and fee policies. One often-overlooked function is budgeting. Budgeting is important so that your therapy business has enough money to pay for your personal expenses and your business expenses.

The finance role also entails cash flow management so you have enough money in the bank for the upcoming bills. The finance function involves saving for taxes, insurance, and any other non-monthly expenses. You also want to make sure that you are saving money for profit, business development (marketing), business expansion, and emergencies. The finance role is responsible for making sure that you, as the clinician, are paid a wage for delivering the therapy services. Regular reviews of balance sheets and profit and loss statements can help the business owner know the exact financial state of the business.

Marketing Role

The business must attract clients for you, the clinician, to be able to provide therapy to them. The goal is to have your therapy business be "top of mind" to potential clients and excellent referral sources. The marketing role includes developing an online and community marketing plan. This is an ongoing function and does not end when your practice is full. At some point, your existing clients will graduate and you will need more clients. This is why we want to always be marketing in a focused and effective way.

Visionary Role

The therapy business owner is also a visionary looking ahead to where they would like the business to go. Is the plan to stay a solo practice? Is the vision to be a small boutique practice that is very high touch, such as a concierge practice? Perhaps you want to help more people in your community than you ever could by yourself and so you will end up adding clinicians to your practice. All the other roles and functions are in service to and will support the vision.

Visions change over time. You may have at one time wanted a part-time practice where you saw a handful of clients two days a week. Then something changed. Maybe your children grew up and you had more time on your hands. Maybe you realized how much you enjoyed being a business owner and making money. Maybe your phone kept ringing and you were tired of referring people out. Spending time on a regular basis with your vision can be a powerful, exciting, and rewarding experience.

Here is the good news: You are already doing most of this!

I shared this discussion of our roles in a recent presentation. One of the attendees said, "This all feels so overwhelming." But it is likely that you are already doing most of this. My goal, though, is to help you identify what you are doing, what you're not doing yet, and help you come up with ways to handle all of these functions in a way that is lighter and easier than you thought possible, and to do so with confidence. Your business deserves a confident CEO.

The Right Questions

Now is the time to take an honest business evaluation and look at which roles are strong and which ones are… well, missing. Just as with a new client, our first step to coming up with an effective treatment plan is to do an assessment. From there, we can identify our treatment goals and the steps and interventions necessary to reach those goals.

Many times when doing a business evaluation, therapy business owners focus on what is *not* working and try to solve it. But what if we looked at what *is* working and focused on how to make the rest of the business work as well? I first learned about this idea from *Breaking the Rules* by Kurt Wright. Kurt shares a process of appreciative inquiry, which can help us assess ourselves using simple questions.

You can easily do a business assessment by asking this set of questions:

- What is working?

- Why is it working?

- What would be ideal?

- What is not quite ideal yet?

- What actions do we need to take to make our situation ideal?

Before tackling our own therapy business assessment, let's take a quick look at our restaurant business owner example.

What is working? Clearly our chef/restaurant owner has a lot of passion for his work. He loves being the chef. After seeing the different roles and functions in his business, he has a new awareness. He cannot be a full-time chef and still take care of the other roles the business needs.

Why is it working? Above all, our chef remembers why he opened this restaurant. He is passionate about food and creating wonderful dining experiences for his patrons. He is willing to examine his personal and business shortcomings and take appropriate action. His enthusiasm is renewed because he sees there is a way out – even if he's not sure yet how he will get there. In other words, he is taking ownership of the problems and is willing to work toward a solution. This empowers him.

What would be ideal? There needs to be clarity on the roles, policies, and procedures. The front of the house (hostess and servers) needs to have systems for how to take reservations, greet patrons, serve people, when to hand out menus, take orders, when to go back and ask about the meal, etc. The back of the house (cooking, administration, finance) needs to have systems and procedures as well. Increasing their profit is the new goal – period! Having tracking metrics identifying how many customers come in, average daily sales, meal costs, etc. would help to set prices. A process to review the finances of the business each month would be valuable. With the knowledge gained from a monthly review, changes can be made quickly and appropriately.

What is not quite right yet? Clearly our restaurant owner is missing some important systems, policies, procedures, and role descriptions. It would appear that the finance function has been mostly avoided. It seems that no one has been looking at the big picture of the restaurant and how each piece helps the restaurant to succeed. In other words, the visionary role is missing.

What actions need to be taken to make the situation ideal? Defining a clear "customer journey" would be an excellent start. What happens when a customer calls for a reservation? How long does the customer have to wait prior to being seated? Developing policies and procedures for both the front and the back of the house could ensure that each customer coming in has a similar and wonderful experience. Returning customers also need to have a consistent experience. Developing a comprehensive daily accounting system with weekly or monthly reports is imperative if the business is to continue making money. Key financial metrics can be identified and tracked. As these metrics are regularly reviewed, the restaurant owner will have the information he needs to continue to improve upon the profitability of his business and add to the experience of his customers.

Above all, our restaurant owner needs to carve out time for the operations, finance, marketing, and visionary roles in his business. From each role, the appropriate systems and policies can be developed, documented, and monitored.

I share this example with you because sometimes it is easier to get the big picture by looking outside our own profession. Now we will begin to look at a therapy business. The service we provide will be different from the restaurateur, but the process to a financially stable and easy to manage business is the same.

As we move through this book, we will review the various roles and functions for you, the therapy business owner CEO. We will identify the missing pieces and suggest policies, systems, and action steps.

This is the first question to start with:

What experience do you want for your clients?

Your clients come to your office because they have a problem they want help with. Most likely it is an uncomfortable or painful situation that can't be ignored any longer. I'm sure you know how you want your clients to perceive you in your clinical role. I am sure you are quite welcoming and use helpful interventions that are congruent with your personality. You are also very consistent with your clients, which helps them feel understood and safe. You may not have thought about creating an experience for the client in your clinical role, but you do it each time you see the client.

Does your physical space or your customer service match the experience you want to create for your clients?

About 10 years ago, I met a therapist colleague at a conference. A week later, she invited me to lunch; we were to meet at her office. I arrived early. As I entered her waiting room, to the left of me I saw a broken printer with cords on top of it. To the right of me I saw a couple of dead plants. She had a therapy dog that tended to shed and it was clear that the space had not been dusted or vacuumed in some time. My allergies were triggered and I started sneezing repeatedly. She finished her session about 15 minutes late. After her client left, she showed me into her inner office, where she saw both

return client plus guilt with?

I can include my improve my clients experience – keeping office cleaner (mine), being on time !, taking credit cards, online paperwork, ? online books children and adults. There were sand tray toys in the middle of the floor. I almost tripped getting to her couch.

The truth? Everything in me wanted to leave. I did not want to be in her space. I made a conscious decision at that moment never to refer to this therapist. She may have been a fabulous therapist, but I did not feel good in her space. I did not feel respected.

Contrast that experience with a car service that I often use to get from my house to the airport. The drivers are always 10 minutes early and wait outside so as not to disturb me. The drivers are quite friendly and dressed in a sharp suit. The cars are clean and bottled water is always waiting for me. I have my choice of magazines. The driver will ask me what type of music I would like on the radio or if I would prefer it to be quiet. Even though this car service costs about double what a cab to the airport would cost, I use them whenever I can. I feel pampered and arrive at the airport refreshed. The bottom line is that I feel treated well and cared for. And that makes me want to use their service again and again.

What experience do you want for your clients?

Our current culture puts great value on experiences. When I opened up the Orange County Relationship Center, I made the decision that I wanted to create a calming and welcoming experience for all of our clients. I wanted them to feel like VIPs.

This value runs throughout our business – from the way that we answer the phones to our minimalistic offices to our beverages and snacks. We have wireless internet in our waiting room in addition to a refrigerator full of soft drinks, juices, vitamin waters, and plain bottled water. Clients are invited to make a hot beverage from a K-cup machine if they would rather have something warm. Many clients will come early to sit in the waiting room, have chocolates or a power bar, and do some work on their computer.

We have a goal of returning all client phone calls within two hours. When possible, we try to have somebody answering the phone in person. We have an online scheduler to help clients book sessions at their convenience. Our intake paperwork as well can be filled out from the client's phone or computer.

This value – treating clients like VIPs – is something that I measure regularly and am always trying to improve.

You may want to create a different experience for your clients. You may want to have a practice that is based around certain hours. This is common for practices that work with adolescents. Or you may wish to create a practice based around equine therapy with all the wonderful experiences that type of therapy brings. Perhaps you want to offer a low-cost counseling option for people with fixed incomes. You don't necessarily have to spend a lot of money to create a great experience.

Several therapists I know work with therapy dogs. They screen the clients carefully to make sure that the client will be okay with the dog in the room. These therapists wish to give the clients an experience of being understood and cared for not just by the therapist, but by the dog too. If you've ever seen a therapy dog nuzzle up to someone who is hurting, you know what an amazing experience this can be for the client.

The experience of visiting your therapy office is more than your waiting room, consulting room, and interacting with you. At some point, your clients are going to need to use the restroom. We've all been in public restrooms that were not pleasant. (Twice I have been in restrooms that had holes in the walls that went through to the other gender's restroom. What's up with that?) You may not have much control over the restroom in your building, but it doesn't hurt to have extra toilet paper on hand or to take a paper towel to the counters if you notice they are untidy.

There are many types of experiences you might want to create.

No one experience is better than another. I'm asking you, though, to be deliberate about your choice.

The type of experience you wish for your counseling practice will reflect your personal beliefs and values. By taking the time to think about the experience you want to create for your clients, your practice will be 100% authentically you. And you will love being a part of it.

So take some time now and think about it. What type of customer service experience do you want to create for your clients?

Next: how will you know if you are successful in giving clients the experience you wish for them? Every good goal deserves to be measured. This will be the first metric I invite you to measure regularly.

I measure my value of *treating clients like VIPs* by tracking monthly:

- How quickly we return phone calls

- How promptly we start and end our sessions

- How soon we can get in new clients

- How they respond regarding our waiting room treats (We take requests. We ask our clients for suggestions for waiting room beverages and snacks. I was surprised to find how many people love mango ice tea and jalapeno power bars!)

We all know that good clinical outcomes are important. And we will talk about how to measure that in a later chapter. But clients will make a decision to return to your practice when they feel good about being there and when they feel respected.

In Summary:

There are five roles for therapy business owners: clinician, marketing, operations, finance, and visionary. For those with group practices or counseling centers, there is the additional role of human resources. Many private practitioners spend most of their time in the clinician role. This means that the operations and the finances of the business suffer. To look at how your business is running, consider doing an "appreciative inquiry," looking first at what is working in your business, why it is working, and what would be ideal. That can help you get a clear picture of which roles may be sleeping and need to be awakened.

Often the place to start is to decide what experience you want for your clients. For example, do you want to offer low-cost, readily available counseling? Do you want to offer a high-touch boutique experience? There is no right or wrong. Once you define what you want for your client's experience, all your roles can be mobilized toward realizing that vision.

Next Steps:

1. Review the five roles and consider which of your roles you have been ignoring.
2. Take two hours and do the appreciative inquiry assessment of your business. (I like to do this quarterly or semi-annually.)
3. Choose the customer service experience you want your clients to have.
4. Decide how you know if you are successfully delivering the experience.
5. Track it monthly.

CHAPTER THREE

The Therapy Business Decision Triangle

In the previous chapter, we discussed the five roles in running a therapy business: the clinician role, the operations role, the finance role, the marketing role, and the visionary role.

When we make decisions for our business, we want to make sure that the decisions are going to be good for all roles and functions of the business, as well as for our clients. So how do we do that?

Take a look at the Therapy Business Decision Triangle. Each point represents an important entity related to your therapy business: the business itself, the client, and the clinician.

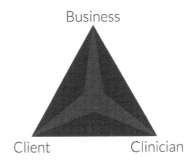

Therapy Business Decision Triangle

Business

Client   Clinician

When you are deciding what policies and procedures to implement, you want to look at how your decisions will impact each component of the triangle. How will this decision affect the business? How will it impact the client? How will it help or hurt the clinician? Decisions that are made for the good of all three components will make your life a lot easier and the business more successful. Let's look at an example.

Imagine it's 6:00 p.m. and your client is not in the waiting room as you expected. You wait. 6:05 p.m. No client. 6:09 p.m. Still no client. On one hand, you are concerned about the client. On the other hand, you're feeling irritated. You could've stayed home and had a little bit more time with your family before venturing out for your evening clients if you had known this particular client wasn't going to show up. At 6:15 p.m., you call the client; your call goes to voicemail. You leave a message saying that you expected to see them at 6:00 p.m. today. You ask them to call you with an update as to what's happening.

What do you do next? Some therapists might decide to immediately enforce their cancellation policy. After all, the client agreed to it, right? Those therapists will take the credit card they have on file for the client and immediately charge it. Momentarily, they feel better. After all, they have now been paid for their time.

But let's look at this situation from the business decision triangle.

How might the client respond to this charge on their credit card? Yes, they had agreed to the cancellation policy in the intake session. When they first came in, they were in a lot of pain with their presenting problem and may not have completely understood the cancellation policy. Or maybe there was simply a miscommunication about the time or date of the session.

When you bill a client without having a conversation about it, the client is likely to feel upset. If they have not had the opportunity to discuss it with you before being charged, a therapeutic break can actually occur. The client might feel a disconnect with the therapist. The client may decide to cancel their next session. Or the client may decide to spread out the treatment. This policy of charging the client without speaking to the client may result in an unhappy client.

You may be reading that and think, "That's my policy." I'm not suggesting that you don't have a stated cancellation policy that you enforce. I am suggesting that when we develop these policies, we first assess how that decision or policy is going to impact each of the three points of the triangle. For example, as a clinician, it might make you feel very good to immediately charge the client because you feel somewhat vindicated for their no-show. You may feel it is in the clinician's best interest to immediately charge the credit card for the no-show so that you are paid for your time.

How might the business be impacted by this policy (of charging the client immediately without having a conversation about why the client no-showed)? If the client, in response, decides to stretch out their treatment or even terminate their treatment because of a therapeutic break over this issue, the business loses. It's as simple as that.

So here is what we see when we examine this policy through the lens of the business decision triangle:

- The clinician might feel good about it;
- The client might feel bad about it; and
- The business might be negatively impacted.

Based on that assessment, this indicates that the policy needs some revision so that it benefits all parties.

How might you revise it? Perhaps you could wait until the client returns and have a discussion in session about the cancellation policy. You could choose to charge the client then or allow them one missed session. By speaking about it in session, you help the client remember and recommit to your policy. My personal belief is that money is a clinical issue and no charges or fee changes should be made before having conversations about it in session.

Again, this is simply an example of how you can use the business decision triangle to evaluate your policies and modify or rewrite them to ensure that they are working the best for all parties.

In the Resource Section, you will find a copy of my cancellation policy procedure. Yours may be different. My point here is not to determine the best cancellation policy. I simply want to share with you how to use the business decision triangle to develop your policies and procedures for the good of all concerned in your business.

Every decision you make for your business can be looked at from these three points of view on the business decision triangle. Perhaps you are considering moving to a new office. Will your existing clients find it close enough to your existing office and want to move with you? If your existing clients don't move with you, how might this impact the business? Would your clients feel there is appropriate parking? Do you, as the clinician, feel the space is conducive to good treatment? Do you want to go to that office every day? Once you look at it from all sides, you can make the best decision for your business, yourself, and your clients.

When the Orange County Relationship Center was one year old, I made the decision to move to a different city pretty far away.

Here's how I made that decision from the three points of the triangle:

Clinician: I wanted to be closer to my home and the new

location was eight miles from my house. (The original location was about 25 miles from my house.)

Business: We were having trouble getting our fees in the original city. While not in a poor area, the original city was less affluent than the new area. Years ago, I had a practice in the area I wanted to move to and I was able to command higher fees, even though it was quite densely populated with therapists.

Clients: This was the hardest for me. Many of the clients would not want to travel an hour to our new location and we would lose them. I knew that.

In the end, we moved. I felt it was the right decision for the long-term viability of the business. I've been much happier closer to home. But looking at the business decision triangle helped me develop a plan to have the least negative impact on our existing clients. We stopped taking on any new clients six months before we moved. Many of the clients finished their treatment with us naturally before our move. We offered weekend appointment times in the new location. This meant some of the clients who wanted to come to the new location could do so in less traffic than they might on a weeknight. And the result? Within two months in our new location, we had doubled our revenues.

Not all decisions will benefit each part of the triangle equally. It is up to the therapy business CEO to weigh the positive and negative impacts and ultimately make each decision. One of the things the triangle does for me is to help me view the decision from the place of each of the parties. And then I, as the CEO, see how I can minimize the negative impacts as I did with the clients and our move.

In Summary:

Sometimes we make decisions from the clinician role only, which tends to hurt the business. The business decision triangle is a tool to use to make sure that all your business decisions are made in the best interests of the client, the clinician, and the business.

Next Steps:

1. Consider your current cancellation policy from the business decision triangle perspective.
2. Is some reshaping of the policy needed? (You will learn more about this in upcoming chapters.)
3. Where else might you employ the business decision triangle in your business?

CHAPTER FOUR

Five Quick Strategies for Immediate Impact

Before we dive into the details of the roles and functions – and how to help you have more time, more money, and more ease, I would like to give you five quick strategies in different roles that can have an immediate positive impact. You may be surprised at how quickly you can see some increased income and more ease when you implement just a couple of these.

1. Answer your phone and return voicemails promptly (Operations Role: front office)

Our profession has a very bad reputation about returning phone calls. We tend to put a priority on working with the clients and less of a priority on responding to their inquiries. Call many therapists and you will hear on their voicemail something like this, "Please note that I return all phone calls within 24 to 48 business hours. If you have an emergency, please call 911 or go to your nearest emergency room." Imagine if you were a client in distress. Perhaps your adolescent was making some bad choices or you and your mate decided you wanted couples' counseling. You put this off for a while and today is the day that you decide to call a therapist. Are you going to wait 24 to 48 hours for this therapist to call you back? Or will you move to the next therapist on your list?

After all, we would recommend that our restaurant owner friend answer his phone when people wanted to make dinner reservations. We would think he was silly if he said, "I can't answer the phone; I am too busy cooking."

Let's look at how much these poor phone habits cost your business. Imagine that you get six new client inquiry calls over the week that you do not answer or return in time. If you had been able to answer the calls, perhaps three of those six inquiries would result in new clients for you. If an average client spends $1,000 with you, then not promptly answering the phone that week cost you $3,000. This can add up to tens of thousands of dollars a year.

Many therapists work hard in their marketing role and their phones are ringing. But if those calls are not answered or returned quickly, all that effort in the marketing role is lost. It breaks my heart.

I can hear you now. "Casey, I have sessions back to back. I can't answer my phone. At the end of the day, I am too tired to return phone calls." This is coming from you in the clinician role. The clinician is feeling tired; the clinician wants to do clinical work – not front office customer service work.

But someone has to do the front office customer service work in order for you, as clinician, to have clients to treat. As a CEO, you need a solution. One option is to recognize that you also wear a front office hat and adjust your treatment schedule so that you have breaks every two or three clients where you can return phone calls. Another option is to hire someone to answer your phone and schedule new and existing clients. Additionally, having an online scheduler can be expedient in that it allows clients to book their own appointments. But an online scheduler does not replace connecting with a live person. The bottom line: the first person to connect with the client gets the client. Will that be you?

2. Take a leadership role with new client inquiries and have a good intake call script (Operations Role: front office)

You want to make sure that whoever is answering the phone, whether that's you or somebody else, has a carefully crafted intake call script. This would be a script that engages the prospective client and helps convert the caller into a client. Too many therapists are extremely passive during an inquiry phone call. They follow the client's lead and just answer questions posed by the client.

I'm not suggesting that you don't want to answer their questions. What I am recommending is that you *join with the client* prior to answering any of their questions. You can see a sample intake call script in the Resource Section of this book.

Until you join with the client and they feel that you care about them and "get them," the client will look for all sorts of reasons not to book an appointment. That is why you want to join with them before answering any of their questions. The first step in responding to a client inquiry is to ask how you can help them. They will then most likely ask you about fees or session lengths or if you take insurance. This is where I encourage you to take a leadership role. You can say to them, "I'm happy to answer those questions, but first can you tell me a little bit about you so that I can make sure that we're the right place for you?"

They will then pause for a second and then be delighted that you actually care about their situation. You can listen to them for a few minutes using your active listening skills.

If you feel that you are a good match for them, you can say,

"Gosh, I'm so sorry that is happening to you. I think it might make sense for us to work together. May I tell you how I work?"

Then you can use this four-point intake call formula:

"My office is located near (a landmark).

"My sessions are 45 minutes in length.

"My fees for each session are $xxx

"I have openings mornings or afternoons. Which would be better for you?"

Your job at this point is to let them process all of this information. If they ask a question, such as "Do you take insurance?" you can then go into your insurance call script if you do not take insurance. (See the Resource Section of this book for a sample.) If you do take insurance, you can get the relevant insurance information.

After the session is booked, you can give the client any "new client instructions," such as directions to your office, how to access their paperwork, and how you accept payment.

Some therapists have told me that they've written the intake call script, had it laminated, and keep it in their day planner or briefcase. Literally hundreds of therapists use this script today and feel very confident as they deliver it. The side benefit is that with you taking the leadership role, the client feels contained and safe, and that you care. Everyone wins!

3. Track your inquiries and conversion rate (Operations Role)

How many inquiry calls do you get each week? How many of those inquiry calls turn into clients? If you don't have actual data on this, please start tracking today. Create a simple spreadsheet, Google Doc, or even put it in your calendar. This data is going to help you decide what to do next in both marketing and visionary roles. (You can see a sample in the Resource Section.)

If you simply aren't getting enough inquiry calls each week, then it's time to increase your marketing efforts. This may mean more marketing, or it may mean improving the marketing you're already doing.

If your phone is ringing, how many of those inquiry calls are turning into clients? This is called your conversion percentage. If ten people call a week, and four become clients, you have a 40% conversion rate. If seven of those ten inquiries become clients, then you have a 70% conversion rate. How do you know what a good conversion rate is? If you have a cash practice, you can expect between 30% and 60% of your callers to become clients. If you have an insurance-based practice, between 70% and 90% is a good conversion rate.

So what does this mean? If your phone is ringing quite a bit but you are not hitting these conversion percentages, then it means you need to improve your intake call script. If you are meeting these conversion percentages but you still don't have enough clients, it means you most likely need to increase your marketing efforts.

4. Have clarity on your fees (Finance Role)

Before you answer the phone, know your fees. Sometimes therapists have a range of fees and they set the fee on the phone with the client rather randomly. In your finance and visionary roles, sit down and decide what your fees will be. Decide if you will or will not have a sliding scale. If you do have a sliding scale, how will it be structured and offered?

When you know your fees before actually getting on the call, it can make the conversation much easier. You can create a script for answering the question, "Do you have a sliding scale?"

Before I had this awareness, I would speak with the clients and if I felt sorry for them, I would drastically reduce my fees without looking at the impact it had on the rest of the operation of my therapy business. I wasn't taking into consideration the finances of the business or how it might impact my feelings as clinician when working week after week for a very low fee. My only goal in the moment – on the phone call – was to help the client feel better.

This is where the business decision triangle comes in. This one decision – about your fees – needs to be viewed from the finance role, the visionary role, and the clinician role. The CEO must give the front office person instructions on the fee policies and exceptions. This is true even if you are the only one in all of these roles.

5. Choose your clients instead of letting them choose you (Clinical and Visionary Role)

Many clinicians come into private practice from other settings where they were required to accept all clients who walked through the door. As the CEO in your business, you get to decide which clients you wish to work with. Always listen to your (intuitive) little voice. If it is telling you during the intake process that this is not the right client for you, let the client go. You never have to sell your services to a potential client. On the intake call and during the intake session, your job is to compassionately join with the client and decide if this is a relationship that you wish to continue with.

I personally tend to take a strong leadership role during the intake session. I learned this early on from Dr. Ellyn Bader of the Couples Institute. (Ellyn offers an excellent Couples Training Program, by the way.)

In the intake session, I listen to the client carefully as I think about whether this is a good match for both of us. If I decide I wish to work with the client, I explain how my therapy works. Taking a leadership role helps contain my clients (in a good way!) and helps us get on the same page regarding our commitment to work together.

My couples counseling clients come weekly for at least ten

sessions. I tell new clients this during the intake session. I explain that in each session, we would be working toward their goals, but that often their old ways of interacting are hard to give up. I tell the couple that they're likely to see some progress in the first couple of sessions, but that we are creatures of habit. We often will go back to our old ways of connecting and interacting with one another, only to find that those ways still don't work.

Then we will make some more progress in the next few sessions, but if they are like most clients, they will go back and try their old ways a second time. We will then get them out of the rut again and about that time they're seeing that the new ways of interacting feel much better.

That is why it takes us at least ten sessions to really get some good traction. I ask them how they feel about that. This is where we see if we are a good match. If the clients expect to come less often than weekly, then we are not a good match for one another. I know I do my best work when people come regularly. Additionally, I don't want to have big holes in my schedule with a caseload of clients of differing frequencies of visits. If the new couple doesn't feel my way of working is right for them, I invite them and help them to find a therapist who would work better for them.

This leaves me with committed clients who understand how I work best. (In case you are wondering… I've been taking this leadership role in my intake sessions for the last two years and have only had three clients decide that it would not work for them.)

You may decide to use a different way of choosing your clients. But you are the CEO of your business. You do get to choose the clients you wish to work with. And we know that working with clients that we don't love really doesn't serve anyone.

In Summary:

Becoming a confident CEO can look daunting at first, which is why I want to give you some wins right out of the gate. By applying the strategies discussed in this chapter, you gain a better understanding of how the various roles in your business interact and the importance of thinking from all perspectives, not just that of the clinician.

I chose these particular five strategies because they are fast and easy to implement and can create a noticeable difference in your bottom line. Small successes lead to big successes.

Next Steps:

1. Pay more attention to returning phone calls. Set a goal to return each call within two hours. If that is not possible, make a deal with yourself that you won't leave the office until you have attempted to reach everyone who called that day.

2. Go to the Resource Section and review my sample intake call script. You can use it as is, or make any changes you feel are appropriate. Print it out and put it by your phone and/or in your planner.

3. Set up a tracking sheet to track your inquiries and conversions. There's a sample tracking sheet in the Resource Section.

4. Take some time to think about your fee structure and how you want to apply it. Become clear on your fee schedule.

5. On inquiry calls, remind yourself that you choose the client. Make sure the person you are talking to is a good fit for you. If they are not, have a list of other therapists you can refer to.

CHAPTER FIVE

Quick Start Guide to Your Therapy Business Finances

When you saw the title of this chapter, did your eyes glaze over? Did you want to skip this section and get to the next? If so, you're not alone. As mentioned earlier, 80% of small business owners fail in the first five years, primarily because they do not know their numbers. So I want to acknowledge you for being open to learning about your finances.

Perhaps you were excited to get to this chapter. Maybe you are already managing your finances pretty well and just want to see if there are any new things you could add to your current systems.

Therapists differ significantly in how they feel about understanding and managing their finances. A lot comes from our family-of-origin beliefs and what we believe we deserve. I have identified five different Money Personality Types. These are default ways that we choose to manage our feelings regarding our finances. See if you recognize yourself in any of these:

1. Alexis Avoider – afraid of looking at your numbers? Worried what you'll find?

2. Oliver Over-Spender – spending to self-soothe or giving it all away?

3. Ursula Under-Earner –always hungry; fearful there is never enough?

4. Hank Hoarder – saving so much that normal living is a struggle?

5. Wendy Wise Money Manager – able to make, save, spend, and enjoy your money?

Knowing your Money Personality Type can help you identify what you need to change to find your way out of your money concerns. I believe that when you know how to manage your money, you manage your destiny.

You may be thinking, "I have a bookkeeper/accountant. I don't need to know this. I can ask them if I have questions." There is some truth to this. They do have the training and the understanding and can create the appropriate financial reports for you.

But as the CEO of your therapy business, you need to understand those reports. You need to be able to make decisions based on the data in those reports for your good and the good of your business.

I want you to have the answers to these questions:

- How much has my business made so far this year?

- How does this compare to my business last year at this time?

- How much do I need to pay myself to live the lifestyle I would like?

- How much do I need to make to live well and pay all my business expenses?

- How much profit did I make last year?

- What percentage of my income is for my business operating expenses?

- Am I spending too much on my business expenses?

- Am I making money? How well am I doing?

- If I'm not doing well, how much more do I need to make to be profitable?

- Can I afford to hire an assistant?

- Will bringing new clinicians into my practice be profitable?

Can you see how knowing the answers to those questions can increase your confidence as a therapy business owner? Even though this is in the finance role, all the roles in your business are impacted by your finances. The visionary wants the business to succeed. The operations role wants things to go smoothly and wants to have the money to make that happen. The efforts of the marketing role can be accurately evaluated when you know your numbers. The clinician will learn how many sessions she needs to complete in order to earn the money that both she and the business want. Your finance role is the glue for your business.

Before we go any further, I want to make two suggestions for this section.

1. Expect mind tricks. In the next few chapters, I am going to be sharing the process where you can learn your numbers and then make decisions based on them. You will learn how to assess the financial success of your business. You'll be given plans for saving money so that unexpected bills won't ever surprise you again. Once you know how to manage your business finances, you will experience such clarity that you will wonder why you shied away

from them before. But the journey can be a little challenging. This is where the mind tricks surface. Please don't let thoughts such as "I don't have a head for numbers" or "I can't do this" take root. You can do this. It is not rocket science. It is not advanced algebra. It is simple counting, tracking, and forecasting.

2. Enter into a "judgment-free zone." As you go through the following materials, please do not make any negative judgments regarding how you are spending money or about how your business is doing. Remember, if this is the first time you've taken a good look at your therapy finances or your personal finances, you may find some surprises. But for now, please don't judge yourself in any way. This is all about learning and exploring. Later, we will learn about how to make decisions regarding your money.

The Quick Start Approach: Six Steps to Getting a Handle on Your Finances

Step One: Calculate what you need to live the lifestyle that you want (your personal expenses).

Step Two: Know how much your business needs to run (your business expenses).

Step Three: Review your expenses to make sure you are spending your money in the way that brings you the most joy. Create your joyful spending plan (aka budget).

Step Four: Calculate your income (revenue) goal. (This is the total of your personal and business expenses, plus additional money saved for taxes and profit.)

Step Five: Decide what you need to do to meet that income goal (Number of sessions or office rental income, for example).

Step Six: Track your income and expenses weekly and monthly

(without judgment) and once you have a full picture, you can then course-correct and modify your spending as needed.

In this and the next chapter, I will explain each of these six steps in detail.

Step One: Calculate what you need to live the lifestyle that you want

Why does your business exist? Yes, you want to help clients to feel better. Yes, you feel called to do this kind of work. But doing so in your own business is so you can earn the money to pay for the lifestyle that you wish to live. Otherwise, you could be working for someone else or in an agency. So our first stop is to calculate how much you need to live on... in other words, your personal expenses. This means calculating how much the business needs to earn for your personal expenses.

You can do step one by looking at your history or you can start tracking your personal expenses today. Looking at your history takes a little longer in the data-gathering phase, but can give you a very clear picture of how you spend your money. You may have an inkling of this already, but most clinicians find it illuminating when they actually go back and look at how they spent their money over the last year.

Gather six months to one year of credit card statements and bank records and separate which expenses were business expenses and which were personal expenses. (In step two, we will be concentrating on your business expenses, but here we are only looking at your personal expenses. If it is helpful for you to do both at the same time, that is perfectly fine.) Group your expenses into categories such as food, housing, etc. When you finish this exercise, you can total the amounts so you see how much you spent in each category.

There is no right or wrong way to categorize your expenses, so pick categories that are meaningful to you. That said, be mindful of how many categories you have. Too few categories and you don't really have a sense of where your money is going and how much you need for any category. Too many categories and the tracking becomes onerous. You may wish to separate categories into subcategories. For example, you may wish to separate groceries from dining out and convenience foods. Later, we will use this data for budgeting.

You might find that you took out a lot of money in cash and you aren't sure what you did with it. Again, just create an "other" category and start going forward tracking your cash expenditures – if the cash went for Starbucks (food), or movies (entertainment), etc.

Sum the categories by month so you know how much you spent monthly in each category.

As you are gathering, categorizing, and tabulating your spending, you can do so on a simple Excel spreadsheet. There are also software programs such as Quicken or QuickBooks. My advice is to keep it simple. I've noticed sometimes therapists will delay in gathering their numbers because they are "researching the best software accounting program." This is a mind trick. It helps us avoid looking at the numbers.

Let's take an example of a fictitious therapy business owner, Chloe Clinician.

Chloe gathered her personal spending data for one year. She went through her January bank records and credit card statements categorizing and totaling her spending for January. She did the same for February and each month of the year. She found her spending was primarily in these categories:

- Housing expense (rent or mortgage, furniture, home insurance)
- Home utilities

- Transportation expense (automobile, fuel, car insurance, bus, or subway pass)
- Food (groceries, dining out, convenience food)
- Medical (doctors and medications)
- Clothing (dry cleaning, shoes, clothes)
- Personal care (hair, nails, gym, spa)
- Education (non-business-related education – this could be for you or your children)
- Entertainment
- Vacation/holiday
- Insurance (life, health, dental, disability, long-term care)
- Technology (home computers, cell phones)
- Gifts
- Pet expenses
- Debt repayment (for any loans or credit cards)
- Savings (retirement, education, emergency)
- Spiritual (worship, tithing, charity)
- Other (for cash withdrawals where she was not sure where the money went)

Since Chloe was looking at a year's worth of data, she found some expenses that came only annually or semi-annually, such as her car insurance. She put those in a column at the end of her spreadsheet. After she totaled what she spent in each month in each category, she added all the monthly totals together, as well as the expenses that she paid irregularly such as her car insurance payments. Once she had the total for all 12 months in each category, she had her annual expenses for each category. She then divided the total annual expense number by 12 to give her a monthly average of what she spent in each category.

Here is what her monthly average looked like after she added all 12 months together and divided by 12:

Personal Expenses	Monthly Average
Housing	500
Home utilities	200
Transportation	330
Food	600
Medical	150
Clothing	150
Personal care	110
Education	90
Entertainment	370
Vacation/holiday	300
Insurance	330
Technology	120
Gifts	120
Pet expenses	40
Debt repayment	150
Savings	200
Spiritual	100
Other	140
Total Personal Expenses	**$4,000**

If you notice, Chloe has housing expense of $500. She has a roommate and they split the rent. $500 is Chloe's share of the rent. If you split your personal expenses with someone else, calculate what percentage you need to cover. For example, if the rent on your home is $1,200 and you split it 50-50 with a partner or roommate, the amount that you would put on the personal expense spreadsheet is $600.

After gathering her data, Chloe sees that to lead the personal life she has been living, she needs to pay herself a salary of at least $4,000. In other words, her business has to earn enough to pay her $4,000, plus cover the business expenses, including taxes on her income.

This is a key metric you have just discovered: how much your business needs to earn and pay you so that you can continue to live this lifestyle. Later, when we get to the budgeting part, you may find that the lifestyle that you lived over the last six months to a year is not ideal. Then you can adjust your spending and earning to make it so. This is where the freedom comes in when you know your numbers. No more guessing.

Some therapy business owners are still co-mingling their business and personal expenses. While not uncommon, it can make managing your therapy business finances messy. I highly recommend that you get separate bank accounts for your personal expenses and your business expenses. This may entail some extra work, but remember this is not your hobby; this is your business. Put on your CEO hat and make sure that you are setting yourself up for success.

Step Two: Know how much your business needs to run (your business expenses)

Now that you know your personal expenses, let's shift to your business. What does it cost your business to open the doors for clients? Again, you want to gather your bank records and credit card statements and by month identify your business expenses – pulling out any that are only paid once or twice a year and documenting them in a column at the end of your spreadsheet. You could start tracking from today, but if you really want to get a handle on this, please go back and grab the last six months to a year. The reason I like a year's worth of statements is that's where you might find some of those expenses that you pay only annually. If you only go back six months, you might miss them.

Just as with our personal expenses, you can categorize your business expenses. Here are the categories I use, although yours may be different:

- Advertising and Promotion *adwords, website, cc, pancl*
- Bank Service Charges
- Bookkeeping
- Business Consulting
- Computer/Internet
- Dues and Subscriptions
- Insurance
- Merchant (Credit Card) Fees
- Payroll Wages
- Payroll Taxes
- Staff (Front Office – A 1099 Contractor)

- Supplies

- Rent

- Research

- Software (Practice Management)

- License

- Telephone

- Training (CEU Programs)

On your spreadsheet, tally the business expenses by month. You will probably have expenses that you pay irregularly, such as an annual malpractice insurance bill. When collecting your data the first time, you can collect these irregular expenses and put them in a column at the end of your spreadsheet.

Add up all of your monthly expenses, including those you pay irregularly, divide by 12 and now you know what it costs for your therapy business to be open to see clients each month.

Here is what Chloe discovered after she totaled a year's worth of business expenses and divided by 12 to come up with her monthly average:

Business Expenses	Monthly Average
Advertising	120
Bank service charges	15
Bookkeeping	215
Computer & Internet	199
Continuing Ed	149
Dues/Subscriptions	15
Insurance and License	50
Merchant Accounting Fees	50
Office Supplies	90
Professional Fees (business coach)	800
Rent (office)	950
Software (practice mgmt. system)	39
Telephone	670
Total Business Expenses	**$3,362**

Chloe now knows that on average, it cost her over the last year $3,362 a month to keep her business open.

She can now calculate the total of her personal and business expenses before taxes. We will discuss taxes and business profit in an upcoming chapter.

Chloe's Personal Expenses (monthly average): $4,000

Chloe's Business Expenses (monthly average): $3,362

Total expenses before taxes and profit: $7,362

You may be tempted (on both the business and the personal side) to adjust your spending once you see how your money is being allocated. I'm going to ask that you don't do this yet. We will be discussing how to create your joyful spending plan in the next chapter.

It takes most people a few hours to a couple of weeks to gather all this data. It can be a bit tedious, I will admit. But that is because you may not ever have done it before. If you build some good habits so that you are tracking going forward, then you won't have to do this catch up again. And if you've taken the time to gather and categorize your personal and business expenses, please congratulate yourself. The finance role in your business is critical to your success and it's one that most likely you've never been trained for. So congratulations on getting this far!

In Summary:

We are jumping into the finance role first. Remember, if this is a role you have avoided so far, expect mind tricks. You may find yourself freezing or judging yourself harshly. Be gentle with yourself – we all need to start somewhere. For me, it is like losing weight… I have to know where I am (get on the scale) before I can move toward my goal.

In this chapter, you have a quick-start approach to getting a handle on your finances. Please don't just turn the page of this book now. Please do these exercises. This is how you learn to become a profitable and knowledgeable CEO.

To start in your finance role, you will look at how much you spent (by category) for both your personal expenses and your business expenses. As you do so, you will calculate how much your business needs to earn to live your life (and run your business) as you have been. This is your preliminary income goal. In the next chapter, you will have the opportunity to create a joyful spending plan, but don't alter your spending just yet. Gather and sum it first.

Next Steps:

1. Start with the first two steps of the six in the quick start approach to getting a handle on your finances by gathering six months to a year's worth of bank records and credit card statements.

2. Categorize your spending by month – separating personal and business expenses. You will have categories for your personal spending such as housing, transportation, food, etc. For your business, you will have categories such as rent, merchant accounting fees, practice management software, supplies, etc. Make sure you separate your business and personal spending.

3. Do this for each month and then add up what you spent in each category. Divide by the number of months you gathered to come up with a monthly amount needed to live life as you have been. This is your preliminary income goal. Next we will see if this is really what you want.

CHAPTER SIX

The Next Step: Your Joyful Budget

In the last chapter, we went over the first two of the six steps to getting a handle on and managing your finances.

Step one was to calculate what you have spent over the last six months to a year for your personal expenses.

Step two was to calculate how much it has cost to run your business over the last six months to a year.

I asked you not to modify your spending until you had first gathered six months' to a year's worth of your spending and itemized it by category. The reason for this suggestion is so you get an accurate representation of how much it took for you to live and run your business last year. If you start to change your spending as you are collecting the data, you end up with a moving target. So please don't jump into spending modifications until you have gathered your spending records for six months to a year.

If you did collect the data as recommended in the previous chapter, you now know how much you need to earn in order to live the lifestyle you've been living before taxes. You have a number. You may find this is a very high number. You may be concerned about earning that amount of money – or spending it.

Step Three: Create your joyful spending plan (aka budget)

Therefore, our next step is to look at your expenses and see if the way that you are spending your money is giving you the greatest joy and value per dollar. Sometimes we spend money without really thinking about it. That can lead us into a hamster wheel of spending more and then needing to earn more to pay for our spending.

The answer to more mindful spending is to create a spending plan so that you spend your money in ways that bring you the most joy. (In later chapters, we will discuss how you can, in your marketing role, work to get more clients and more income if you're not making enough now or want to make more.)

When thinking about the word budgeting, most people feel uncomfortable. My friend Chellie Campbell defines b-u-d-g-e-t as "baby you deserve to get everything." I believe that you can have what you want, although you may not be able to have everything you want at the same time. It's about choices.

I like the words "spending plan" as opposed to budget. You work hard to earn your income each month. You have choices as to how to spend that money. Some expenses won't feel like a choice, such as housing. But you really do have a choice as to how much money you want to spend on housing. You can choose to live in a tiny home in a rural area or you can choose to live in a luxury high-rise in an expensive area. Most likely, the tiny home is going to cost less per month. This means you work fewer hours to pay for that tiny home than you might for the larger, more expensive option. This is why you want to spend some time determining what expenditures give you the most joy and plan accordingly.

In the book, *Your Money or Your Life*, by Joe Dominguez and Vicki Robin, the authors discuss how to prioritize your spending so that you're getting the most joy for every dollar that you spend. But how do you do that? I believe it takes conscious spending.

There are four steps to creating a conscious, joyful spending plan:

1. List your expenses from the most expensive to the least expensive

Take the expense categories for both your business and your personal expenses that you gathered in the previous chapter. Sort them from the most expensive category to the most inexpensive. Let's look at your personal expenses first. Housing might be the most expensive, followed by transportation, food, or debt repayment. The lowest might be pet expenses. Everyone's totals will be different. Just use your numbers and create the list starting with the most expensive category down to the least. Do the same for your business. The highest business expense is likely your rent. The lowest of mine is bank service charges.

Now you should have two lists – one for personal and one for business. Each list has your expense categories in order from the one you spend the most on to the category you spend the least on.

2. Identify your expense line items as "needs" or "wants"

Now you are going to take each list – the business and personal expenses – and identify each category as a "want" or a "need."

This is a very personal choice. In my area of southern California, an automobile is a need. Well, for me that is. Your story may be different. You may have the option of getting around without a car, so for you, a car may be more of a "want." For my friend Christel, travel with her family is a need. This is also true of my sister who visits her grandchildren across the country as often as she can. Many clinicians could consider the online practice management system we use at my counseling center a "want." For us, it is a need because of our values of being a paperless office. There is no right or wrong here. Just quickly review each expense line item and mark it as a want or a need.

Our office magazine subscriptions are clearly a "want." When I first opened our counseling center, I subscribed to 12 magazines – including *Wired, Popular Science, Golf, Oprah, More, Martha Stewart Living, Entrepreneur, Sports Illustrated, People,* and others. I even bought a wall rack to display the 12 magazines. The magazines look stunning; they looked like wall art. I thought our clients would enjoy reading the magazines before their appointments. But you know what? We are so prompt for our sessions, that most people spend less than five minutes in our waiting room. And you know what they do in those five minutes? They're on their phone texting or emailing. I spent $300 that first year on magazines and that expenditure turned out to not be joyful for the clients or bring us revenue.

So go ahead, take the ordered list (from high to low) of business expenses and the list of personal expenses and identify each category as a "want" or a "need."

3. Rank your needs and wants from what is most important to you to what is least important

This is the fun part. Look at the categories on both your lists. What are the big joyful expense categories for you? Take a few minutes and rank from high to low how important the categories are to you and your quality of life (and business). Remember, our goal is to create a spending plan that will help ensure you are spending in ways that serve you in the life you want to live.

Remember our judgment-free zone agreement, right? When I spent the time to prioritize my expense categories, I realized cable

TV is a "strong want" for me and I rank it very high – even higher than some expenses I thought I "needed." You may be laughing at me right now if you are not an HGTV fanatic like me. The point is that your priorities will be unique to you.

4. Look at your list to see if there are places you wish to make spending cuts

You can begin to evaluate your spending after you've looked at a year's worth of your data, identified needs versus wants, and prioritized both your needs and your wants. You now have enough information to see how you wish to rearrange your spending.

After you look at your needs vs. wants (and which are most important), you may find that you can make some changes in your spending that will bring you more joy.

Let's go back to Chloe Clinician for a moment. After looking at her numbers, Chloe identified four areas where she was overspending according to her priorities. She was spending, on average, $600 a month for food. More than half of this was convenience food that she picked up on her way home from the office. She did not really find much joy in that, as evidenced by her low priority on the list. She decided to cook several dinners on the weekends and freeze them. She now has meals available in the freezer to heat up for a quick and easy dinner. She was able to cut her food spending in half to $300 a month. She also decided to give up her home telephone landline, which reduced her share of the household utilities by $100 a month. She called her insurance agent and found there was a discount for health-care providers that shaved $100 off her monthly insurance premiums. Chloe decided that her entertainment bill could also be cut by $170 since some of her weekend partying wasn't so "entertaining" anymore.

When she reviewed her "wants," Chloe also realized that

having a massage or pedicure more often was a very high "want." She decided to add $100 to the personal care spending category.

As she made these adjustments, she was able to shave a net of $570 off her monthly living expenses! Now the monthly total for her personal living expenses is $3,430, as compared to the original $4,000.

Chloe did the same review process with her business expenses. She was able to reduce her telephone bill by a whopping $513 by removing some of the landlines (and associated features) that were in her office. This reduced her average monthly business expenses to $2,849.

Now the new total of Chloe's personal and business spending plan before taxes totals $6,279, as opposed to the original $7,362, and the expenditures are more in line with her personal priorities.

After looking at the prioritization of your "needs" vs. "wants," do you see any areas where you wish to rearrange your spending? Perhaps you can renegotiate your cell phone plan. Perhaps there is a gym membership you are still paying but never using. I used to spend $100 a month for fresh flowers for the office, even though I was only there three days a week. I was constantly throwing away dead flowers. I chose to stop that expense.

Cutting back on your expenses will reduce your income goal. This means that you don't have to work as many hours to meet your income goal. Or it can mean that there is more money to spend in ways that bring you more joy. Perhaps you'd like to take a gourmet cooking class, but feel you "can't afford it." When you look at your priorities, you can see that reducing a couple of "low want" expenses will give you the money for the class.

Stop the bleeding and then move forward

My suggestion is that you quickly identify some places to cut your expenses to be more in line with your wants and needs and then walk away from your budget for a week. Come back a week later and look at it again. In these two reviews, you can make some initial cuts based on your personal choices, but please be careful not to cut too much. Our goal is to help you live the life that you want easily. Sometimes people cut too much and end up binge-spending later.

As each week, month, and year goes by, continue to track your spending, evaluate how you feel about your purchases, and adjust as needed. Your needs, wants, and goals will change over the years. This is not a "one and done" activity. This is one of the main activities of the finance role of your business. Embrace it. It is the secret to living life on your terms.

Spending plans for the therapy business owner that has a center or group practice

Some entrepreneurial therapy business owners will decide to expand their business by adding additional clinicians to their practice. There are additional expenses with running a center. You may have additional office support. You may have additional expenses for marketing each of your clinicians. As you evaluate your expenses, ask yourself, "Does this expense contribute to the joy of our clinicians, our clients, and/or does it contribute to the bottom line?" This will help you decide what to spend and what to cut.

One group practice owner that I was coaching was paying $3,000 a month for several telephone landlines. She had a front office receptionist who answered the phone and then she had landlines in every office and a few extra in a conference room. She had an expensive voicemail system with voice mailboxes for each clinician.

In her operations role, she wanted all the new client inquiries to come into the main phone line for the center. This central scheduling allowed her front office person to answer the phones more quickly than the individual therapist might, and get new appointments scheduled faster. The practice owner interviewed the clinicians in her practice and found that most ended up giving their cell phone numbers to their clients for emergencies. (Actually, they had digital phone numbers that forwarded to their cell phones so that their cell phones were still private numbers.) Simply put, those landlines were going to waste. It took some negotiating, but she was able to cut out almost two-thirds of that bill by getting rid of most of those landlines – adding nearly $25,000 to the center's profit.

As we will discuss in an upcoming chapter, central scheduling for counseling centers is almost always going to make the center more profitable. So by reviewing her front office operations procedures as well as her finances, she was able to make a business decision that helped the clinicians, had no impact on the clients, and improved the profitability of the business significantly. Win-Win-Win!

Step Four: Calculate your Income (Revenue) Goal

Your Income (Revenue) Goal is the total of your personal and business expenses plus additional money saved for taxes and profit.

Calculate your Income Goal with this simple formula

You now know how much you need to earn to support your personal life (as you've been living it) and your business (as you've been running it), using the numbers you gathered in the first two steps above.

So far, though, we did not include any amounts for taxes or

profit. We must not forget those! After all, most of us are required to pay taxes. That is a no-brainer.

And your business needs to be profitable. I like to think of profit as PRO-FIT. It is the measure of your financial fitness for your professional business. Profit is your reward for taking the entrepreneurial risk of opening your own business. Once you have money saved in your profit account for at least two months of operating expenses, then if you like, you can bonus yourself with some of your profit! How cool is that! So let's make a "profit goal" and start putting money away before we spend it.

In the book *Profit First,* author Mike Michalowicz recommends reserving 5% of total revenue earned for profit and 15% of total revenue earned for taxes in businesses under $250,000 annual revenues. (He explains this in incredible simplicity. I have been teaching percentages for your finances for a while now and he makes it easy-peasy to understand. I strongly encourage you to read his book. You can check it out here: http://BeAWealthyTherapist. net/profitfirst.)

Let's look back at Chloe Clinician's monthly numbers and see if we can back into how much she needs to earn (her income goal):

Personal expenses: $3,430 (This is how much Chloe needs to pay herself from her business earnings.)
Business expenses: $2,849 (This is how much her business needs to run.)
Total expenses: $6,279

Let's add to that expense total 15% for taxes:
$6,279 * .15 = $942
Let's add to that expense total 5% for profit:
$6,279 * .05 = $314

Now we can find Chloe's true income goal:
Income Goal = Profit + Taxes + Personal Expenses +
Business Expenses

For Chloe then, her monthly income goal would be $7,535. I calculated that with this formula:

Profit ($314) + taxes ($942) + personal expenses ($3,430) + business expenses ($2,849) = Monthly Income goal: ($7,535)

Do you see the beauty of this? You now have an income (revenue) goal that is based on what you actually need to be happy in your personal life and to run a successful business that you want. Plus you will be running a profitable business with money saved for taxes! How cool is that?

To get *your* income goal, add the personal and business expenses that you gathered in the earlier steps… then add in an additional 5% of your total expenses for profit and 15% for taxes. If you feel that 5% is too high, start with 2% or even 1%. But start somewhere. You will enjoy the feeling of running a profitable business.

Step Five: Decide how you're going to meet that revenue goal

Most therapists will meet their income (revenue) goal by offering x number of sessions at y dollars per session. For example, Chloe has a monthly income goal calculated in step 4 as $7,535. If her average session fee collected is $155, then she needs to be paid for at least 49 sessions a month.

Assuming a 20% cancellation or no-show rate, this means

that Chloe would need to book 62 sessions a month in order to be paid for doing 49 client sessions (number of sessions you want to complete x 1.25). You may not have 20% of your clients cancel with notice or no-show, but add something in here for sessions you book but aren't completed. I learned this from one of our therapist clients. She had a goal of booking 20 clients a week with the assumption that 100% of them would show up and pay for the session in order for her to meet her goal. When they would want to change to a different week, she would begin to panic because she wasn't going to meet her goal. Once she started adding in some padding, she began to relax and hit her goals.

There are other ways to meet your income or revenue goal as well. Perhaps you have an interior office that you wish to sublease to another therapist. Or maybe you do workshops. It doesn't matter how you earn the income; you just want to create a plan. If your income goal is $7,535 a month and $1,000 a month comes from renting out a couple of interior offices, then you only need to make $6,535 a month from one-to-one sessions. This would reduce the number of sessions you need to do per month.

Step Six: Track your weekly and monthly business and personal expenses without judgment and course-correct as necessary

This is where the fun comes in. You may decide after tracking for a while that you have to work an extra hour or two a month to pay for some movie channels that you never watch. This is where you can begin to evaluate if each expenditure is bringing you enough pleasure to continue paying for that expense.

For example, I love watching cable TV. Our cable bill is not inexpensive, but I am happy to work the time it takes to pay for that bill. When I first did this exercise, I realized how much I was spending going out to a nice restaurant every day for lunch. Most of the time, I was tired and read my book during lunch; I didn't really pay attention to the quality of the food. I decided that I would much rather go to the local salad place and pay half as much. I could rearrange my spending and spend that money on a very nice dinner out once a week or I could choose to work less.

A personal note: my spending plan process

After I reviewed my personal spending expenses with these exercises and came up with my joyful spending plan, I decided to go one step further. You see, I was shocked by how much money I was spending on my credit and debit cards. I love internet shopping. (And Amazon loves me.) It was very easy for me to get online and spend $130 on things I "needed." And then do it again a couple of days later.

In my personal spending plan, I have categories for things like gas, vitamins, clothes, eating out, and gifts. And these are all things that I put on my credit cards. I even got a refillable debit card for more online shopping. I was hoping this would keep money off of my credit cards. The problem was that the refillable debit card would auto refill and I felt like I had an unlimited supply of money.

You've probably heard my story by now. I wasn't always very good with money. I went $45,000 in debt when I started my first counseling practice because I didn't market my business. I was warm prey for any advertising people who told me "This will get you money and clients!" It took me a few years to get out of debt, and then I actually went and did it again to the tune of $13,000 because I was convinced I needed a new logo and a very expensive website. Once I paid off that credit card, I made a commitment that

I would pay off my credit cards every single month and have done so for the past 15 years.

So even though I was doing a fair amount of internet shopping and mindless spending, I was paying those bills in full every month. But the problem was, I would have to come up with several hundred – sometimes even a couple thousand dollars – each month. There was no association between the large amount I was paying on my credit card and the joy I was receiving on any individual purchases.

In my business, I was on track with my spending for the counseling center. My business expenses are almost the same every single month and I've honed them down to expenses that give my clients, the clinicians in my practice, or me either joy or additional income.

I wanted more connection and control over my personal spending. My personal expenses seem to vary each month. During the times of my annual conference, I would spend more on clothes. Other months, I may spend more on books or crafting materials. I thought the personal expenses budgeting software would help to manage the spending plan, but I kept moving amounts from category to category each month. I felt like I was chasing my tail. I still wasn't able to associate an amount I was spending on each purchase and decide if it was worth it. This is partially because all my personal expenses were lumped together on one credit card payment. And it was also because the payment was made well after the expenses were incurred or the experience was enjoyed.

Enter Monica, my bookkeeper. Monica had been doing my QuickBooks for about a year. One day, I was discussing this problem with her… that I was constantly moving money around in the budgeting software from category to category without having a sense of whether each purchase was "worth it."

The Envelope System?

Monica had some ideas for me. She suggested a new system that has completely solved this problem for me.

Monica explained to me that the reason I had difficulty assessing the value of any purchase was because I was using credit instead of cash. "When you pay cash, you can immediately associate the amount you're spending with the product or service you are buying. You can quickly do the evaluation and make the choice so that you are spending in ways that serve you and feel good."

"Let's create a cash system for your spending. It's the old *envelope system*. Each week, you will take a certain amount of cash out and place it into category envelopes. You will have an envelope for spending and eating out, clothes, personal care, gas and car wash, and slush. Based on the spending plan you've already created, you will put that amount of cash into your envelopes. Then you spend from your envelopes. When you are out of money, you stop spending. The slush envelope will contain some extra money for things that you might not expect, such as going out for a special dinner when a friend comes to town."

Personally, I thought this was ridiculous. That envelope (aka category) allocation was basically what I was doing in my budgeting software program. And who uses cash anyway? Besides, I love the credit card reward points.

I would love to say that I took Monica up on the offer the first time. I did not. I went another few months trying to get my budgeting software to balance each month. I noticed that when I had a really hard week, I would spend more on books and fun stuff on Amazon than I did during other weeks. But I still had difficulty assessing if what I was purchasing was worth what I was paying for it.

A few months later, I went back to Monica and said I would give her envelope system a try. We set up envelopes with the categories I mentioned before: spending and eating out, personal care, clothes, gas/car wash, and slush. Actual envelopes! But now that I think about it, I find it ironic that I bought the physical envelopes (that I store my cash in) on Amazon. Amazon still loves me.

Each week now, I pay myself my "owner's pay" from my business account. That money is deposited into my personal account. I then withdraw cash (from my personal account) for the amounts for each envelope.

I have a standard amount that is to go in each envelope. For example, the amount going into the gas/car wash envelope is $40 a week. If in any given week I spend more than that, I take it out of my slush fund envelope. (I put $50 in the slush fund envelope weekly.) I also put money each week in a personal savings account for irregular expenses, such as car insurance and gifts.

There are still some things that I buy online. And when I do, the amount for that expense envelope gets reduced the following week. For example, if I buy some makeup online for $30, my personal care envelope amount will be reduced the following week by $30. So even though I'm paying for the makeup with a credit card, I'm keenly aware that my envelope in that category will be reduced by $30 next week. It gives me a place to really decide if this purchase is worth the $30. My mindless internet shopping now becomes a choice when evaluating the value each time I make a purchase.

For example, yesterday I was looking for some colored markers for a personal art project on Amazon. There is quite a varied price range for colored markers. Did you know that they could range in price from $15 a set to over $300 a set? Who knew? Well, everything in me wanted those $300 markers. It was like the giant crayon box I had as a kid. I was salivating over those 72 different colored markers.

Instead of hitting the "buy now with one click" button, I paused. I don't have a $300 colored marker budget. It would need to come out of my weekly spending or slush fund budget. I do have about $300 in my slush fund envelope right now… But did I want to spend it on those markers? After all, this personal art project is a new one and I may not like working on it. I may decide not to finish it. Then what would I do with a set of $300 markers?

In the end, I went for the $15 set, thinking that if I like doing this particular craft, and I see myself doing a lot more of it in the future, I will save up some of my spending money to purchase the more expensive set. I'm excited to see what unfolds. I know this may seem like a trivial example, but it has helped me reconnect to the value of what I spend and has literally saved me thousands of dollars this year.

The other fascinating suggestion from Monica is that I pay my credit cards weekly instead of monthly. So the total amount going to my credit cards plus the cash going in my envelopes each week add up to my budgeted amounts for each category. This means that I am paying my credit card closer to the time of purchase. I never end up with these huge bills where I can't remember what I purchased.

I also have similar habits for my businesses. I wanted to systematize saving money for taxes as well as making sure I was running profitable businesses. So, each week I take out 15% of what I earned that week and put it in a separate tax savings account. I also pull out from my business checking account a percentage of what I earn (10%) and put it into a separate profit savings account. (I used to save 5% for profit as suggested earlier, but now that the business is doing better, I tuck away 10% in the profit account. This way, I have money saved for future business expansion.) I do this for both of my businesses – Be A Wealthy Therapist and the Orange County Relationship Center. This way, I'm always ensuring that my business is profitable and that I have money saved for taxes. Further, it helps me pay attention to my business spending. Before I did this,

I always felt there was more money available to spend and then I'd be scrambling when tax time came. And quite honestly, before I started doing this, I was not very profitable because I was spending what was in the bank account.

I also pull out additional money each week to save for business expenses I pay irregularly or am saving for – such as future business coaching or a new computer. This way, there is almost always money when I need it for my important business expenditures.

With these habits, I have created more profitable businesses and saved more money than I ever have before. My spending is joyful and in line with my wants and needs.

In the next chapter, we will continue helping you understand the finance role with one more "know your numbers" step: Your Profit and Loss Statement. Armed with this information, you can move from confused to aware of how well your business is doing at any given time. Once you understand the data on your Profit and Loss statement, your operations, marketing, and visionary roles can come up with new plans and action steps to make your business easier to run and more profitable.

This is how you become the confident CEO of your therapy business.

In Summary:

You work hard for your money. Make sure you spend it in ways that are the most rewarding to you. Some call it a budget, but I call it your joyful spending plan.

Next Steps:

1. Let's create your joyful spending plan.
2. Start by prioritizing your expenses and then ranking the categories from most spent in that category to the least spent.
3. Next look at your categories and identify each as a "need" or a "want."
4. Rank your needs from highest need to lowest need. Do the same for your wants. You now have a picture of your current spending plan. Does it bring you joy?
5. If not, consider rearranging your spending based on what you learned. Where might you adjust your spending to be more in line with your needs and wants?
6. Calculate your income goal by adding a percentage for profit and for taxes to your expenses.
7. Continue to track your expenses and review your spending plan from time to time to make sure you are spending more in ways that bring you the most joy and ease.

CHAPTER SEVEN

Profit and Loss Statement

A therapist told me recently that she thought she was doing well in her business as long as she was "above the red line in her QuickBooks program." I had never heard that expression, so I asked what she meant. And guess what? I am not sure she really knew either! But she was shocked to find out that she did not have enough to meet payroll that week – even though she was *above the red line.*

This is a common problem. Many therapy business owners think they know how well their business is doing by looking at their bank balances or by the number of sessions they do per month.

Often when I ask therapists how they define success for their businesses, they will quote a number of sessions per week: "I want to do four sessions, four days a week." And that can be a fine goal for the clinician role in your business. But you, as CEO in your finance and visionary roles, need to take the clinician's desires and see how to set the fees to make that work. Finally, you, in the marketing role, need to take that goal and create and implement the marketing plans to meet that goal. And then the operations and finance roles need to make sure that there is money saved for the months when the caseload dwindles or there are additional expenses.

Other therapists define the success of their business by their bank account balance. Your bank balance alone does not tell you the financial status of your business. You may have $1,000 in your bank account, but if you have bills totaling $1,500, then you will lose money this month. Your bank balance alone can't tell you if you are making money at being a therapist or owning a therapy center. It does not tell you if you are bringing in more income than you did last year at this time. It only tells you how much you have not yet spent at this moment in time.

So, if number of sessions completed or our bank balances don't tell us how well our businesses are doing, what will?

We need a measure – a report that tells us if we made any money – and if so, how much. We need a report that can compare your revenue to your expenses and see how much, if anything, is left over.

The best report for you to understand how well your business is doing is the profit and loss (P&L) statement. Your P&L statement is a summary of the financial performance of your business over a particular period of time. You can look at your profit and loss report month by month, quarter by quarter, year to date, and annually. It is the most common report used by business owners to assess their business finances and how well things are going. In the financial role of your business, you want to learn how to look at your profit and loss statement and interpret what it is telling you.

In the introduction of this book, I mentioned how one year not very long ago, I ended the year with only $1,000. Had I been looking at my profit and loss statements each month in that year, I would have seen that I was either overspending or under-earning (or both) and made adjustments. Since I was an Alexis Avoider at that time, I just looked at my bank balance. If there was money in the account, I felt I had money to randomly spend or invest back into my business. But the reality was that I did not have that money to spend or invest. At that time, I was lucky enough to have other income and was not relying on this business income to support me. If I had been solely dependent on this business's income, I would not have been able to survive on fifty cents an hour.

I don't think I'm the only one who has been confused by their finances. While some therapists are very good at understanding their finances, many of us have very little education and understanding in this area. This is sad because your profit and loss reports are actually very easy to create and read. I'm going to show you how to create and read/interpret your report in this section.

How to Create Your Profit and Loss Statement

Let's start with the good news. If you already have an accountant or bookkeeper, they are able to get these reports to you. Just make sure that this person has your income and expenses each month and they will create this report for you. While some clinicians wait until the end of the year to accumulate their income and expenses, I recommend you do this monthly, quarterly, and annually. Then you can create your profit and loss report with each month's and season's data. That way you, in both your financial role and your visionary role, have the opportunity to read your P&L report, interpret it, compare it to this time (or season) last year, and decide if you want to make any changes to the way you are running your business.

There are four steps to creating your profit and loss statement:

1. Collect all your business revenue
2. Collect your business expenses
3. Subtract your expenses from your revenue
4. The remainder is your Income from Business Operations (or Income before Taxes)

Let's review these steps in more detail.

Collect your business revenue

The profit and loss statement starts with a top line of what we call Revenue. This is all the money that comes into your business from sessions that you do, from workshops you might have, or from rental income if you rent out one of the interior offices in your suite. Your revenue is any income that your business generates.

Subtract your business expenses

From that revenue, you want to subtract your business expenses such as rent, malpractice insurance, internet, telephones, and salary for an assistant if you have one, and any of your remaining business expenses.

Income from your business (Business Income before Taxes)

Your revenue minus your business expenses gives you your income from your business. If it is a positive number, it means you spent less than you made. After you pay your business taxes, you will then have a very real and clear picture of whether you made a profit or had a loss for that time frame.

Here is a sample P&L for Chloe Clinician:

Income for January

Counseling Sessions	$7,500.00
Interior Office Rent	$700.00
Workshops/Speaking	$320.00
TOTAL INCOME	$8,520.00

Expenses for January	
Advertising	120.00
Bank service charges	15.00
Bookkeeping	213.30
Computer & Internet	199.00
Continuing Ed	149.00
Dues/Subscriptions	15.00
Merchant Accounting Fees	195.00
Office Supplies	80.70
Owner's Payroll Wages	3,500.00
Owner's Payroll Taxes	315.00
Professional Fees (business coach)	800.00
Rent (office)	1,000.00
Software (practice mgmt. system)	39.00
Telephone	157.30
TOTAL EXPENSE	$6,798.30

Net Business Income	$1,721.70

Saved for profit (5% of total income)	$426.00
Saved for taxes (15% of total income)	$1,278.00
Net after taxes and profit saved	$17.70

Let's review Chloe Clinician's January P&L statement

You can see that she has three types of income: counseling sessions, rental income from renting an office in her suite to another therapist, and income from a speaking engagement totaling $8,520. Her business expenses of $6,798.30 include her normal office expenses, as well as payroll for herself. In this example, Chloe is an employee of her therapy business and pays both payroll wages and payroll taxes on her owner's salary. She pays herself $3,500 a month and her payroll taxes (state and FICA taxes) are $315 for a total payroll amount of $3,815.

Each week, Chloe took out money for profit (for a monthly total of $426) and taxes (for a monthly total of $1,278) and put that money in business savings accounts.

At the end of this month, Chloe breaks a little better than even after she saves for profit and taxes, pays her business expenses, and pays herself. So this month was a good one for Chloe. If she has similar or better P&Ls every month, she will have a solid and stable business.

What can you learn from a profit and loss statement?

In this example, Chloe brought in $8,520 of revenue for the month of January. Think about that for a moment. Do you consider that a good month? If you saw that number alone without looking at her expenses, would you think that Chloe's business was doing well? If she makes that amount (or more) every month, then she has a better than "six-figure" practice. Great, right?

Well, as your mama said, it depends. How much your business brings in is only part of the equation.

If Chloe spends more than she brings in, then her business is running at a loss, regardless of her income. You can begin to see why practice income alone cannot be the only measure of success of a therapy business. Income alone is only part of the equation. We need to make sure that the expenses are paid and the owner is paid. We want to make sure that we have money saved in the bank for taxes and future business expansion.

In my work coaching therapy business owners, I find that many of them talk about their income only. "I made $5,000 last month!" Of course, a great income is important, but we need to really understand the complete financial position of the business. If you are unclear regarding how well (or not well) your practice is doing – and why – I hope this chapter will help. The great news is that your P&L report will give you the information you need. Once you have the P&L and know how to interpret it, you can either celebrate or course-correct as necessary.

Now back to Chloe. We see that her expenses for this month are $6,798.30.

Since her income this month is $8,520, right away we can see that Chloe is spending less than she is making. So far, so good. We can also see that Chloe paid herself $3,500 in January. (This number came from her personal spending plan.) Because she is an employee in her business, she pays payroll taxes, so the total amount going to pay for her owner's wage is $3,815.

This is a very good sign. Chloe is paying herself a salary to support her personal needs and wants – and she is spending less than she is making in her business. This is another sign that she is doing well in business.

After she pays her owner's wage and her other expenses for the month of January, Chloe has $1,721.70 left over on her P&L report. This is called net business income. It is the amount that her business made for the month after she paid herself her owner's salary. But remember she has taken out her profit and taxes, amounts totaling $1,704.

Some clinicians will look at the amount left over after paying expenses and assume it is available for spending... either for the business or to put into their pocket.

But Chloe knows that she wants to run a profitable business as well as save for taxes. In the last chapter, we learned that Chloe's goal is to save 5% of all income earned and place it in a profit account. This month that number totaled $426 ($8,520 * .05 = $426). Chloe has put that into a business savings account. Her goal is to build up at least two months of operating expenses in her profit account. This will give her a good cushion against anything unforeseen in her business. It can be used for business expansion at some point if she'd like. She can even bonus herself as business owner in the form of a dividend if she wants.

She also saves 15% of her total income each month for taxes. Then, when tax time comes, she has the money saved and can easily pay her taxes. Chloe's total income for this month is $8,520 and her tax savings of 15% equals $1,278.

Some of you may look at that and think, "15% for taxes? I am in a *much* higher tax bracket!" And you might be. But remember, Chloe is saving 15% of her total income and she will only be paying taxes on her business income *after expenses*. But please ask your accountant what percentage of your total income you should be saving for taxes. It is an amazing feeling to have it right there at tax time and not worry about where you will get the money!

Sometimes there is some confusion between "owner's pay" and "business profit." Your owner's pay is what you pay yourself. It is your salary. Therapists often ask me, "How much should I pay myself?" If you have done the earlier exercises (identifying your personal expenses and creating your spending plan), then you know how much you need (and want) to earn to support your lifestyle. You will have an amount you wish to pay yourself based on your needs and wants. Chloe's personal expenses on her spending plan totaled $3,430, so she is giving herself a monthly salary of $3,500.

Most accountants would say that business profit is what is left over after you pay all the expenses, including your owner's pay. The profit of the business does belong to you as the owner and you *could* pay yourself all of it immediately. My recommendation is that you don't do that because you want to show that your business is making a profit. This is important if you ever apply for a business loan or want to sell your business. You want to show that you have a profitable business. Plus, as noted, you want to have money saved for emergencies. In the book I mentioned earlier, *Profit First*, the author, Mike Michalowicz, advises us to take our profit percentage immediately from our income. Mike notes that the "old" accounting formula is:

Income minus expenses = profit

But left to our own devices (and spending habits), many of us end up with little or no profit. He recommends the following formula instead:

Income minus profit = amount available for expenses

This is genius when you think about it. We then curb our spending to be in line with what is available and there is money saved for future business expansion – or bonuses to us, the owner! Our friend Chloe has taken his advice and stashed it away before spending any money on any of her business expenses. This means she will always run a profitable business.

Once again, I highly recommend the book if you'd like to take a more detailed look at your finances. To read more about *Profit First*, check out Mike's book here: http://BeAWealthyTherapist.net/profitfirst.

Summary of Chloe's P&L for this month:
1. Income was $8,520.
2. She spent less than she made. (Yay!)
3. She paid herself an owner's wage of $3,500 + $315 for payroll taxes = $3,815. This means her owner's wage was 45% of her total income.
4. Her business operating expenses (expenses minus her owner's wage and payroll taxes) were $2,983 ($6,798 - $3,815= $2,983). This means her business expenses were 35% of her total income.
5. She saved 15% of her total income available for taxes. (Great!)
6. She saved 5% available as business profit, which she will save to get two months' operating expenses. (Very good!)
7. After saving for taxes and profit, paying her owner's salary, and paying her business expenses this month, Chloe essentially broke even. Next month, she might try to get a couple of additional clients so she has more "padding" in her numbers.

Even though she basically broke even, this is a very good month for Chloe. Her business is financially very healthy and she is paying herself the amount she budgeted. And there is money saved for profit and taxes!

Comparison to her spending plan

Chloe set a monthly income goal (when she created her spending plans) of $7,535. This month, she exceeded that number. Since therapists tend to have a "seasonal business," there will be months when your income is higher than others – and vice versa. My advice is to assume you only have 44 weeks of a full caseload each year. This leaves two weeks for vacation, and extra time for continuing education, holidays, illness, and times – when for some unknown reason – your caseload empties out for an entire week. Expect and accept this fact. And work toward building two months of operating expenses in your profit account. This can help you have extra money when your caseload is lighter. It is even better if you save an additional amount for 'light months' so that you are not raiding your profit account.

There may also be months when your expenses are more. This month, Chloe's business expenses are right in line with her spending plan.

Let's take a look at her expenses as a percentage of Chloe's income for this month

Owner's Pay = 45% of total income ($3,815/$8,520 = 45%)

Business Operating Expenses (Expenses minus owner's pay) = 35% of total income ($2,983/$8,520 = 35%)

Taxes = 15% of total income ($1,278/$8,520 = 15%)

Profit = 5% of total income ($426/$8,520 = 5%)

These can be great percentages to shoot for, although you can talk to your accountant about what would be right for you personally. You may have found when you did your spending plans that your percentages were different. You may want your business to earn more for your personal life. Or you may want to run a leaner business so there *is* more for your personal life. Your job is to find the right balance for you.

After you create your P&L statement, you can calculate what your owner's pay, business operating expenses, taxes, and profit percentages are. You can also set goals. For example, if this quarter you were only able to put away 1% for profit, why not try for 2% next month?

What if there is a negative number at the end of your P&L statement for this time period?

If you have spent more than you've made, you had a loss during the time period of this report. This may or may not be a problem. Let's look at the reasons for a loss.

1. <u>One-time or irregular expenses</u>. If you are only look-ing at a one-month time period for your profit and loss statement, there may be an expense that you had been saving for and paid for in this month. For example, when I expanded our office space, there were furniture and tenant improvement expenses for January and February. These were one-time expenses, but for those months, my expenses were more than my income. Since this was planned for, I did not panic when I saw that the "income from business" bottom lines on the P&L reports were negative. Looking at a longer time frame helped. I could see that over the last six months (or projecting forward the next six months), things started to even out.

2. <u>Overspending.</u> Sometimes we simply spend more than we have. In our example, Chloe budgets 35% of her total

income for business operating expenses. She is actually
running pretty lean. Many clinicians spend 50% or more
on their businesses. Some who are uneducated on their finances think that if they make $2,000 a month, then they
have $2,000 a month to spend. They don't understand
that the money is earmarked for four purposes: Owner's
pay, operating expenses, taxes, and profit. We want to
make sure there is money saved for the lean times. We
have seasonal businesses as private practitioners. There
are some seasons where we make more than others. If we
are always spending all that we make, we will come up
short sometimes. That is not a good feeling and can be
prevented or planned for. If you are overspending, it is
the responsibility of the finance role and the operations
role (even if you are both) to assess the situation and
course-correct as needed. This may mean reducing your
spending, increasing your income with more sessions or
other income, or maybe even getting a loan.

3. Under-earning. There are many reasons for under-earning. It could mean that the marketing needs to be increased so the business gets more prospective clients
inquiring about services. It may mean that the operations
role needs to have a better intake call script and conversion percentage. It may mean that the clinician wants
to do fewer sessions than can support the personal and
business lifestyle she wants.

The P&L reports will tell you if you are under-
earning. Then all the roles in your business will get
together and come up with your next steps: More
marketing? Better response to phone calls? Improved
conversation with prospective clients when they

call in so the conversion percentage increases? Even though it is discomforting to learn that you might be under-earning, it gives you the data you need so you can decide what you want to do next. As I said before, it can take two to seven years to build a full and financially sustainable private practice. Some people find that a part-time job while they are building a business can be a welcome relief from money pressures due to under-earning.

I know this chapter is full of numbers and for my Alexis Avoider colleagues, you may be tempted to move quickly to the upcoming chapters and learn about how to create policies, procedures, and systems or increase and improve your marketing efforts. But I am going to beg you (I am not above begging!) to review this chapter so that you become clear on what a jewel your P&L report is. This report gives you the data to know how well your business is doing. If you have a feeling that things are not going well, you can look at your year-to-date numbers. You can compare this season (month or quarter) to the same season last year. You can also pair looking at your P&L reports with your call tracking logs. You can see that x number of calls resulted in y amount of income. You can project into the future. You can predict what might happen to your income and bottom line if you increase your calls by a certain percentage.

This is where the ease comes in. As you look ahead, you can predict your income and your expenses. You have money saved for the lean times and for future expansion. This knowledge is the foundation for your confidence as a CEO.

Getting Started

Most clinicians who study the profit and loss reports for the first time may find they are not doing as well as Chloe in our example. This is because nobody ever explained all of this to you before. Remember our judgment-free zone, okay? You have to start somewhere and that is by getting the data and looking at your P&L for last year (if you have it) and each month this year.

Once you know the state of your business, there are many, many actions you can take. And you can do so from all of your roles: the clinical role, the operations role, the finance role, the marketing role, and the visionary role.

Here are some examples: The therapy business owner in her clinician role may decide that, for the time being, she needs to do more sessions so as to increase the income. In the operations role, the therapy business owner may decide to start doing her billing more regularly so that more income is coming in faster. In the marketing role, the therapy business owner may decide to increase her number of networking contacts per week. In the finance role, the fees for new people may be reviewed and increased. In the visionary role, the therapy business owner may decide that she needs to rent out her office one day a week while she grows her practice. Or if her caseload is full and she doesn't want more clients, it might be time to add clinicians, which would bring more income into her business. See what is possible when you know your numbers?

What About Business Debt?

Recently, a new private practice owner said she did not have enough money to pay for a business checking account – and so she planned to comingle her personal and business expenses.

First of all, please have a business checking account for your business income and expenses. I recommend also that you have a business savings account for profit and taxes. (I have a business savings account for profit and a business savings account for taxes).

Second, I advised this new private practitioner to get additional funding before trying to really make a go of her private practice. When we are running that close to the bone, where a $15 a month bank charge causes concern, then every potential client looks like lunch money. We may accidentally appear desperate for business. You can receive funding by working another job as you are growing your practice, from family members or outside investors, or you can get a small business loan. Business debt is not *always* a bad thing. But make sure that you allocate it in your expenses and have a plan for paying it back.

Please don't burden yourself with so much debt that it is impossible to pay it back. My dentist is a great example. When she wanted to expand, she saved her money and was able to expand with no additional loans. Even though the clinician or visionary in her might have wanted to expand earlier, the finance role knew that saving was the right option for her.

For Center Owners with Associates in Your Practice

If you own a center (where you are earning income by billing for associate clinicians), your P&L reports will have one significant difference from Chloe's. You will want to take out the amount you pay your associate(s) from your total income. In other words, you will do your percentages based on your income *after you pay your associates*. In the future chapter, we will discuss compensation for your associates. So stay tuned.

In Summary:

Your profit and loss statements are key resources for you to assess the state of your business. From the data on that report, you can determine what will be the next steps to improve the financial stability of your business.

Next Steps:

1. Make a plan to create your P&L reports monthly. Will you have a bookkeeper or accountant prepare them or will you do it yourself? If you do it yourself, you can do it simply with a spreadsheet or with accounting software. Let's start this month.
2. Review your P&L reports for last year. See what the numbers tell you.
   a. Did you spend more than you earned? If you made a profit (after paying your taxes), how much was the profit?
   b. What percentage of your total income were your operating expenses? Your personal expenses?
   c. Based on what you learn from your P&L reports, what actions are you considering?

CHAPTER EIGHT

Therapy Business Essentials for Your Operations Role

The operations role gives therapy business owners the most difficulty. Perhaps it's because we don't save enough time for it. Simple tasks like finishing treatment notes, handling rescheduling requests, and returning new client calls – and especially the finances – can feel exhausting. And when we are this tired, who has time for anything else?

When I hear private practice owners complaining about operations tasks, I am very clear that I am speaking to the practice owner in their clinician role – and not to the practice owner in the CEO role. The clinician, as we have mentioned, is usually more interested in doing clinical work. This may lead to no one doing the operations role. And *someone* needs to pay attention to the operations of the business to make it run smoothly.

There are four steps to improving the operations of your business:

1. Define your policies as discussed earlier using the business decision triangle.

2. Create action steps (also called procedures or systems) delineating how you want to implement or enforce those policies.
3. Document your policies, procedures, and systems in your Operations Manual.
4. Assign responsibility for the implementation of those procedures. (In a solo practice, all responsibilities may be yours, so make sure you allocate time to do so.)

Someone asked me recently, "Why do we need policies and procedures? That sounds like a lot of corporate nonsense to me." I understand the sentiment as we all have seen dusty policy and procedures manuals that have no usefulness. But let's look at your practice. You understand that you need some type of cancellation/no-show policy. Why is that? The purpose of that policy is to take care of the business while providing consistent expectations for the client.

In fact, this is the goal for all your policies. When you document what you expect (your policies) and how you want your policies implemented, you have identified the very structure of how you want your business to run. There is no more guessing. You know *exactly* how you want your practice to run.

This structure is what gives you the ease in managing your business. You don't have to wonder how to handle various situations since you have identified and documented them ahead of time. This saves you time, and can lead to an increase in profit – all while helping your clients have a consistent experience. As we mentioned earlier, people love to return to places that give them good, consistent experiences. For example, if your policy is to return phone calls in two hours, your clients will come to expect this and feel well cared for.

There are three ways that therapists get in trouble with setting and implementing their policies. Let's use the cancellation policy as an example.

1. Inconsistency. Many kindhearted clinicians feel very uncomfortable about billing for sessions when clients have an illness or emergency and are unable to give appropriate notice before missing a session. What often happens is that these kindhearted therapists don't charge the client on the first few missed sessions. But at some point, these clinicians start to feel taken advantage of. They realize how much money the business is losing because of those missed appointments. They feel a bit disrespected by the client. Then they will charge for the next missed session. The problem with this is that the client assumes they're not going to be charged and to be charged intermittently can cause confusion, discontent, and distrust. And this can lead to a therapeutic break.

2. Leniency. Other clinicians have a very lax cancellation policy. They will allow the clients to cancel whenever needed. At some point, the sleeping CEO wakes up and notices that this leniency is leading to open blocks of time that could be filled by paying clients. If you have a 48-hour notice policy and you get it, you can often fill that slot. This results in additional income to the business. Therapists who are too lenient, and then want to change their policies with existing clients, often run into the same problems as a therapist who is inconsistent with her policies.

3. Unclear Policies. As noted, clients coming in for the first time are usually very focused on their pain and not very focused on your intake paperwork. I know you went over

it with them. I know you had them sign a copy of it. But three or four months later, when an emergency arises, most of them are not going to remember. It's important to expect and accept that you are going to need to remind your clients of your office policies and get a recommitment to those policies as you go through the course of treatment with them. This is not a power struggle here. It is simply about helping them to understand what you need, and maintaining the therapeutic alliance as you do so.

With the structure in place (knowing how you want things to run and having the steps documented), you can really begin to experience the joy of a smooth-running therapy business. For example, you can develop systems for answering the phone and assessing clients for appropriateness. When you are away from the office, your substitute will know what to do. When you decide to expand and take on new team members, you will do this from a place of calm rather than chaos. I have coached many therapists who came to me describing their business as a "hot mess." They have been so busy getting and seeing clients that they have largely ignored the operations role. All their practice policies and procedures (if they had them) were in their heads. But they would forget how to do something such as billing and they'd have to relearn it every time, costing them hours of wasted time.

On top of that, these busy clinicians often inconsistently implemented the few policies they did have. No time had been spent really planning how they'd like their business to run. Because they were so tired (from the clinician and marketing roles), they ended up hiring the first person who seemed helpful and then abdicated most if not all of the non-clinical policies to the new person. "You decide – just take it off my plate." These clinicians often complained they couldn't find anyone "competent" when actually what they meant was that they couldn't get anyone who could *read their minds*!

Recently, a therapy business owner told me that he had a practice management system that was not cloud-based. This turned out to be quite a problem when the computer died with all the schedules and records on it (and with a very old backup). When I asked the therapy business owner why he had made the decision to have a non-cloud-based practice management system, his response was, "Frank, our part-time tech guy hates cloud-based systems." When I tried to dig deeper, the therapy business owner had no answer as to why this significant business decision was left to Frank.

I'm not suggesting that you have to be an expert in technology. Of course you can ask experts for their opinion. But please make sure you understand the policies that you have in your business, as they are the foundation of that business. In this case, it turned out that Frank, the part-time tech guy, was unaware of some of the great, encrypted cloud-based practice management systems available. His choice of keeping it local with no regular backup cost the practice owner dearly.

Once you define your policies in the major areas of your business, such as front office, banking, finance, facilities, etc., you can define the steps you want done to implement those policies. Some call this a procedure; I call it a system.

A system is a set of action steps organized in a certain way so they can be executed in the same order each time, ensuring a consistent result.

We live in a world that runs on systems. When we drive a car, we follow a set of action steps designed to give us a consistent result every time. We stop at red lights, turn only when safe, watch for pedestrians, etc. Deviate from those systems – or worse, imagine not even having any driving policies or systems – and chaos ensues.

By documenting how you accomplish the tasks in your business, you create order. You save time, increase efficiency, provide a better experience for your clients, and increase your profitability.

You probably have a lot of systems in your business – or rather in your head – already.

For example, you have a certain set of tasks that you perform when you go on vacation. You may not be aware of how many steps go into closing your office for vacation. They may be something like these:

<u>Office Closing for Vacation Procedure</u>

Two weeks prior to the vacation:

- Get agreement from a colleague to be on call for you

- Discuss with the on-call colleague any concerns you have for current clients

- Explain to the on-call colleague how you would like him/her to handle calls from current clients

- Explain to the on-call colleague how you would like him/her to handle new client inquiries

- Get the colleague's phone number for your outgoing voicemail message

- Notify your clients x days in advance (and explain the on-call procedure)

Three days before vacation:

- Make sure all bills that might come due while you are away are paid in advance or scheduled while you are gone

- Address any housekeeping tasks such as mail delivery, banking, or plant watering that need to be done while you are away

- Make sure any clinical matters (billing or adjunct referral inquiries) that are due are completed

Last day before vacation:
- Connect with the on-call colleague with any last minute instructions and your contact info while away

- Change your voicemail greeting to include:
  "Thanks so much for calling the counseling office of xx. I am away from the office and will be returning on mm/dd. I look forward to returning your call upon my return. If you would like to speak to a counselor before then, please call my colleague, (name), at (number)…that is (name) at (number). Again, I look forward to speaking to you when I return. Take care."

- Close the office door and have fun!

When you return
- Connect with the colleague on-call and get updates on anything that happened while you were away.

Every time you go on vacation, you perform this simple set of routines. But when this routine – your system – is documented in the form of a simple checklist or as a flowchart, you do not have to reinvent the wheel every time. You don't have to worry about "what am I forgetting?" You simply pull out your system and check off the tasks as you complete them. The clinician on call for you knows what to do and you can relax on your vacation.

Imagine if you had systems for other tasks in your business – such as how you handle new intake calls, or schedule clients, handle client terminations, even save for taxes. As you create systems for your therapy business, several amazing things happen:

- You begin to relax – you do not have to keep so much in your head all the time.

- You find that systematizing your tasks allows you to get more done in less time.

- Your clients begin to have a consistent experience. They know what to expect and feel good and safe.

- You can someday (maybe someday soon!) bring in someone to help you manage your practice – and they will know exactly how you want things done since the system is documented. (Then the client gets a consistent experience regardless of who helps them.)

- You spend less time and effort struggling to manage your business.

- Your business becomes more profitable as your financial systems become systematized, too. You stop accidentally leaving money on the table. Simple systems and procedures, implemented regularly and consistently around cancellations and no-shows, can increase the bottom line by between $2,000 and $4,000 a year!

The logical place to document your policies and procedures is in an Operations Manual. This is not a one-and-done process. You will be growing and implementing your policies as you grow your business. Your visionary role will invite you to stretch and offer something new. Your operations role will then need to decide how to systematize and implement that policy.

Here is the start of a sample table of contents for your therapy business operations manual:

- Client Journey Policies, Procedures, and Systems
- Clinical Policies and Procedures

- Quality Assurance Policies and Procedures
- Finance Policies and Action Plans
- Marketing Action Plans
- CEO Dashboard (Tracking) Action Steps
- Facilities Action Plans
- Systems for Centers/Group Practices

Let's get started.

In Summary:

The operations role is one often ignored by therapy business owners. In fact, if you find yourself irritated at something in your business, it is likely that you are missing a system. What is a system? A system is a set of action steps that when executed in a particular order each time, provides a consistent result. Systems are the key to making the operations role easier and lighter and more profitable. Documenting your procedures in an Operations Manual can increase your confidence as well. Remember, as long as you own your business, you will be creating and improving your systems. Don't try to do this all at once. In the next chapter, we will talk about the Client Journey. That is a great place to start.

Next Steps:

1. Review the suggested table of contents for your Operations Manual.
2. Identify at least three policies that you want to develop within the next two months.
3. Document the steps (system) you will use to implement.

CHAPTER NINE

Policies, Procedures, and Systems for the "Client Journey"

Earlier you identified the type of experience that you want for your clients – both with you clinically, as well as with your front office operations and your physical space. Now we can look at what action steps you need to take to ensure that experience as the client moves through your business, from their first inquiry contact through treatment termination. I call this the "client journey." This is what your business is here for – to facilitate the client's healing journey.

The first step is to identify the unique steps in the client journey. Once you have defined the journey, you can then document your policies, procedures, and systems to smooth that journey for both the client and the business. By creating systems, our goal is to provide a consistent experience for each and every client.

Here are the steps for a typical client journey:

- The client inquires about services via phone, email, text, or web form.

- The client is contacted as soon as possible – preferably immediately.

- An intake conversation takes place where the client is assessed for appropriateness for the practice.

- In the conversation, the client is given information about fees and payment.

- If the client decides to come in for a session, the client is given options of dates and times (and therapist in the case of a group practice).

- The client is given information about paperwork and the office location.

- The treating clinician is notified of the new client. (This is especially important if the person answering the phone is not the treating clinician, as in the case of a front office receptionist, or if there are multiple clinicians in the practice.)

- Client appointment reminders may be sent out.

- The clinician welcomes the client on the first day of treatment.

- Treatment continues until the client and therapist agree the client has met his goals and is ready to end treatment.

- Client is given any appropriate community resources upon discharge.

- Termination notes are written and the case is closed for now.

- In six months, client's file or case is reviewed for check-in call, if appropriate.

You may have a few additional steps, but I think that is the gist of the client journey.

Now let's look at how we can create and implement policies and systems for the client journey.

1. Develop an intake call script

We discussed this as one of the Five Quick Strategies in Chapter Four and you can review my intake call script in the Resource Section of this book. There, you will find samples for both solo practices and group practices.

How you manage the intake call is one of the most important decisions you make. Do it well and your business will prosper. Here are some suggestions for a great intake call.

As I suggested in Chapter 4, I urge you to take a leadership role on the call. This will help your prospective client feel like they are in good hands.

The client will naturally have questions when they call. Show that you are interested in their questions and happy to help them. That said, my recommendation is that you redirect the conversation to their presenting problem prior to answering their questions. You want to know if they are an ideal client for you. If you don't want them as a client, answering their questions won't be necessary. In other words, it makes no sense to tell them what you charge before assessing if they are a good client for you.

Plus, when you take even a few minutes to listen to their presenting problem, it gives you the opportunity to join with them… to help them feel cared for. Do not underestimate the impact of this. I have had many clients tell me that feeling cared for on the intake call was the primary reason they decided to choose our center. This is true even though we are more expensive than many other therapists in the area and we don't take insurance.

If you do decide you want them as a client, of course you want to answer their questions. To be helpful and prepared, write out standard responses to the common questions such as, "Do you have a sliding scale?" and "Do you take insurance?"

The intake call and entire scheduling process becomes even more important when you have additional clinicians in your practice. You added additional associates so you could serve more people than you could by yourself. A central scheduling function that can help book the new client with the correct clinician (and schedule an appointment as soon as possible) is critical. We will discuss this more in Chapter 19, Expand Your Reach.

Consider your answers to the questions below when creating your intake call policy. After you create your answers, you can document the intake system for you or your team to use when answering the phone. (Mine is a giant flowchart form, but you could just as easily use checklists or print yours out.)

How will you answer the call?
How will you assess for appropriateness?
If not appropriate, to whom will you refer them?
How will you join with them?
How will you transition to telling them "how you work"
(your location and fees)?
What concerns (barriers to coming in) are they likely to have?
And how can you be helpful and responsive to those concerns?
What are the most frequently asked questions by new clients?

You may want to also create a policy and system for responding to text inquiries or email inquiries. For example, we know that a phone connection converts better than something via email. So when people email, I have a standard email ready to go that I personalize a bit based on their inquiry. If they ask, for example, about fees in the email, I tell them I am happy to answer their questions about fees if they give me a call. That way, I can make sure we are the right place for them – and if we aren't, I will be happy to help them find the right place. (You can see a copy of my email in the Resource Section of this book. I start with that and personalize it to the request.)

2. Identify who is an appropriate client for your therapy business

The client journey begins with the initial inquiry. But not every inquiry will be a perfect client for you. Make a list of the types of situations or diagnoses that you do not want to work with. In your intake call script, you can listen for these types of clients and have responses prepared for referring them elsewhere. When you have this process documented, and a client calls who is not your ideal client, you have the right words to say and the right resources for this caller. That benefits everyone.

I am sure you can immediately think of some diagnoses or populations that you don't enjoy working with, so let's actually build your business around clients you do enjoy. Take a moment and look at the clients in your current caseload. How is your energy level after your session with each client? One of the first things we do with the therapy business owners we coach is to ask them to evaluate their clients in terms of how much they enjoy working with them and feel energized by their work together. You do your best work when you are energized so if you aren't, look at why that might be.

You may be thinking, "I don't really need to spend the time documenting this. I know who I want and don't want in my practice."

But as your practice grows, you may not be the one answering the phone. Build your systems now so that when you hire front office support, they can easily move into the job and know whom you wish and don't wish to treat.

Besides, sometimes we "forget" whom we don't want as clients when the bank account gets a bit low. I often ask therapists when they knew that their difficult clients would be a bad match for them. A common answer is "on the intake call, but I was worried about money, so I thought I'd better take this client."

I understand that when finances are tight, we may be less discriminating about our "ideal client." But one of my favorite expressions is "the cheap comes out expensive." By taking on a client that you know from the beginning is not right for you, you do not serve the client. Let them (or help them) find a clinician who is a better match. You will do them and yourself a big favor.

3. Document Your Intake Call Script/Procedure

Earlier, I discussed how the intake call can be scripted to help you join with the client and help reduce the barriers to them coming into your office. You can review my intake call script in the Resource Section of this book.

How will *you* take a leadership role when a client calls to book an appointment with you? As mentioned, I recommend that you join with the client first before answering any of their questions regarding fees or insurance. You can answer all those questions after you have decided you want them as a client. If you do decide you want them as a client, how will you answer their questions about insurance or how much you charge, or if you take a sliding scale? To whom will you refer them if they are not ideal for you? All this becomes part of your intake call procedure.

Document your intake call script/procedure and the answers to questions you think prospective clients might ask. Have this near you when you answer the phone. Therapists around the world tell me how much this one system has increased their confidence and income!

4. Track Your Inquiries and Conversions

In the Five Quick Strategies section, I also encouraged you to track your inquiries and conversions. Now let's create a system to document your number of inquiries and how many of those inquiries become clients. Perhaps you will create a Google document or maybe collect the data simply in a notebook by the phone. Remember, knowing how many calls come in and how many are converted to clients gives the marketing role powerful information on how to improve the outreach. Develop a consistent system/procedure for tracking these numbers. Then whoever answers the phone can simply follow your documented system. A sample system could be:

    a. Create a Google spreadsheet with columns for
        Date
        Time of day
        Type of inquiry (Phone, email, text, web form)
        Prospect's name and phone number
        Presenting problem
        Referral source (if stated)
        Did they schedule an appointment? (Y or N)
        If so, date of scheduled appointment
        If not, why not? (if known)
        Intake paperwork sent or process explained (Y or N)

And, in the case of a group practice:
Which therapist the client was scheduled with
Therapist and practice owner *(if desired)* notified of
new client (Y or N)

b. When new clients inquire, fill in the sheet.

That is it – a simple system for tracking your inquiries. In a bit, we will talk about what other metrics you will want to track and how to review and assess those metrics. But the first step is to gather the data, and now you have a system to do so.

Follow the system and you will have the data to analyze. From that analysis, you will know what steps to take next for more income and more ease. More on that soon – let's finish defining the systems needed for the client journey.

5. Client Scheduling, Including Appointment Confirmation and Reminders

After the intake procedure, the next biggest operations task in the client journey is helping the client get in to see you! I advised you before to choose your clients rather than having them choose you. This starts with choosing the days and times you wish to work.

When I first started my practice, if you had asked me, "When do you see clients?" I would have said, "Whenever they want." I even left a movie theater midway through a movie once because a new client called and indicated they were ready to see me then. That is no way to run a practice with ease. Document the times you wish to work before you get on the phone with a client and only offer those times.

Beware of scheduling first-time clients too far in advance.

Often, if people schedule their first appointment more than seven days from the time of their initial call, they are more likely to no-show. One of our procedures at my center is to try to book the appointment as soon as possible. That said, we find that many "same-day" appointments end up as no-shows as well. These people tend to be very anxious and call to book an appointment for that evening. But by the time the evening comes, they've changed their minds and they are a no-show. So we have a policy that we try to book them within one to four days and, at this time, we're not taking same-day appointments.

You may have a different experience or desire for your client journey. I have a colleague who loves same-day, new clients and differentiates herself from others by indicating that she can "see you within 12 hours of your initial call."

My objective is not to have you adopt my policy, but to share with you how we use our tracking data to shape our systems. By knowing how many same-day, first-time clients no-showed, we were able to reshape our policy. The clinicians in my center were MUCH happier when we stopped scheduling same-day appointments since the cancellation rate was so high. If a client needs a same-day appointment, I simply refer them to my colleague. Win-Win.

How will you *confirm* appointments for new clients? Will you remind them prior to the session? Many therapists simply give the appointment confirmation information over the phone (or whenever they schedule the appointment) and do not send reminders. One clinician told me that her clients were adults and ought to remember on their own. I used to think that, too. But we are living in a world of alarms and reminders, so I thought I'd test it. Unsurprisingly, it turns out that reminders do reduce no-shows and late cancels. (Well, they reduce late cancels as long the client gets the reminder before the cancellation window. At first I made the mistake of sending out the reminders 24 hours before the appointment when we had a 48-hour cancellation window. I have since changed that so the reminder goes out two business days before the session. That gives people enough time to cancel with notice. And it gives me enough time to offer the opening to someone else.)

Here is a sample (documented) scheduling procedure:

- Clients can schedule an appointment at the Orange County Relationship Center either via our online scheduler or by talking to the Client Ambassador.

- If new clients call in for their first appointment, the Client Ambassador assesses for appropriateness using the intake call script procedure.

- Part of the intake call script is to ask the new client if they would rather see a male or female therapist. We also ask them when they would like to book their session.

- We then look at the calendar and book the next available time with that therapist.

- If they have no preference on therapist, we give them two or three options for times within the next one to four days and the appointment time they select is put into the calendar.

- Immediately after the appointment is scheduled, the clients are sent a confirmation email with directions to the office and a link to their online paperwork. The treating therapist is notified via email or text that they have a new client.

- The clients are advised that they can fill out the paperwork over their phone or computer via an online site.

- Then two days before their appointment, the clients are sent an appointment reminder text or email, depending on how they'd like to be reminded. These reminders come out automatically from our practice management software.

This scheduling procedure is well documented so that any new administrative staff is usually up and running and booking appointments very quickly.

6. Client Intake "Paperwork" System

How will your client receive the intake paperwork from you, fill it out, and return it to you? When documented, your process may look something like this:

When a new client schedules their first appointment, they are instructed to visit the page XXX on our website and download the intake forms. They are asked to fill those out and return those at the time of their first session. An additional copy is placed on a clipboard in the waiting room in the event that the client forgets to fill this out or bring it.

Or your process may look like this:

When the client schedules their first appointment either via the online scheduler or the front office receptionist, they are instructed to visit our HIPAA-compliant, cloud-based system where they can fill out their intake paperwork via phone or computer. When this is filled out, the cloud-based system sends an email to the clinician and the client letting them know the paperwork has been received. If the client does not fill out the paperwork, the front office person reaches out to the client the day before this session, asking them if they need the link again to fill out the paperwork.

7. Client Payment and Billing Policies

What is your business policy in terms of who pays you? Will you always be paid by the client? Or will you be billing third-party payers? Might you be billing employers, insurance companies, or other family members for your clients' treatment? The answer to those questions shapes your policies. In Chapter 11, Finance Policies, Procedures, and Action Plans, I share sample systems/procedures for how you can document your fee collection and billing process. Even if you use software or an outside biller, document what you expect to be done and when.

For now, just decide on your policy.

(a) From whom will you accept payment?

(b) Will you expect to be paid at the time of service or will you be billing for service later?

8. Client Termination

What is your process when a client terminates? What forms are there to fill out? Do you have a set of community resources that you refer them to? Do you have any recommendations for six-month follow-up visits? Documenting this reminds you of all the steps you need to take when a client terminates. Additionally, if you expand your practice and bring on any pre-licensed or licensed associates, you've already documented how you like to perform client termination.

9. Client Reactivation

What happens when a former client wants to return to work with you? How do you handle your fees with that client? Do you have them fill out new intake paperwork? Again, documenting these policies can help you clarify how you want your practice run and also help you save time. It can be as simple as having a checklist and just checking the tasks off as you do them. Less falls through the cracks and you have less to try to keep in your head! The older I get, the more important that is to me.

Documenting the client journey seems like a fair amount of work. And I won't kid you – it can be. But if you spend just a few hours, you would have the basics of your policies and your Operations Manual. You would have created a strong foundation and structure for the operations of your business.

And with it, your confidence as a CEO will expand exponentially.

Finally, remember that creating your client journey policies and documenting them in your Operations Manual is an ongoing project. Don't worry about getting it perfect the first time. You will hone and shape your policies over time.

In Summary:

Each client will have a journey into and through your practice. You want this to be a wonderful and consistent experience. The way to ensure this is to define the steps in the client journey, and develop clinical and operations policies, procedures, and systems, to make the journey smooth for both you and the client.

Next Steps:

1. Review this section for policies you might need to create for your client journey.
2. Take a few moments and envision your client journey. Really visualize it. Imagine the first time the prospective client contacts you. How do you want them to experience that connection? How do you assess whether they are right for you and your practice? How do you schedule? How do you get the intake paperwork to them?
3. Do a quick outline or mind map of what you just envisioned.
4. Document your client journey. You can do so in a mind map, checklist, narrative format, or a flowchart. Do what works best for you.
5. Understand this is an ongoing process. You will make modifications to your systems as you continue to grow and develop.

CHAPTER TEN

Policies and Procedures/Systems for Your Clinical Role

Remember, you want to identify your policies and systematize your procedures so that you make things easier on yourself and provide a consistent experience for your clients. In the previous section, we discussed how to best do this for the client journey into and through your practice. Now it is time to do the same for your clinical policies and procedures.

Whether you are a solo practitioner or have a group practice with multiple associates and locations, you will want to document the steps you take to do the following tasks. I'm sure you do many of these without thinking, but let's see if we can articulate and document your clinical policies and procedures.

1. Intake Session Procedure

Think for a moment. What is the purpose of the intake session? What is it you want to accomplish during the session? And how do you go about accomplishing your goal for the intake session?

Documenting the intake session procedure can help you feel more confident, the client gets a consistent experience, and the business will be more profitable and easier to run.

I am sure that different clinicians have different goals for the intake session. Here are some of the things that are important to me in an intake session:

- Assess and decide if I want this client and if I am the best therapist for this client

- If I decide I want to work with this client, I want to join with the client

- Discuss expectations and commitment – what I expect is an average length of treatment

- Review informed consent and office policies

- Discuss the "secrets policy" and confidentiality

- Obtain payment arrangements

- Schedule for future sessions

Once you are clear on your goals, you can develop an intake session procedures system to make sure that the session is designed to meet those goals.

The first step in your procedure might be to make sure that you are on time and welcoming to your new client. I personally use a technique called "the old friend" technique. As I am centering myself before seeing a new client for the first time, I imagine what it would be like to meet a dear friend I hadn't seen in years. When I go into the waiting room to meet the new client, I look at them with that feeling of meeting my old friend. I'm happy to see them. I'm warm and welcoming. I have a big smile on my face.

Other clinicians prefer to be more reserved when meeting their clients for the first time. A clinician once told me, "I don't want them to think I'm going to be their mother until I decide that. And often that is not for a few sessions. So I tend to be very reserved in the beginning."

The first step, then, is to figure out how you are going to present yourself as you meet new clients. Will you need a few minutes to relax, breathe, and ground yourself before you go to the waiting room? Will you be very friendly or more reserved at that first meeting? You may never have thought about this before. But if you want everyone to have a consistent and pleasant experience into and through your practice, I think it's time to think about it. Those first few seconds upon meeting set the stage for the relationship. What do you want that to look like? I have to tell you there was a time when I did not pay attention to this. Some new clients would get a relaxed welcoming version of me. On days when I was scheduled back-to-back without taking breaks, new clients might get a harried, not very present version of me. As I began to think more about this, I realized what version I wanted new clients to see and took steps to make sure that I was grounded and centered and on time.

Next, you'll bring them back to your consulting room. What will you do first? Do you take a history first or do you ask them why they are there? Or maybe you start with some other questions. Consider how you like to open your intake sessions. There are probably as many ways to do this as there are therapists in the world. What works best for you?

I like to hear the clients' story first. I like to hear why they are seeking therapy at this time. During those first 30 minutes or so, I am assessing the clients' strengths and deciding if I am the right therapist to help them. I want them to feel heard and respected. If I decide that I would like to take these clients into my caseload, I go over the office policies (including the "secrets" policy) and get their

117

commitment. I explain how I work and that we will probably be in weekly therapy together for at least three months. I also discuss the session lengths. As I work with couples, some couples come for 45 minutes, but many come for 90 minutes. I discuss the options and we decide on a session length.

I explain that we do things differently than many therapists in that we want feedback from our clients as to how well the clients perceive their therapy is going – and we would like that feedback at every session. That way, we can course-correct as needed. I discuss the outcome rating scale and the session rating scale (feedback informed treatment) as taught by Scott D. Miller and let them know that their input to me is very important. (You can read more about feedback informed treatment in the next section on Quality Assurance.)

At the end of this first session, I obtain payment arrangements for this session and for future sessions. I make it a point to be clear on fees and methods of payment. We also schedule at least the next three appointments.

In the Resource Section of this book is a sample Intake Session Procedure that I recommend for our clinicians at OC Relationship Center. Yours may be similar or very different. I encourage you to document how you want to organize that first session. In my experience, I have found that by documenting what you want to accomplish and listing the steps, you will feel more relaxed in session, and more confident as both a clinician and a business owner. Recently, one of the therapists at my center reported that these recommendations helped her to be of even more value to her clients.

If you like, you can also document how you do subsequent sessions and even termination sessions.

After you consider how you want to do the intake session, let's address some of the other clinical policies, procedures, and systems in your therapy business.

2. Scheduling for Future Sessions

What is your philosophy on appointments? Some clinicians consider weekly sessions best and work with clients to schedule standing appointment times each week. Others let the client take the lead. Spend some time thinking this out so that you do what is best for you, the client, and the business.

I work best when people come in weekly. This way, we don't lose traction. As mentioned, most of my couples come in for double sessions each week. That way, we get a lot accomplished and both parties have the opportunity to share their experiences and feel heard.

We can look at the business decision triangle to make this decision. What scheduling options work best for you as the clinician? For me, if they come too infrequently, I tend to lose track of the goals. I find that the clients do, too. The gains from the session before sometimes have trouble taking root if we spread out the treatment. And from the business' point of view? If clients come on an irregular schedule, it can become a scheduling nightmare. If a client is coming every other week, I cannot fill the open weeks with a new client because they won't have that time available on a weekly basis – so the business loses money. (Some of my colleagues tell me that they will take two clients who are on every-other-week frequencies and try to schedule them at the same time. When I tried this, one of the clients would inevitably ask to skip a week and the schedule became messed up quickly.)

Standing appointments (such as Mondays at 3 p.m.) work well for us when we take on new clients at the center. If a new client is unable to book a standing appointment, we try to get the next few sessions on the books. That way, if they need to miss a session, we know we have another session scheduled and don't have to play telephone tag to schedule it.

Now, what is your ideal policy on scheduling appointments?

3. Cancellation and No-Show Procedure

In an earlier chapter, I wrote that inconsistent policies can result in thousands of dollars lost each year. If you were going to spend time creating only one policy, start with your cancellation and no-show policy. Here are some things to consider:

- In general, what is the policy – 24 or 48 hours?

- What if the client is sick?

- What if they have an emergency? If you are going to allow emergencies, what constitutes an emergency?

- How will you handle the first missed appointment? And others after that?

- When will you actually bill them?

- How and when will you get a recommitment to the policy from them?

- How can you reduce future cancellations (if possible)?

- What if you are sick?

The choice of 24 vs. 48 hours for your cancellation policy is an interesting one. I find that 24 hours usually turn into 12… meaning the client sees "24 hours" as cancelling "the day before," regardless of the hour. So they may cancel at 8:00 p.m. for an 8:00 a.m. appointment on the following day. This means that you most likely could not fill that 8:00 a.m. slot with a new client. So for ease, we use 48 hours at my center.

Therapists vary about how they wish to treat the situation when a client late-cancels due to illness. Some therapists "forgive" late cancellations appointments if the client is ill. I understand this if you do not wish to sit in a small room with a client continuously coughing. That said, it could be an "easy out" for people who decide they don't wish to come into session.

Some therapists do not charge for missing an appointment due to illness if the client can reschedule in the same week. While this may be a nice policy for the client, the business suffers. A new client who would come regularly could have filled the open slot that the ill client takes that week.

I feel strongly that all clients get one late-cancellation or no-show appointment at no penalty. This gives me a chance to review the policy in session with them and get their recommitment to the policy.

What if you, the therapist, need to cancel on short notice? To me, the client's time is as valuable as mine. So if I need to miss, I give them one free session. When my husband, Bob, was in the hospital, he unexpectedly had to stay in for one more day. I found out the day before (less than my 48 hours) so I moved all my clients one day later. Then it happened again! So I had to move them all again. Since it was less than 48-hours notice both times (and since I had done it twice), they all got two free sessions. Yes, that month's profits took a hit, but those clients felt so respected. There were no therapeutic breaks and treatment continued easily and well with each of them.

As noted, a sample cancellation policy is in the Resource Section of this book.

One more point about no-shows and late-cancellations: I have found that often no-shows or late cancellation appointments are the result of a therapeutic break. Sometimes the clients don't have words to express that something doesn't feel quite right and they tend to act out by missing appointments. In many cases, I will invite the wayward client back for a session "on the house" just to reconnect. This free session has resulted in several clients recommitting to treatment. This helped the client, me as clinician, and served the bottom line of the business.

4. Progress Notes

Most of the time, we love our clinician role. The one part of the role that many of us don't care that much for is writing our treatment and progress notes. Decide how and when you wish to document your clients' progress. Committing to a policy and system for doing your treatment notes will save you a lot of time and stress.

Your progress note system or policy could be as simple as "I complete at least a short note of important data for each client session before I leave for the day." Or you could have a template note that you fill in quickly and regularly.

A key indicator of how your system for progress notes is working is how you feel about doing them. If you feel anxious or avoidant, ask, "How could I do this lighter and more easily?" Often it is just a missing or broken system that is causing the problem. And imagine how you will feel when your notes are complete each day and you don't have to spend weekends "catching up."

5. Vacation Coverage

What are the steps you take when going on vacation? Do you have someone you regularly connect with? In the beginning of this chapter, you saw a sample vacation coverage policy. While admittedly this is not the most important procedure you have, documenting it can save you time and worry.

The coach in me really encourages you to find someone to be on call for you during your time off. Taking your cell phone and triaging client calls when you are on vacation or at a conference is not ideal. The whole point of getting away is for you to get some *space* from your clients and business. Give yourself this gift. Start going to association meetings if you don't know any other therapists. Meet other clinicians and see who might be available to be on call for you. Or see if there are others in your building who might be willing to share on-call responsibilities. Just make sure you help them understand what type of call you classify as an emergency and how you want them to handle emergencies (and non-emergencies), as well as new clients. Oh, and bring the on-call person a small gift when you return. It (and you) will be appreciated.

6. Incapacitation Coverage

What happens if you are unable to do the work? What happens if you are suddenly taken ill or pass away? Who notifies your clients and how are the records handled? To whom are the clients referred? As we therapists age, this is something that is vital to our practices. Please don't leave the disbanding of your practice – everything from notifying your clients to handling the art on your walls – to people who love you and are devastated by the loss. Professional wills can help, but can be problematic. What if the person you appointed to close your practice in the event of your death changes his mind or predeceases you?

I am proud to be on the board of Practice Legacy Program, a company that takes into consideration all the legal and ethical issues involved in practice closings – for retirement, incapacitation, or even death. For a monthly subscription fee, your practice will have the correct legal and ethical procedures in place. A trained therapist will come in and close your practice when it is time. It is not something we like to talk about, but we all will die – and many of us hope to do so after seeing one last client!

Let's not put our loved ones – who may not understand the legal ramifications of our work – in the awkward position of closing our practice. You can check out Practice Legacy Program at http://www.practice-legacy.com.

7. Quality Assurance Procedures: How to Best Serve Your Clients with Feedback Informed Treatment

How will you assess how well your clients are doing in their treatment? You can do so in several ways. Some therapists send out anonymous surveys. Some do thorough exit interviews.

I am quite partial to Scott D. Miller's Feedback Informed Treatment Model. If you are not familiar with it, the concept is quite simple. Scott and his colleagues discovered that 50% of clients leave therapy before their treatment goals are met.

FIFTY PERCENT! This has huge implications for the clinician, client, and the business.

In your clinical role, of course, you want all your clients to have positive outcomes. You want them to stay committed to treatment until their goals are met. You want to make sure that, in your work, you are actually helpful to them.

In graduate school, I learned that the best predictor of positive outcomes for therapy is the quality of the relationship between the therapist and the client. Scott D. Miller said it is actually the quality of the relationship between the therapist and the client *as*

124

perceived by the client. (I don't know about you, but I have been in relationships that I thought were going well only to be surprised when the other person ended the relationship. So of course, this would be true in our therapeutic relationships, too.)

I think exit surveys are too late. I also think asking the client, "So, how do you think therapy is going?" may lead to people-pleasing behavior on the part of some clients. That is why I love the Feedback Informed Treatment Model.

Scott Miller and his colleagues developed a set of measures to help you get at the client's perception of the therapy and the therapeutic relationship. It consists of two very short, four-question surveys that are given at each session. The four questions have a Likert scale next to each so that answering them requires just a pencil and an X at the appropriate spot. They each take about a minute to administer.

The first one is called the ORS (Outcome Rating Scale). The questions are regarding how the last week went. It is given to the client when she comes in the office. Over time, you can see if the client is reporting on the ORS that her weeks (between sessions) are improving. If not, then perhaps some different interventions (or a different therapist) may be needed.

The second inventory is called the SRS (Session Rating Scale). This too is a four-question survey with a Likert-scale answering grid. Given to the client at the end of the session, this instrument measures how well the client thought this session went. It helps you, the therapist, know if you were able to meet the client's needs this session.

Scott told me that the goal of these instruments is not to try to get perfect scores. The goal is to help you – session to session – evaluate how well the client perceives your work together. The goal is continued improvement. If you do not see that, then as noted, another therapist or set of interventions may be best for this client.

What I love about this model is that you get immediate feedback. One time I thought I did a particularly brilliant session with a man, only to have him report on the SRS at the end of the session that he was not pleased. I am not sure he would have shared that if I had asked him to articulate it – or asked as he was leaving, "So was this a good session for you?" The Likert scale gave him the freedom to put the X at the "not so great" area.

The intent, as I understand it, is not to fully process the SRS at the end of the session but to have (and show) compassion toward the client – and be willing to change to help meet their needs. When I read it, I said to him, "I see I wasn't as helpful today. I am sorry about that. Is there something you wish to share now that will help me do better next time?" He shyly told me that I had given him too many things to think about this session. "I like it when you give me just one." Who knew? My brilliant-yet-overstuffed-session that I was so proud of was not that helpful to the client.

And the best part? Had I not created the space to look at it from *his* perception, I may have done the same in the next session. I predict that he might have left treatment – and done so feeling bad that he couldn't take in all I was offering him. I was so grateful and the client has continued in treatment, meeting his goals.

Not all clients will be able to articulate what did not go well. Again, the point is for them to help you be aware of it so that you can nimbly change course as needed.

I am not a trainer for Feedback Informed Treatment, but I encourage you to learn how to use these measures. You can Google Center for Clinical Excellence or even Scott D. Miller ORS SRS to find out more.

In Summary:

The clinical role is the role we are most familiar with. You could probably be a great clinician without ever creating or documenting your procedures. But remember: the point of policies and procedures is two-fold: (1) to create a consistent experience for each and every client and (2) to make things easier for you.

Next Steps:

1. Start with your intake session goals and create a checklist or system so you can cover the important aspects of the session in a consistent manner.

2. Review the cancellation policy questions in this section (and, if you like, my sample procedure in the Resource Section) and document your cancellation and no-show policy. Include the process as to how you will handle it the first time the client is a no-show. And what about subsequent sessions? Thinking about this (and documenting it for yourself) can save you time, frustration, and money later.

3. Review this section for other policies and procedures you may wish to create.

CHAPTER ELEVEN

Finance Policies, Procedures, and Action Plans

In earlier chapters, we went through the steps of understanding:

- How you are spending your money now
- How to set revenue goals
- How to create a joyful budget and
- How to measure if your budget is on track using your profit & loss report.

Since our goal is to help your business be financially sustainable, let's continue with the finance role and take a look at your finance policies and procedures. These are your desires and plans regarding fee setting, negotiating, and collecting. They include billing and banking.

When I was a newbie private practitioner, I was not good at setting or collecting fees. My supervisor (a very wise man) said to me, "You don't have to charge people for your services. Why not set up shop downtown on a curb and help people as they pass by?"

Arrogantly, I retorted, "I don't want to do that! I want a nice office where people come to see me!" His response has stayed with me for nearly 20 years. "Then you better get good at setting and collecting your fee."

1. Setting Your Fees

Determining your fees should be done with thought and planning from your visionary, finance, and clinical roles. The fees you charge should feel authentic and right for you. Please have clarity about your fees — even if you have a sliding scale — before you answer the phone. You will be much more confident on the intake call and you will convey that to your clients. Documenting your fee policy in your Operations Manual can help you have conviction in your fees — help you "own" them. (NOTE: *To be clear — when you document your fee policies and procedures in your Operations Manual, it is for YOU and your team only — not for publication to the general public.*)

As with most of your policies, there is no one right way to do things. But the more that you clarify how you want things done, the easier managing your business will be. At the same time, know that there will always be new situations where you will add to your policies and procedures.

Here are a few sample fee setting and collecting policies to guide you in creating your own.

Sample #1: "My fee is $xxx per 45 minute session. I have two low-fee slots. I am not on any insurance panels and I don't accept third-party reimbursement. My clients are expected to pay at each session. I do provide a receipt of money collected. If the receipt contains a diagnosis, the client and I have a discussion about that diagnosis. I do not bill any third parties of non-minors. For example, if my client is a college-aged young adult, the client brings payment to each session. If the parent has agreed to pay for the session, the client and the parent can work out the reimbursement between them."

Sample #2: "I accept insurance panel and managed care reimbursement: (list of third-party payers). For those who do not have or do not want to use insurance, my rate is $xxx per 45-minute session."

Sample for a Center: "Our fees range between $xxx and $yyy as the associates in our practice set their own fees. We provide clients with a statement of services with a diagnosis–that we discuss with the client first. The client can choose to submit it to his insurance company if he likes, but we are not a party to that agreement."

Questions to ask yourself when setting your fee policies:

- Will you be accepting third party payments? If so, from whom? (Insurance companies, EAPs, employers, family members, places of worship?)

- What is your "fee-for-service"? (Non-third-party rate)

- Will you have a sliding scale? If so, what is the range of the scale? And when will you slide? (Meaning what are the requirements?)

- Do you have an intake session fee that is different in terms of session length and/or fee? If so, what is the time/fee for that?

- Do you offer different fees for different types of services?

2. Payment Collection (including billing)

Will the clients pay their fee (or co-pay) at the beginning of each session? Will you be billing? If so, whom do you bill and when? Will you offer to bill parents or employers or do you require the client to pay at each session (and be reimbursed by the other party)?

Recently in my center, a young couple came in for couples counseling. The young woman gave her mother's credit card for us to bill. At first, since they had similar names, we thought the card was our client's card. When the card was declined, we called the client and she told us to call the mother, as it was the mother's card. That presented a rather awkward situation. Since then, we are clear that we only accept payments from our clients.

As a reminder, your business needs fuel and that fuel is cash and clients. Many therapists could increase their income simply by being more careful and thoughtful about how they *collect* fees. Your clients owe you for your time. Please do not let clients build up a debt. Building up a debt actually puts you in a dual relationship in that now you are both their therapist and their creditor.

To develop your fee collection policy, consider:

- Will you expect your client to pay all or part of the fee at each session? If so, when during the session will you expect the client to pay? (Beginning? End?)

- What types of payment will you accept? Cash, credit cards, checks? Will you accept payment from relatives of a non-minor client? (ex: parents of young adults)

- What if your client "forgets" to bring her/his payment?

- What if your client asks you to bill him monthly?

Below are some sample fee collection policies; you can merge several pieces from each to create your own. If you use a billing or practice management system, it would be important to have a separate set of action steps (a system) documented to show how you input the data into the system and how you review payments.

Sample Fee Collection Policy for Fee-for-Service Practice: "The fee is expected at the time of service." This is written into my informed consent so the client is aware of it. At the first session, I clarify my policies and explain that after the first session, I collect the fee at the beginning of the session. Since I use a credit card capture device on my smart phone, when the client comes in, I say, "Let's check you in. Did you want to bill this session to your card today?" If yes, I swipe their card. If a client pays by check, I invite them to write their check ahead of time so that we spend the whole session on their issues and the finances are taken care of. Cash is also accepted. By having them pay at the beginning, I save time at the end of the session as all the "finance" details are taken care of. This also allows me to address any clinical issues around the client not having their method of payment available. The clients themselves must make payment – I do not accept credit cards or checks that are in the name of family members.

Sample Fee Collection Policy for an Insurance-Based Practice: When a client first schedules an appointment with us, we verify her benefits and know what to explain to the client about her benefits. At each session, we collect her co-pay. At the end of each day, we do online submission of the claims for the clients who were seen that day. If the client arrives without her co-payment, she is allowed to continue the session and be "one-behind." At the next session, she is expected to have the co-payment she owes as well as the co-payment for this session. If she does not have the co-payment at that time, the session is spent on dealing with why she thinks that might be happening... or the client is invited to go to the nearby ATM. Twice a month, I go through the outstanding insurance claims to see what has not been paid and take appropriate action.

<u>Another Sample Fee Collection Policy for Out-of-Network Fee-for-Service Practice:</u> In my practice, we do no insurance billing. We accept payment at the beginning of each session. Should the client request it, we will create a receipt for the client indicating the amount he paid, the CPT code, and diagnosis. The diagnosis and related implications are discussed in detail with the client. He has the option to submit that to his insurance provider. I explain that I am not a party to his insurance contract and do not know if and/or how much he might be reimbursed. We accept credit cards, cash, and checks. Any bounced check or declined credit card issues are considered clinical matters and are discussed with the client at the beginning of the following session – and not via email, phone, or text.

3. Fee Increase Policy

We can look at fee increases in two ways –for new clients and for existing clients. It is perfectly fine to have different policies for each. For new clients, you can choose to set your fee as you like.

Existing Clients: As we've discussed, all policies should be made with the best intentions for the business decision triangle: the business, the clinician, and the client. Fee increases for existing clients are a perfect example of where we must look at all three before deciding on a policy.

At first glance, it appears that increasing the fee will bring additional income into the practice. However, some studies show that increasing the fee for a client while in treatment – even if stated in the informed consent – can cause a therapeutic break. And if that happens (and the client leaves treatment), it can actually reduce the income for the practice.

I know that many clinicians have annual fee increases. And here is the thing about that: it makes sense to both you and the client that you would do this. *Cognitively.* But what about emotionally? You have agreed to "love" them (aka treat them) for a certain amount of money per session. Now you are saying that you will continue to do so, but want to be paid more for it. Again, clients will rarely argue with an annual fee increase – after all, they know they agreed to it in your informed consent. But if you do this, I invite you to track how many clients end up "cured" and terminate treatment within a few weeks of the increase. Again, there is no right and wrong and you must do what is right in your heart. Just please look at it from all your roles and consider the potential negative consequences if your plan is to have annual fee increases.

That said, if you are in any way resenting the client for the fee that you set, you could think of this as a "gift in dirty paper," meaning that client has given you the gift (reminder) that you won't offer a fee you will resent again. If you cannot get past your resentment on your own, get consultation about the alternatives. Perhaps you tell the client you will be increasing your fee for them in three months by x%. That gives you time to either finish your work together or help them find another therapist for whom they would be a better match.

To develop your fee increase policy, decide:

- Will you keep the clients at the same fee throughout their treatment or will you have regular fee increases for existing clients?

- Will you increase the fee if a client sees you for some period of time, terminates treatment, and then returns when you have a higher fee?

Sample Fee Increase Policy: All clients will pay the fee they agreed to throughout their treatment. If a client terminates therapy for a year or more and wants to return, I will explain the new fee. I might consider taking them at the old rate if I will not resent them. If ever I find I am resenting any client due to the fee that I agreed to, I will get consultation and decide if I can reduce my resentment and do good work with this client, or if I need to tell them the fee is going up in three months by x%, or if I need to transfer them to someone who would work better with this client at this budget. I will consult with a peer supervisor before discussing any options with the client.

4. Fee Decrease Policy

What if a client tells you, "I cannot afford this any longer" and you wish to continue to work with the client? You could lower your fee for this client of course – as long as you will not resent the client. If you would resent the client, consider getting consultation to see if referring the client to another therapist who could work within the client's budget would be in the best interests of the client, you, and the business.

Consider how you will handle it if a situation occurs where the client is out of money for a while due to an event (such as a job loss) but wants (or needs) to continue with therapy. I caution you against deciding to lower or eliminate the fee until the resolution of the event. I once said I'd reduce a client's fee to $0 until she got a new job. She did not get a new job for THREE YEARS.

If your client wants or needs a fee decrease, one option is to reduce the fee for a period of time and explain to the client, "Let's reduce your fee to $xxx for three months. At the end of three months, one of four things will likely have happened. Either our work here will be done – you'll graduate, or the situation will be resolved (you'll have a new job), or we will revisit this agreement to see how we both feel about it and possibly extend it a short while more, or we will transfer you to a therapist who might work better within your budget. What do you think?"

Another option is to continue to see the client and let them accrue a bill. Please note there is a possible problem with this in that the bill might become a real burden to the client based on all the other financial stressors they have. It might impact treatment in that they might be afraid to face you. Plus, you now have a dual relationship in that you are the therapist and creditor. You may experience some unexpected countertransference.

There are any number of ways you can handle this, but addressing it now will help you prepare for this eventuality.

5. Banking Procedures

When will you get any checks or cash to the bank? I used to only bank every other week. Most people paid me via credit card so there weren't a lot of checks. I'd wait a couple of weeks until I had accumulated about 10 checks before going to the bank. I stored them in my wallet. Well, my wallet was stolen. I had to call all the clients and ask them to stop payments and reissue checks.

My recommendation is to get your checks into the bank as soon as you can. Smartphone banking can save a trip to the bank.

What about depositing your cash? A while back at a therapist conference, a clinician asked several of us, "Do you claim all your cash as income?" He indicated that a lot of his peers did not. First of all, I highly recommend you follow the tax laws about reporting all your income. Second, if you do not record the cash your business brings in, your profit & loss reports won't be accurate. You can't make informed decisions with only part of your income reported. It is simply a bad business decision not to deposit your cash.

Some clinicians do record cash deposits in their accounting systems, but do not deposit the cash in the bank. They use any cash received for personal spending. Again, please don't do this. Deposit your cash and then pay yourself the wage you have calculated in your budgeting process.

In Summary:

In this chapter, we discussed the intersection of the finance role and the operations role. Several policies regarding fees need to be established and my recommendation is to do so before you NEED to do so. Fee setting, collecting, (and renegotiating) are part of the very foundation for the success of your business. As you go through the questions in this chapter, consider developing your procedures through the lens of the business decision triangle. How can you make sure your policies work for the good of all concerned?

Next Steps:

1. Review the questions in this section to develop your policies. You want to know how much you charge, who pays you, when they pay you, and how they pay you.
2. What is your policy on fee increases and decreases?
3. What is your banking plan? Remember, you don't have the money until it is physically in your account.

CHAPTER TWELVE

Facilities, Technology, and Hiring Practices

Let's just pause here and look at what we have addressed so far. You have designed the journey that you want your client to take into and through your practice. You have developed policies, procedures, and systems to make that journey smooth and relatively seamless. You have identified your business and clinical policies to help your business run with more ease. You have addressed the financial measures and reporting so you can build a business that is profitable. Can you see how amazing this is? Some clinicians tell me, "It is like I have been running my business in the dark! Now I have found the light switch!"

There are a few more areas to address to continue to create ease in your business. Let's start with your physical space and your facilities procedures.

Facilities Procedures

If you are a solo-practice and there are no renters in your suite, you may not need a detailed facilities procedure. On the other hand, if others are in your space, it is a good idea to document how you want the place to be maintained.

Below is the procedure I have for our counseling center. Before I created this policy, I was continually mentioning parts of it to different clinicians, but they were busy and would forget. My goal was to make sure that at the end of the day, the center was ready for clients the next day. Here is what I created for them:

1. Supplies
Extra snacks and drinks are stored in the kitchen cabinets. There you will also find extra business cards, a first aid kit, cough drops, headache remedies, paper for the printer, and pens, etc.

You will also find a basic tool kit there with a hammer and screwdriver, as well as extra batteries for the clocks.

There are laptops available in both the kitchen and hallway for booking clients and checking email. Please make sure you log out of the practice management system when you end your session at either computer.

The refrigerator will be cleaned of any perishable items on a weekly basis. Please be aware that there is no freezer in the refrigerator.

Please let Casey or the Client Ambassador know when any supplies are running low.

2. <u>Wi-Fi</u>

We have two Wi-Fi networks available: one for clients (Relationship Center Guest) and one for our therapists (Netgear 62-5G).

    a. The login password for **therapists** on Netgear 62-5G network is: **(password here)**

    b. The login for clients on the Relationship Center Guest network is: vacation

    c. (This is printed on small cards in the waiting room for our clients.)

3. <u>Entry Codes for the Restrooms</u>

Men's room– yyy

Women's room –xxx

(These are also printed on small cards in the waiting room for our clients.)

4. <u>Facility Contact Info</u>

Property Manager: (name and phone number)

<u>Electrician: (name and phone number)</u>

I list here any other people we need to contact or any other vendors we hire.

5. <u>Air/Heat Policy</u>

While we work very hard to equalize the temperature in the waiting and consulting rooms, there will be variations. The thermostat is in Room B. It is set at a temperature that will be best for regulating the temperature in all the rooms.

If you find you are too cold or hot, please discuss with the person in Room B. Please talk with Casey about adjusting the temperature, as it is on a timer and, if that is changed, it can affect the people who come in after you.

6. Office Opening and Closing Procedures
We want our clients to feel welcome and appreciated. Part of this is being on time and having the office clean for them.

   a. Please arrive 30 minutes before your first session. This gives you a chance to settle in and prepare for your client's arrival. Since some clients arrive early (especially on their first session), we want to have the door open and the office ready.

   b. When opening the office for the day...
There are two keys to the office – one for the outer door, the other for the inner door that leads to the therapy offices and kitchen. Upon entering the office:

- Unlock the lower handle lock on the main office door.
  Turn on the lights.
- Make sure the call light switches are all facing the same way and that the call lights are out in the individual offices.
- Please remove any overflowing trash left over from the night before.
- Turn on the music in the waiting room:
  - Open the MacBook Pro in the hallway
  - Pair with the speaker in the waiting room
  - Turn on the Zingg music for the waiting room
- Turn on the K-Cup coffee machine in the waiting room, fill the reservoir with bottled water, set cups out and make sure that all supplies and snacks are

stocked. (Extra supplies are stored in the kitchen cabinets.)

- Turn on sound machines.

c. Choose your room for the day

Except in extreme situations, OCRC consulting rooms are not reserved so you may choose any available room when you arrive.

- Choose your room for the day and put your larger nameplate in the sign outside the room you choose. *(Office nameplates are kept in the kitchen drawer if not already in use.)*
- Put your small nameplate in the call-light system next to the room you will use. (For more on this, see the call light system process.)
- When you are using a room, please move the room status slider (in the sign) to say "In session."
- When seeing clients, keep inner waiting room door locked for your safety.
- ALWAYS take keys with you if you step out.

d. When leaving your counseling room for the day, please...

- Remove trash from the end or coffee tables.
- Straighten pillows on couches/chairs.
- Look for anything that needs to be cleaned up – rings on glass table from drinks or chocolate/lint in couches. (Windex in kitchen.)
- Please empty wastebasket if it is full.
- Replace tissue boxes if needed.
- Open blinds.
- Turn out lights.
- Leave door open with sign identifying the room as "available."

- Please notice if anything in the waiting room needs restocking.

e. If you are the last to leave in the evening, please...

- Refill waiting room fridge with water, tea, and soda – this should be completely full when the next person comes in.
- Make sure all call-light switches are facing the same way and turned off in each room; otherwise they burn out.
- Refill coffee/tea supplies (cups, sweetener, lids, K-cups, creamer, stir sticks).
- Make sure there are no used K-cups in the machines.
- Turn off the K-cup machines.
- Remove any trash or spilled creamer so the next person has a clean area to get their drink.
- Please make sure side tables are full with candy/ power bars.
- Please make sure everyone is logged out of the practice management system on both computers. (This is a security issue and we need to make sure we don't have sensitive data available after hours.)
- The inner door can be left open if you are the last to leave.
- Please lock the outside door top bolt lock if you are the last to leave.

Technology Procedures

The old joke is that there are only two types of people in the world – those that have had a hard drive crash and those that are *going to* have a hard drive crash.

So, your three most important words? Backup. Backup. Backup.

Here are some things to consider with your technology policies:

- Email – What will be the email address that you use? Will you encourage email contact with your clients? Do you need encrypted email?

- Practice Management and/or Scheduling Software – Will you use this? How? Make sure you export your data at least monthly.

- Phone System – How will clients reach you (during and after hours)?

- Laptop or desktop computer – What data will be on them? Passwords? Who has access? Backups?

- Backups – Schedule backups for everything: your website, online locator copy, any cloud-based records, etc. It doesn't hurt to have two types of backup – a cloud based backup and a hard drive backup.

- Passwords – There will come a day when someone needs a password. Decide early on where these will be stored and updated when changed.

Hiring Policies: For Center Owners, Group Practices, or Any Hiring You Might Do!

Many therapy business owners wait too long to hire additional staff. Often this results in hiring the first person available. Please take some time with (a) what services or tasks you need the person to do and (b) what type of person would be best.

Here are some things to consider:

- Creating Role Descriptions – What functions do you need performed? (Don't just hire someone because you are busy and then offload your work onto him or her. Create role descriptions first – then you can assign them one or more roles.)

- Recruiting – Where will you look? What is the application process?

- Hiring – Interview process, questions, and references. Will you do background checks?

- Training – What systems does the additional team member need to learn? Who will train them?

- Systems Setup for New Staff – What do you need to do to add new team members to your email system, practice management system, phone system?

If you document this ahead of time, the hiring process will go MUCH more easily and probably be more successful. If you have questions about this, consider getting a mentor – one who has done it before. It will save you a lot of time in the end.

In Summary:

As you can see, you can set up systems and procedures for every part of your business. Even though "facilities" seems like an odd choice for a procedure, the nightly office closing procedure listed in this chapter has improved the experience each client has when they enter our waiting room. Additionally, since the expectations were clear and documented, everyone easily follows it without struggle and inconsistencies.

Don't forget to pay attention to your technology needs – especially in terms of backups, passwords, and your client calendars and data.

And if you decide to hire clinicians in your practice (something we will talk more about in Chapter 19), consider documenting your hiring procedures. It will save you a lot of time later.

As a clinician and a business owner, you need policies. Policies are the choices you make regarding the principles of your business. You implement your policies with procedures called systems. Systems are repeated action steps that, when performed in the same order every time, provide a consistent result. Systems allow you to save time and provide a consistent experience for your clients and any additional staff members.

Documenting your policies, procedures, and systems in an Operations Manual means that you have a central repository for how your business runs. You can reach for it whenever you need to repeat a system (such as billing) and want a quick checklist for all the steps. It becomes very helpful when you hire additional team members. You know how you want things done and can get the new hire up to speed quickly. Plus, you are no longer abdicating how you run your business to a new hire!

Creating your Operations Manual is an ongoing process. The

point is to create a manual that helps you – not something you create and put on the shelf.

Next Steps:

1. Identify a table of contents for your Operations Manual.
2. Prioritize – Perhaps start with the client journey and your finance action plans.
3. Plan Time – This is the responsibility of the operations role and often gets overlooked. Yet, clarity in your policies and procedures is what the clinician role needs to make things easier to manage.

CHAPTER THIRTEEN

Tracking Systems
(Your CEO Dashboard)

CEOs are busy people. There is a lot of switching into different roles throughout the day. So how do CEOs "check the pulse" of the business on a daily, weekly, or monthly basis?

There is a term in the corporate world called "CEO Dashboard," which is a real time assessment of the key performance indicators of a business. In big corporations, there is fancy (and expensive) software that brings in all the data for the CEO to assess how things are going.

We don't need fancy software, but we do need to know what metrics are important for you to track. I have listed some suggestions for you below. The key to knowing how well your business is doing is to measure and then compare how you are doing in relation to other time periods. By taking a regular look at your metrics, you can interpret the data and decide on appropriate actions steps.

Below are some things you can track or measure. How do you collect the data? Most of it is simply counting and recording. You can do so with tick marks on a paper or in your calendar. You can do so with an Excel spreadsheet or Google doc, as discussed earlier in the client journey systems.

Some practice management systems will help you track several of these indicators. But please understand that you will probably not find one single piece of software that will collect all of this data. I tell you this so you don't waste time trying to find the Holy Grail of metrics-collection systems.

Beware of tracking just to track. The idea is to track and then interpret what the data are telling you. This way, you can use the data to make better business decisions and help you be a better business owner. So, if you are going to track *your* key performance indicators, decide right now that you will regularly (weekly and monthly) review the data so you can interpret what it means and decide your next steps based on the data.

1. New to tracking? Try quick start tracking by gathering these seven metrics for your CEO Dashboard

There are dozens of things you could track, but if you haven't done so before, start with just a few. This way, you can learn how to track and to intelligently interpret what the data are telling you. So, if you are just starting out, track these metrics:

1. **Income** you bring in each month.
2. The **expenses** you have in your business each month. (This will help you see if you are profitable.)
3. Amount saved this month for profit.
4. Amount saved this month for taxes.
5. **Number of inquiries you receive**. How many calls did you get? How many emails? How many texts? Track daily and total it for the month.

6. **Number of inquiries that turned into clients**. Track the number of new clients daily and total it for the month.

7. **Conversion percentage**. To find your conversion percentage, divide the number of new clients by the number of inquiries. (3 new clients from 10 calls: 3 divided by 10 = 30% conversion rate.

CEO DASHBOARD			
MM/YYYY	#	Comparison to last year	Notes
1. Income			
2. Expenses			
3. Saved for Profit			
4. Saved for Taxes			
5. Inquiries Rec'd.			
6. New Clients			
7. Conversion %			

Track your data by month and by season so you can compare season to season. For example, you may feel like this is a slow month as compared to last month. But if you look at last year during the same one-month time frame, you may find you are really doing well! I am writing this in the month of June. When I compared my June revenue for this year to June of last year, I see that our revenue has increased 104%.

153

2. The review process: How to interpret the call and conversion data and decide your next steps to improve your results

- An insurance-based practice should aim for 70-90% conversion. A cash-based practice should aim for 30-60% conversion. If your conversion rates are lower than that, you need to improve your intake call script/connection with them.

- If you convert a high percentage but don't have a lot of inquiries, then you need to improve your marketing. Learn what works, get more focused, or increase your efforts. If you aren't successful doing this on your own, get a coach who knows how to market a therapy business to help you figure out what to do – or not do.

3. Set goals based on the data

After you compile some baseline data, you can set goals to increase your number of inquiries, conversion percentage, number of sessions per month, and income. You may find that you now get 20 calls a month and convert 30% of them (or six of them) to clients. You may set a goal to increase your marketing so that you get 24 calls a month and convert 50% (or 12) of them to clients.

4. Advanced Metrics

Once you have been tracking and using the data above consistently, add these indicators to your tracking process:
- Average length of stay of a client
- Average amount a client spends with you
- Number of clients who no-show for the first session

- Number of clients who come for one session and don't return

- Marketing efforts (where are your clients coming from?)

- If you have third-party payers, how much do you make each month from each third party?

- For center owners: Number of new clients given to each provider and how long each provider keeps clients

- With your finance data, you can track the amount saved for profit or taxes

Plan a monthly, quarterly, and annual review. With this additional data, you can see how your therapy business is doing and set goals as desired. Again, it is better to track less and actually use the data than to track too much and never look at the data.

Then, in your review process, you can ask, "What are the data telling me?" Here are some examples:

a. Review of Your Marketing Activities and Investment: Let's say your marketing efforts cost $500 and bring you two clients. If you know that an average client spends $2,000 with you (for a total of $4,000), then that $500 investment was well spent. You may choose to increase your budget to see if you can attract more clients with that strategy.

On the other hand, if you invest that $500 and get no clients, then that may not have been a good strategy. Don't throw it out right away, though. Continue to ask questions such as "Did I give it enough time?" and "Is there some way it could be improved and work better?" If you have given it at least three to five months and are still getting poor results, then perhaps it is time to improve it or stop that activity.

b. Review of your intake and scheduling (front office role): If a significant portion of clients no-show for the first session (more than 20%), then you can infer that there is something wrong in the intake process. Try to improve the connection when you speak to the client. Perhaps you need to add reminders to your client journey system.

c. Review of client retention: What if you find that people show for the first time, but only come a couple of times after that? Perhaps you haven't helped them understand the commitment to therapy. It could be that you might not have joined with them well enough. Or maybe you took on a client that truly could not afford weekly therapy.

One clinician told me, "The client knows what is best for them. I let them decide how often they need to come in. Many of my clients come every other week or even monthly." I asked her, "Do you do your best work with irregular frequencies like that?" She admitted she did not.

Clients come to therapy because *you* are the expert on the problem they have. If they were complete experts on their own issues, they wouldn't need your counsel. Clients want and need your expert opinion on how often they should come in. You do not serve them if you do not give them your expert opinion on what they need. If they cannot afford the frequency in which you do your best work, in my opinion, we need to help them find the therapist that is a better match for them.

d. <u>Review of Income by Third-Party Payers:</u> Say you decide you want to move from managed care panels to a cash practice. (My recommendations for the steps to do this are in a later chapter.) You can expect that move to take at least a year and most likely, two or three years. The first place to start is to build and consistently implement your marketing plan. At first you will attract managed care clients as well as cash clients. That is fine. You want to track your marketing efforts to know when it is time to start removing yourself from the panels. You will start removing yourself from one panel at a time. When you know how much each pays you, you can make decisions on which to drop first.

Do you see how the tracking data (your CEO Dashboard) can help you make better-informed decisions? Your data can show you what is working – and what is not working. From there, you can course-correct and continue tracking and measuring your results. This is just one more set of activities to help you be the confident CEO your business needs. Whenever I share this with therapists and they see their data for the first time, they feel a whole new clarity. Even though they may not be completely happy with what they see, they know what needs to happen. I love it when this happens!

In Summary:

Track your income, expenses, inquiries, and conversions in order for the finance and marketing roles to know which steps to take next. I also encourage you to track how much you have saved for taxes and profit. It can feel great to see that you are really running a financially stable business. And if your numbers don't look great, you can use the data to assess what is wrong and adjust. These numbers – your CEO Dashboard – can help you make sound decisions for the future of your business.

Next Steps:

1. Create your own CEO Dashboard and decide what you will track. Start with just a few, and add as you grow more comfortable with the process. Don't overwhelm yourself with too many metrics to start.
2. At the end of each month, review your data and ask, "What is this data telling me?" Get help if you don't understand. Tracking without a review is a waste of time. The point of tracking is so you can determine which actions to take next *based on what you learned from the data.* You can do this!

In the next chapter, we're going to move into the marketing role of your therapy business.

CHAPTER FOURTEEN

Marketing Action Plans

Unless you have had a full practice for years, you will most likely need to market your practice consistently to stay in business. Otherwise, how are people going to find you? Many therapists assume that word of mouth (or even insurance panels) will be enough. The bottom line is word of mouth is wonderful and I consider it dessert. I enjoy it, but I can't count on it to provide me the basic fuel I need. And we know your business needs fuel – and that means new clients and income.

There is a lot of crazy information and many misconceptions about marketing. So I want to share with you in upcoming chapters what works now (and why) and what does NOT work to attract clients into your practice.

Your marketing role will design the marketing plan. As with your policies and procedures, you will want to document some of the repetitive actions in your Operations Manual. You do this so that you know what to do, how to do it, and when. Before we create your personal marketing plan, let's take a look at some sample action plans. I break up my marketing into two sectors, offline or community marketing and online marketing.

1. Community Marketing Plan Action Plans

You want to choose at least some community marketing to continue to be known in the community. The community is filled with people who truly want to refer to a therapist, but don't know anyone in particular.

That said, community marketing takes a while to produce results. The sole goal of community marketing is to build relationships. As you do so, people will be inclined to refer to you. Please be careful and remember – you are not selling you or your services. You are in the process of building relationships. Above all remember: relationship before request. In other words, please don't ask for referrals. Build relationships and people will want to refer to you.

Below are some samples of community marketing actions. Please note that this is only a sample of how to document your procedures; it's not meant to teach you all about marketing. We will go in-depth on how to choose your marketing strategies in the future chapters.

After reviewing your own community marketing strategies, create your own marketing procedures with the activity, steps to do the activity, and the frequency of the action.

Sample #1 Community Marketing: Speaking
Goal: to speak at least once a month in the community

Initially:
Create three to five fun, fresh, and unique talk titles and "blurbs."
Identify 10 (or 20) places to speak.
Create intro letter to send to program directors. (See a

sample in the Resource Section.)
Get contact information for the program directors for
the 10 (or 20) places to speak.

Weekly:
Send intro letters to at least five people on this list.
Follow up in one week with emails or calls to those five.
Look for five more places to speak.

Within 12 to 24 hours after each talk:
Follow up with those who wanted more information.
Schedule any consultations.
Track my efforts and conversion. (How many people
from the talk requested a consultation and how many of
those became clients?)

Quarterly:
Review list of those I have reached out to and identify any
follow up actions.
Identify 10 (or 20) more places to speak.
Get contact information for the program directors for the
10 (or 20) places to speak.
Plan to reach out to these contacts. Schedule this into the
calendar.

Sample #2: Community Marketing: Networking
Goal: Build relationships with existing referral sources
and potential referral sources.

Initially or Annually:
Create a list of at least 20 (and up to 90) existing referral

sources or potential referral sources. These could be
people I know or people I'd like to get to know.
Get contact information for my list.

Daily:
Reach out to between three to five people on my list using
a variety of methods: email, phone, handwritten note or
card, small gift, or in-person meeting.

With each interaction, plan to share my compassion, my
knowledge, or my network. (See Tim Sanders' *Love is the
Killer App* book for more on this, as well as the upcoming
chapters on marketing.)

Document who I reached out to, how I did so (what
contact method), and, if I like them, put them on my
calendar for the next time I wish to reach out. Record
any personal information they gave that I can reference
later such as an important upcoming event. If I don't like
them, eliminate them from my ongoing "reach-out" list.

2. Online Marketing Action Plans

Just as with community marketing, there are many ways to market
your practice via the internet and we will discuss some of these
in the upcoming chapters. But, as with community marketing, I
recommend you document your process. It is too easy to forget the
marketing role if you have not documented what you plan to do.

There are two primary methods of online marketing that work
for therapists.

The first is to have a good basic website with four pages:

- A Homepage that speaks to the clients' needs
- An About page that shows the therapist understands the clients' needs and is looking forward to working with them
- A Frequently Asked Questions page
- A Contact page
- Optionally: A Services Page
- (We will discuss what to put on those pages in our up-coming chapters on marketing.)

The second way to market a therapy practice online is to put listings on at least two to four online therapy directories such as Psychology Today. Again, you want to make the content similar to your homepage where you speak to the concerns of the client.

In Summary:

Unless you have had a full practice for several years, you are going to need to market your practice until you close it or retire. Make peace with this. Once you have reviewed the marketing strategies in the next few chapters, consider which marketing activities will work best with your personality and your ideal clients. Then build and document your marketing action plans. By documenting these, you will be reminding yourself that you have a marketing role and your business success depends on attracting new clients. Develop consistent and focused marketing activities and follow your action plans.

Next Steps:

1. Decide what marketing activities work best for you, your prospective clients, and your personality. You can read more in the next few chapters.
2. Create procedures with step one, step two, etc., and then indicate the frequency at which you will do them.
3. Put those action plans in your Operations Manual.

CHAPTER FIFTEEN

The Empathy Map

Remember in the beginning of the book, I spoke of the idea of having a business strategy? The concept that you need to decide who you want to serve and how you want to help them? We'll cover that further in this chapter, through the lens of a helpful tool called The Empathy Map.

If you want to download your copy of the Empathy Map, you can do so here:

http://beawealthytherapist.net/resources

Your Empathy Map can help you discover whom your business is called to serve. You might think of your business strategy as starting with your specialty or niche. While this is important, we must go further. What help do the people in your niche want? What is in their heads and their hearts? We must go beyond a generic definition and really understand what they want and need.

Clients come to therapy because they have a problem they want solved. We want to look at this problem through the eyes of the client. We also want to know if they would pay for help with this problem.

Your Empathy Map

WRITE DOWN WHAT YOUR
IDEAL CLIENTS...

SAY	THINK BUT DON'T SAY

WANT/ DON'T WANT	DO AND DO NOT DO

FEEL	FEAR

For example, anxious women can be a great niche. And women with anxiety will often pay for help to reduce their symptoms. Now consider a niche of cancer patients. Obviously, cancer is a difficult diagnosis and situation. At the same time, there are a lot of free resources available to cancer patients. So it may be a bit more difficult (although not impossible) to find clients who are willing to pay a private practice fee to deal with the emotional issues surrounding the cancer diagnosis. When I opened my counseling center in Orange County, California, we decided to focus on relationships. We know people pay for help with relationships.

Once we have the broad vision of our niche market, we want to dig deep and get, as I said, into the heads and hearts of our ideal clients. We want to be very clear on how they see their problems. Why is this important? In order for clients to decide that we are the right place for them, they must know that we truly understand them.

The Empathy Map is the tool I recommend for really fleshing out the picture of what your ideal client is thinking when they are looking for a therapist. It is a tool used by designers for everything from cars to luxury items.

The Empathy Map is one of the most important tools that you can use throughout your business. In this step, you are using it to ensure you are clear about your target market's concerns. You can also use it to create any of your marketing materials. Some therapists even use it when they are conceptualizing treatment plans.

The beauty of the Empathy Map is that it gives you the language from the client's perspective about what they think they need. When you can speak to potential clients in the language that they use, it will help them to know that you understand them. It sounds simple, but please don't underestimate the value of this. You will stand head and shoulders above your local colleagues when you are able to show potential clients how well you understand them.

You can see in the diagram that the Empathy Map is a series of questions to understand the problems *as perceived by the client.*

What does the ideal client say about his problem (on the intake call or when he complains to others)?

What does the ideal client think but not say about his problem?

What does the ideal client want or not want as related to his problem?

What does the ideal client do or not do in regard to his problem?

What does the ideal client feel when thinking about his problem?

What is he afraid of?

Certainly you can add additional questions here. The idea is that you understand how the client refers to the problem that he would pay you to help him with. This knowledge and descriptive language is gold. I call it "languaging their situation." (People much smarter than I tell me that "languaging" is not a verb. I figure that we humans are good at taking nouns and turning them into verbs, so I am doing that here.)

You will use this Empathy Map to build your client-focused website copy and other marketing messages.

This is how you differentiate yourself from the other hundreds or thousands of therapists in your area. When people are searching for a therapist, the first thing that they look for is someone who understands them. And now you know your ideal client. You are clear on how they talk about their problems and what they want. When you reflect that understanding in your marketing, yours is the phone number they will dial.

A while back, one of our Be A Wealthy Therapist Elite coaches, Helen Odessky, and I were role playing the process of filling out the Empathy Map. Besides being on our coaching team, Helen is a psychologist with a vibrant counseling practice outside of Chicago, Illinois. In her psychotherapy practice, Helen specializes in treating anxiety and panic disorder.

As we went through the Empathy Map, Helen got in touch with her ideal client. Here is how she filled in the Empathy Map for the anxious client:

<u>What does the ideal client say on the intake call (about her problem)?</u>
"I've been anxious for a really long time, and I've been able to deal with it up until now. I just want it to stop."

<u>What does the ideal client think but not say (about her problem)?</u>
"I'm losing my mind; I think I'm going crazy. There's got to be something wrong with me. I'm either really different and people just don't get it, or they haven't discovered what's wrong with me, or I'm just going crazy. People think I'm nuts."

<u>What does the ideal client want – really want?</u>
She wants to get back to a time when she had very little anxiety or to find to way to lessen her anxiety or, optimally, make it stop. She also wants to be the person she used to be. She feels like she used to be okay; things were going well once upon a time. She'd like to have that relief.

<u>What does the ideal client NOT want (as related to the problem)?</u>

She does not want a therapist – or anyone – to tell her it's just in her head. She doesn't want to be told that she has to take medication in order to fix everything. She doesn't want to be told that it's going to take years and years to fix this because she is ready to do something about it now.

What does the ideal client do about her problem?
She researches anxiety online. She has read all the books in the self-help aisle. She has tried every suggestion on earth that her friends, family, doctor, and health magazines have suggested. Nothing has worked, and yet, she is constantly working so hard to have the anxiety stop.

What does the ideal client not do about her problem?
She might avoid doing the things that could heighten her anxiety. She might start avoiding certain places or certain activities until her anxiety is less. She may choose only driving on safe routes that she knows really well. Or she may not travel outside a certain radius.

What does the ideal client feel? What is she afraid of?
She feels ashamed. She feels embarrassed to tell her friends or even sometimes really close confidants, such as a significant other or her parents, about it. She feels judged, even when not telling anybody about the problem. She feels sad because it doesn't seem like the solutions are working. She tried, and it doesn't seem like it's getting solved, and it's been a long time. She feels scared. ("What if this never ends?") She is tired – she's working really, really hard at trying to change this, and it's not working. She is afraid that maybe she IS crazy or

she did something to cause this. She feels out of control. Some days she even worries she won't know what to do if she does NOT have the anxiety.

That is a sample Empathy Map of Helen's ideal client. This may not be your ideal client at all. In fact, you may specialize in anxiety, but be more focused on stress and not panic disorder. The point is to dive deep and paint a very clear picture of your ideal client. In this example, can't you just feel this client's pain? Every time I do an Empathy Map, I find myself with so much compassion for the clients I am called to serve.

Additionally, it is clear from the Empathy Map that this client wants help and will pay for help. This is a "seeker."

When you have reached the clarity about your prospective client with the Empathy Map, you can begin to think about how and where she is looking for help. Is she looking for help online? Are there other professionals she confides in about her problems? Does she attend community lectures?

This will take some work to uncover, but once you do, the Empathy Map is the pathway that will connect you to your clients – and have you stand out among your colleagues.

Frequently Asked Questions about the Empathy Map

1. How long should the process take to create an Empathy Map?

Many clinicians get stuck here. They perseverate over EXACTLY the right client and worry that what they are doing isn't right or good enough. Here is a strong recommendation. Give yourself no more than one hour to take your first cut at your Empathy Map. Set a timer for 60 minutes and walk away when it goes off. Come back in a day or two and review. Add anything else that comes up.

There is no perfect way to complete this exercise and the part of your brain that strives for perfection will keep you hostage if you don't push through the resistance. So, as Nike says, just do it.

2. What if you have multiple units of treatment? For example, you treat adolescents, but the parents pay the bill.

Write an Empathy Map for each one – the parents individually and the teen. See what they have in common. Having the perspective of both will make your marketing copy really stand out and be strong.

3. What if you want to market multiple specialties?

If they are complementary niches or specialties, create an Empathy Map for an ideal client in each specialty and see where there is overlap in how they describe their problem. For example: couples and families or teens and younger children.

Beware of trying to market specialties that do not seem to go together. Marriage counseling and divorce coaching are one example. I know several clinicians who do both. Yet, if you were a client seeking marriage counseling, you may have concerns that the clinician might be "pro-divorce." My favorite example of dueling niches was a therapy business owner who said she specialized in adolescents and sex therapy. I know she did not do sex therapy for adolescents, but the pairing made that assumption possible.

After you complete your Empathy Map (60 minutes – remember?), the next step is to build the marketing plan to attract that ideal client into your therapy business.

In Summary:

The Empathy Map is the best tool I know of to make your marketing easier. By answering the questions *from the client's point of view,* you will know exactly what to say to encourage prospective clients to call you (and not the clinician next door). Take some time creating your Empathy Map, but don't get stuck. It is a tool and a guide. Some clinicians work so hard to create a perfect Empathy Map that they end up never marketing their business.

Next Steps:

1. Take a moment to visualize the ideal client you are called to serve.
2. Draft your Empathy Map. (Take no more than an hour to do this. Set it aside and review it a few days later. Then move on to developing your marketing plan! (You may wish perhaps to reward yourself with some chocolate first!)

CHAPTER SIXTEEN

Building a Client-Attractive
Online Presence

I am pleased to say that the marketing role is one that many clinicians are willing to do these days. That wasn't the case eight years ago when I wrote my first book, *Be A Wealthy Therapist: Finally you can make a living while making a difference*. Back then, most clinicians felt that marketing one's practice was unseemly – similar to ambulance chasing. As a profession, we have come quite far in those eight years; most therapy business owners now recognize that they have at least two roles: as clinician who delivers the service and the marketing role. And yet, as you've seen throughout this book, the operations role, the finance role, and the visionary role are equally important. For those of you who have centers (group practices), you know that human resources is also a major function in terms of how you're going to hire the clinicians coming in and how you're going to mentor them.

Let's take a look at the marketing role and how to best attract clients.

The need to market one's practice is new to the last decade

or so. Fifty or sixty years ago, therapists did not need to market their businesses. Referrals came easy. In fact, in the 1960s, being in therapy was a badge of honor. Everybody wanted to be in therapy. Indemnity insurance paid very well and both clients and therapists were happy with the reimbursement. In the 1970s, we went through the Vietnam War, which impacted our culture significantly. Coming out of the war was the value that "business is bad." Therapists quietly ran their practices and referrals came from word of mouth or other health-care providers.

In the 1980s, in the US, managed care companies entered the picture. The goal was to "manage" behavioral health care. The future of private practice was changed. Employers signed up with the managed care companies in the 1990s and therapists were now forced to get on these panels or lose the clients they were seeing. In the 2000s, many of the managed care panels in the United States were full, and therapists were unable to get in. Today, well into the 21st century, clinicians are choosing to stand up as proud business owners and not rely on the insurance or managed care companies to get their phones ringing. As I have said many times, if you do not already have a full practice, you will need to market your business for the rest of your career.

There is a lot of opportunity for private practice owners today. You have an opportunity to help a lot of people who need you. In many countries, one in four people are diagnosed with a mental illness each year. One in four, and that doesn't even include relationship issues or V-codes. Think about that for a moment. That is a significant number of people who need you!

And there is great news for therapy business owners! Right now, those people are looking online and in their community for help. In fact, I've read reports that there are 1.5 million online searches a month for counseling. Think about that for a moment. 1.5 million searches a month from people looking for the services you offer. And that is only online searches – it doesn't include the people who ask others for referrals to a therapist. So once and for all, we need to let go of the idea that there aren't enough clients to go around. That scarcity mentality is not helpful and simply not true.

Your job as a therapy business owner is to build enough credibility and visibility online and in the community so that your name is at the top of their mind when someone is looking for a therapist… so that you seem like the "go-to" option for them.

Some clinicians still feel uncomfortable with the idea of marketing because they interpret it as selling their services. But you are not selling your services. All you are doing is letting people know what kind of hope and help you have for people who have certain kinds of problems. I like to think of it this way. You are doing a community service by letting people in your community know you are available, help with certain types of pain, and want to help those who need you. When you approach marketing from a "how can I serve you" place, you then become instantly attractive to people, and coming from a place of service might make marketing easier on you, too.

Marketing starts with the Empathy Map. We discussed this in the last chapter. It is the foundation of all your marketing. It helps you really get into the head and the heart of your ideal client. You want to understand what they are thinking, and saying, and wanting, and afraid of, and hopeful for. When you do that, you can then show them – in all of your marketing materials, whether written or verbal – that you understand their particular problem. You are showing that you understand them and want to help. You are a service to those who are hurting.

I am often asked, "Do I need to continue to market, even if I have an insurance-based practice?" Yes, if you want more clients.

Yes, if you want a stable caseload over the long haul. Therapists have an average length of stay for their clients. What I mean by this is that most therapists will have clients come, on average, for a particular length of time. For you, it may be 15 sessions, or it may be a year. But at some point, when your clients reach that length of treatment, they will begin to organically fall off. This means that you are going to need more clients to replace them.

This normal attrition can be predicted if you know *your* average length of stay. But when therapy business owners do not know these metrics, it can lead to a problem I call *binge marketing*. This is where therapy business owners do a lot of marketing and are rewarded with new clients. Then, when their caseload is full again, they stop marketing. They are relieved and relaxed, and they go back into the clinician role, and the marketing role is put on the shelf for a bit.

Since each of us has an average length of stay for clients, and many of the new clients came in at the same time because of the marketing effort, those new clients will tend to graduate treatment at the same time. This results in a decreased caseload again and the therapist doing another round of *binge marketing*. This is not a sustainable way to run a business. You want to create a marketing plan that you work consistently and regularly throughout your business.

A common question is, "How much time should I allocate for marketing?" If you have a full caseload, then most likely, you're going to want to spend at least three to five hours a week marketing your business so you can continue to add new clients as your current clients terminate treatment. However, if you need more clients than you currently have, you want to market your practice more hours per week. For example, if you want to see 15 clients a week, and you're seeing five, then you have ten hours available to market your business.

Now that you have an idea of how many hours you have to market your practice, how are you going to spend those hours? What is the most effective way to build a marketing plan? Next we will explore the two types of marketing plans you want to create.

A solid plan to create growth contains an online marketing plan, which includes a client-attractive website and a listing on two to four online therapy directories. It also consists of a community marketing plan, which includes networking and speaking. You don't have to waste money buying all sorts of ads, trying various media, or turn yourself into a marketing shill. Consistent effort in the following areas will take you to where you need to be.

Your client-attractive website

Sometimes when I talk about a client-attractive website, people think I mean an attractive design. And while design is nice, what I mean is using language on your website that speaks directly to the ideal client's pain. Many clinicians make the mistake of trying to show how much of an expert they are. This actually can be off-putting to a potential client. The only thing the client cares about (at first, anyway) is "Do you understand my pain?"

Before we go into detail about the format of a client-attractive website, let's first discuss the business purpose of your website. Some clinicians would say that the purpose of your website is to educate your clients. These clinicians will put lots of links leading off their site to helpful resources such as books or public health resources.

The problem with sending people off your site is, well, now they have left your site! They don't have your number or contact information in front of them and now they are less likely to make an appointment with you. In your attempt to educate them or give them helpful resources, you have inadvertently told them they would be better served by another resource.

So our goal is to keep them *on* your site and help them to make an appointment. That is the business purpose of your website. Please keep that in mind while you are creating your website.

If you do not yet have a website, and you're unfamiliar with what a website entails, it's really not complicated. You need a domain name or URL. That is your website address and how people find you. Then, your website is hosted, usually for a monthly fee, on a server maintained by a hosting company. You can often buy your domain name (which is a yearly fee, usually around $10 to $20) and host it with the same service, such as GoDaddy or LunarPages. If you hire someone to create your website, you want to make sure that you own the domain name and have your own account with the hosting company. While it seems easier to have your web designer "just take care of everything," you need to have control of your website, meaning having the user names and passwords for your domain company and hosting company. Then, if you want to change designers or work on the site yourself, you can.

Your online presence starts with a domain name. It is a good idea to have a domain name that would appeal to your ideal client. For example, mine is OCRelationshipCenter.com. You also want to purchase a domain name with your name without all the degree-and-license letters after it, if possible. (e.g.: chloeclinician.com or caseytruffo.com). You want to own your own name rather than let somebody else have it.

Next, you will need hosting services for your website. Make sure your contact information is correct at your domain service and your hosting service. Make sure **you** are the contact person and not some web designer that you hired originally. In 2014, I lost our Be A Wealthy Therapist domain name due to just this problem.

The domain service had an old email address on file for me. When the domain came up for renewal, my credit card had expired. The domain service emailed me (at the old email address) asking for a new credit card. They emailed three times to that old email address and of course, I never responded since I didn't have access to that email address anymore. The domain went to auction and was sold within seconds. The only way we found out was when we went to our website, it was gone. So, I beg you, make sure that you annually check that your contact information is correct at your domain and hosting service companies.

You may want to physically build the website yourself with do-it-yourself platforms such as WordPress or hire WordPress experts/designers to do it for you. If you hire someone else to actually create the structure, please do not give up creative control. Please do not let someone else write your website copy (text). No one else will ever know your ideal client as well as you do. And with the Empathy Map, you will have the client-attractive language you need.

What makes a website attractive to prospective clients? A client-attractive website will be approximately 80% about the client (and their pain and your hope for them) and only about 20% about you, your mission, experience, and credentials. Many therapists open their home page with their mission and the discussion of how they help people. Others open with a laundry list of 17 different specialties and their credentials. Neither are considered client attractive. After all, remember, something has just happened that is making the client seek a therapist. Their first criterion is to make sure that somebody understands them.

If you have done the Empathy Map, creating client attractive website copy (or text) will be a very easy task. You will just take the language that you've written on the Empathy Map, and put it into the format for your website pages.

How many pages should you have? On your website, my recommendation is that you have four or five pages. You will have a home page, an about the therapist(s) page, a contact page, a frequently asked questions (FAQ) page, and a services page. A blog page is also a nice addition.

Your Home Page

Your home page will have a headline that is a statement of a benefit, or some statement or question that shows that you understand their pain. For example, "Worried about your children's choices?" Or, "Tired of having the same old argument again?" Or, "It's time to feel better." This type of headline gives them a sense of what is coming and invites them to read further. The purpose of your headline is to encourage people to read the first paragraph. If you can grab their attention with a statement of a benefit, they will want to know more.

My recommendation is that there are three sections to your home page:

- Connect with their pain

- Transition to hope

- Introduce you and give a call to action

In the first section, you connect with them around their pain as they conceptualize it. This is where you use your Empathy Map language to show you understand them; you are keenly aware of what they are thinking, feeling, and wanting.

If we take the anxious client from Helen's example in the last chapter, the headline and first section might read:

> You are not going crazy. You have anxiety.
> Let's see if we can make it stop.

There was a time when you didn't feel like this. Things used to be easier. You didn't have to worry about when the anxiety would hit. You didn't worry about traveling or visiting with people. And I know you want to go back to that person you used to be.

And it is hard because not many people really understand. And the ones who do have all kinds of ideas for you. But you have tried every suggestion on earth that your friends, family, doctor, and health magazines have suggested. It doesn't work, which is so frustrating because you are working so hard to have the anxiety stop.

If you notice, almost every word came exactly from the Empathy Map. This is true for the headline and the first section.

Let's look at another example. Say you were creating the text for a website for parents and teens. Your headline might be, "Worried about your teen's choices?" Then in your home page first paragraph, again, working from your Empathy Map, you might say something like, "Clearly, you love your child. You want the best for your teen, and yet sometimes it's simply confusing to know when their behavior is normal rebellion or a cry for help. You worry that the choices they might be making – the ones you know about and especially the ones you don't know about – might hurt them. You may be wondering how to get your teenager to talk to you more. You want them to grow up to be happy and healthy people in the world, and yet what you're looking at right now is causing you concern."

Those phrases may have come directly from different sections in the Empathy Map from the parents' point of view. See how easy that was? See how much more compelling it is than simply talking about you and your years of experience? (Well, for the client anyway.)

The next section on your home page is literally about the transition from where they are now to hope. Let's look at the two examples again – the first is our anxious client and the second is the web page for the teen client. The second section may read something like this:

(For the anxious client website)

I know that having anxiety is not easy. I want you to feel the freedom to do what you want in your life without fear of an anxiety attack. And I have some good news. What I know is there are some proven strategies to help you feel better – and without medication. Yes, it is time to find your way back to the you that you were without the anxiety. And you don't have to do it alone.

(For the teen and parent client website)

This can be a difficult time for parents and teens. What I know is that, often, the teen needs someone to talk to who can understand their point of view, as well as help you understand what is normal adolescent rebellion and what is concerning.

Then the final section is where you introduce yourself and put in the call to action. The call to action is a direct instruction – what you would like them to do next. Your third section may read:

(For the anxious client website)

Hi, my name is Tim Therapist and I want to help you reduce your anxiety right now. You've tried everything on your own and it hasn't given you the results you want. Let's see if I can help you feel better – and sooner rather than later. Please call me today at xxx-xxx-xxxx or schedule an appointment on my online scheduler (link here.) *If you want them to text you, you can add,* Or text me at xxx-xxx-xxxx. *If you wanted them to email you, you can do that, as well.*

(For the teen and parent client website)

Hi, my name is Chloe Clinician and I have been helping families like yours for seven years. Please don't wait one more day. I want to hear your story. I want to be there to support you and your teen. Please call me at xxx-xxx-xxxx or schedule an appointment on my online scheduler (link here.) *If you want them to text you, you can add,* Or text me at xxx-xxx-xxxx. *If you wanted them to email you, you can do that, as well.*

Your Contact Us Page

On each page, including your contact page, you want to be welcoming to the client. On your contact page, you will be inviting them to call you. Consider having a professional picture for your contact page. The copy on your contact page might read:

Let's get started. Let's see if I can help you make things better for you (or for your teen and you). Please contact me today at (fill in the ways you wish to be contacted).

I don't recommend having a contact form on your website contact page. Web designers love using contact forms, but I think about this from the prospective client's point of view. If I am the parent of a teen worried about my child and trying to find a therapist, I want to talk to one quickly or make an appointment quickly. It's the same if I am the anxious client. Probably it is the same for most clients. If I cannot contact you right now, I'm going to find somebody I can contact in an easier and more direct way than filling out a contact form.

Now you have completed your home page and your contact page. That is the minimum needed for an online presence. And you did so using the language you put on the Empathy Map. That is why I so strongly recommend that you spend a little bit of time creating the Empathy Map. It saves so much time later when you're working on your website copy.

You might want to consider adding some additional pages to your website.

Your About You Page ("About Chloe")

The purpose of the about page is to further help the prospective client know that you understand them and their problem. There are two ways to go about writing your about page.

If you have experienced the problem that you are helping people with and feel comfortable sharing it, prospective clients might resonate with it. Should you decide to do this, make sure your story is fully processed and you're only sharing that which is appropriate to helping the client know you understand them.

For example, on our About You (the therapist) page on the parent-teen website, one could say:

When our children were little, I thought the most difficult problem I would have is healing skinned knees. But as my children moved into their teens, I recognized that they had more distractions than I ever did. The choices that they made on a daily basis had very scary consequences.

Truth be told, at that time, I did not know what was normal teenage behavior and what could be a problem. Our family found a wonderful family therapist and I am happy to say that today, all my kids have grown into amazing human beings and I couldn't be prouder. But back then, I really needed support and so did my children.

After that amazing therapy experience, I decided that I wanted to help other families like ours. I returned to school and became a licensed family therapist. And I have the best job in the world. Every day, I get to help parents and teens move through the difficult stage of adolescence and come out the other side. I'd like to meet your family and see if I can help. Please call me at xxx-xxx-xxxx (or link to online scheduler).

Very often, the details of a therapist's personal story are inappropriate to share on their website. Perhaps you treat our anxious client and had a relative who struggled with panic disorder. Perhaps your relative does not want you to share the story about her difficulties. If, for personal or ethical reasons, you do not wish to share your story, you can share a story of how you helped someone with the problem that they have. In the case of our anxious client, the about page might read:

Early in my career, I met an amazing, accomplished woman I'll call Roberta. Roberta had advanced well in her career and was quite well liked. But she had these moments where her anxiety overwhelmed her. She mentioned that one time at a party, she became so anxious she felt the room start spinning. She barely made it to the bathroom before throwing up. After that, Roberta started to avoid all parties and social gatherings. This was difficult, as her work demanded these types of social activities.

Roberta had tried many things to help reduce her anxiety and when she came to me, she had just about given up. Her physician had offered her medication, but she did not want to take it due to the side effects. She said seeing me was her last hope.

Roberta and I worked with some very specific strategies to help her manage her thinking around the anxiety. I helped her with some slight behavioral changes too – things that would help her float through a panic attack. Within a few weeks, Roberta reported that the anxiety episodes were much fewer and farther between. Not long after that, she said she no longer felt controlled by her anxiety. In fact, I heard from her recently and she reported that she had recently hosted a large social gathering with ease. It had reminded her of how far she had come and she thanked me for our work together.

As I mentioned, this was at the early part of my career. I decided to devote my professional life to helping other anxious clients like Roberta reduce the stranglehold of panic and help them return to the person they used to be. And I have the greatest job in the world! I so enjoy seeing people find peace again.

I'd love to help you too. Shall we connect?

At the bottom of the about page, you can add, "P.S. For those who care about the credentials," and then you can put your education, your license, any associations, any publications, or media appearances. The reason you put this after your story is because people want to know you understand their pain first. Then they care about your credentials.

Your Contact Page

The contact page is once again giving people ways to contact you. A common mistake made on the contact page is to say, "I know contacting a therapist is a really hard thing to do." You might actually be discouraging them from calling – reminding them how difficult reaching out for help is. They might read that and close the computer without calling due to their anxiety. My advice is to make your contact page warm and light:

Let's get started! It is easy to reach me (insert ways). I look forward to helping you (or you and your family).

You may also put a map or pictures of your office on this page.

Your Frequently Asked Questions Page

The frequently asked questions page is one of the places where I think most therapists accidentally cause themselves some problems. This is due to a misconception of the purpose of the frequently asked questions page.

Remember, the goal of your website is to get prospective clients to contact you for an appointment. The frequently asked questions page is to help them by answering any questions that they may have that would prevent them from reaching out to you.

Your frequently asked questions include something like, "Are you going to tell us what to do?" Or if you're doing couples counseling, they may ask, "What if my partner doesn't want to come in?" Or in the case of our anxious client, "Are you going to tell me it is all in my head?" and "Are you going tell me I need medication?" Again, the frequently asked questions are the questions that would keep the client from picking up the phone or making an appointment with you. As you answer them, you do two things. You help them see how clearly you understand them and you lower their resistance to calling you.

The error that many therapists make is having questions on the FAQ page such as, "What is therapy?" or "Will therapy help me?" The problem with these questions is that if somebody is already on your website, about 95% of the time they already have an idea what therapy is, and they already have decided it's going to be helpful. You are preaching to the choir. It is not really helping them to make that decision to contact *you*. What I would do instead is use questions that allow you to give answers that address their concerns and make it easier for them to contact you. And guess what? Your Empathy Map has the content for this page. What are they afraid of? What are they afraid might happen if they come in? Put that in the form of a question on your FAQ page.

Also, the last question on your frequently asked questions page can be, "How do I get started?" Then put your contact info there.

Your Services Page

Your services page can indicate the different types of services you have, whether it's individual counseling, family counseling, or couples counseling, etc. I would tend to stay away from the word *psychotherapy* unless your clients would be searching for that. In my opinion, the services page is primarily to help the search engines, but it also can give your clients a little bit of information. On your services page, make sure you're writing it from the client's perspective. Make it non-psychobabble. Help them see how you might help in each service.

Video on Your Website

A welcome video is a nice touch. If you do this, make it short – fifteen seconds up to a maximum of two minutes. Less is more here. Speak to the client, showing them you understand them. In the case of our teen therapist, your video might have this as a script for the parent-teen website:

> "I bet I know why you're here. You are a concerned parent and you just want the best for your family. Hi, my name is Chloe Clinician and I really want to help you and your family. Please give me a call. Let's see if we can make it better."

Short and sweet. We simply want the video long enough so they can hear you speak and get a sense of your presence. A welcome video, however, is not mandatory. So if you are completely freaked out when the camera is on you, relax. It is simply an option.

There you have all you need to create a client-attractive website. You only need four to five pages: home, about, contact us, frequently asked questions, and services.

A Blog

Another subject people ask me a lot about is blogging. Blogging can be a very good option for client engagement. Your prospective clients can read about your ideas and thoughts, and get helpful hints. It can also be good for search engine optimization if the keywords and tags are set up correctly.

If you like writing, blogging can be a good way to create client engagement, but I don't think that blogging alone (at this time) is a very effective way to attract brand new clients. They will call you if they feel connected with you from your entire presence on your website. A blog can help with this. But focus on your home page and the about page first. If those are not client attractive, it is unlikely that your blog will make them decide differently about you.

Common Website Errors

As noted, a common mistake is to have links off the website. The social share links are one example. They look cute and I am sure you'd like people to like your Facebook page. But the point of your website is to have them see you as the one they wish to contact and to make an appointment. Every link off your website tells the visitor there is another (and better) thing to do rather than contact you. Every time you offer them a link, whether it's to a resource, a book, or a social media page, you have now taken the client off of your site.

Another mistake that therapists make is that they don't make their websites mobile-friendly. I imagine as soon as I write this, technology will change. But right now, you want to make sure your website can be easily navigated on a mobile device. You want your phone number to show up easily in the first couple of scrolls on a mobile device. Please make sure your contact information is at the top of your page, and maybe even in each of those three sections of your home page. Early on, I made the mistake of putting my phone number only at the end of each page. Those looking at my website on a mobile device had to scroll all the way down to the bottom. It felt like 100 scrolls to get there and no one is going to do that. Also, you want to make sure to have it set up so that when I touch the phone number, it comes up and asks me if I would like to call that number.

Online Therapist Directories (Online Therapist Locators)

Additionally, in your online marketing plan, you're going to want to be listed on two to four online therapist directories. These are subscription services that have high search engine optimization ranking. This gives you more back links into your site, as well as giving you more places where people might find you.

How do you know which are the right therapist directories for you? First of all, enter into your search engine what you think somebody in your area would be looking for. An example would be, "marriage counseling, Madison, Wisconsin." Then see which of these paid services (online directories) come up. Many different ones might come up, such as Psychology Today, Theravive, goodtherapy. org, Network Therapy, or find-a-therapist.com.

From there, you can look at each directory and see how many therapists are listed for your area. If they have thousands in your area, it may not be the right one for you.

A common question is, "Is it worth it to be on an online

directory if I only get two to three clients a year?" Let's go into our finance role and look at the return on investment. If you get two to three clients a year, and you know that an average client spends $1,500 with you, then that's between $3,000 and $4,500 a year you're making from that $400 investment. I think that's a pretty good return on investment.

Your copy (text) on your online therapy directory listing can simply be your home page copy. Make sure you do not put too many specialties on your listing or else people might think you are exaggerating your expertise. And make sure the specialties go together (are complementary). The same is true with your treatment approach. Remember, clients are there to see if you might be a good fit for them.

Beware of newcomers to the online therapy directories arena. Very often there are entrepreneurial people who have decided that they would like to offer a new subscription service for therapists "to help them get clients online." Many of these new online directories do not have good search engine optimization yet. They will get that after they sell a bunch of subscriptions. Beware of being an early adopter. When you get calls from these new vendors, ask about their search engine optimization position. Do your due diligence. Google what you think an ideal client would be searching on and see if the new directory comes up. Some of these vendors will tell you that they are not optimized yet in your area because they have no other therapists and you would be the only one. This may or may not be true. So consider a trial for a few months before committing too much to a new service.

Beware of the shiny

Every day, new ideas for marketing are being developed and salespeople will be calling you. I love testing new ideas. But in your role as confident CEO, please don't try some new, untested marketing strategy until you have developed a good online and community marketing plan as described here.

What about social media? (Facebook, Twitter, Instagram, Pinterest, etc.)

At the time of this writing, social media has not been proven to be a great way to get new therapy clients. After all, who was the last health-care provider that you hired based on their social media profile? Perhaps in the next edition, I will report that this has changed. For now though, please focus on the basics. As I said, the basics aren't always sexy, but they work.

Beware of spending too much time on your online presence. Once it is "good enough," you can move on to your community marketing. We will explore that in the next chapter!

In Summary:

You do need an online marketing plan which can include a website and two to four online therapist locator directories. Speak to the client in your online marketing; they want to know that you understand them. Your client-attractive text for both the website and your online directory listings can come almost directly from your Empathy Map. All you need is a home, about, contact us, frequently asked questions, and services pages. Make sure your website is mobile-friendly. Put your contact information on your site in several places. Make sure that you don't accidentally lose potential clients by sending them off your site to a different resource or to your social media pages.

Beware of spending too much time on your website. It is easy to procrastinate on the rest of your marketing due to spending too much time on your online presence. Don't chase after every new, "shiny object" marketing idea. Focus on putting up your website and your directory listings and making sure they are working for you.

Next Steps:

Your next steps to creating a great online presence:

1. Review your Empathy Map to make sure you really understand the problem from your client's perspective.
2. Write the client-engaging copy (text) for a four to five page website that is 80% about the client and only 20% about you. You have a lot of the content for your website text already on your Empathy Map. In fact, you could probably write all four pages of your website in about 90 minutes after you have completed the Empathy Map. (NOTE: If you do not have a website yet, you will need a domain name, hosting services, and a platform such as WordPress. You can do the physical building of it yourself and input your client-attractive copy or you can hire someone else to build it for you and give them your client-attractive copy to put on the site.)
3. Create listings on two to four online therapy directories.

CHAPTER SEVENTEEN

Building Visibility and Credibility in the Community (Community Marketing)

Most therapy business owners would love to become better known in the community. Imagine having well-respected, influential people in the community sharing your name and contact information as a trusted referral source? Or imagine giving a speaking engagement and having several of the audience members ask you "Are you taking new clients?"

There are two primary ways to get the word out to your community about you and your therapy business: speaking and networking. In this chapter, I will share some of our secrets to community marketing – even if you are shy like I am.

I started my first private practice before the household use of the internet. (Yes, there was a time when Google was not a verb.) At that time, I had no option to let people know about my practice other than to meet them in the community – either through networking or speaking. Since I really, really wanted to be successful, I knew I had to develop marketing activities that I could and would do. So if you are shy like I am – and even if you aren't – here is what I found works even today.

Community Presentations (aka Speaking)

Giving presentations to a roomful of wonderful, prospective clients or referral sources can be an effective way to build your visibility. Many people shy away from speaking because they have unrealistic ideas about what a community speaking engagement is. To me, it is simply facilitating a group discussion on a topic you enjoy and treat. For example, let's look at our clinician who specializes in parents and teens. This therapist in her marketing role could do a talk on "How to raise great teens when their idols are pop stars" or "How to get your teen to talk to you." This could be done at a church, school, youth group, or any place that parents of teens might congregate.

You may have heard me talk about the structure of these community presentations. They are very interactive. The talk consists of three parts (or questions):

- Why is it hard to (your talk title here)?
- What does not work to (fill in your talk title here)?
- What does work to (fill in your talk title here)?

So for this clinician, the three parts of the talk might be:

- Why is it hard to raise great kids when a primary influence is a pop star?
- What does not work when you want to influence them more than the pop star?
- What does work to become more influential in your teen's life and help them with their choices?

The interactive part then gets fun. You engage the audience by asking them those questions. There will always be at least one person who will speak up. You validate them. "Great answer! You are right about that!" You may expand a bit, share a story or a point, and then ask, "Who is next? Why is it hard?" and continue the same validating and expanding.

You will be perceived as the approachable expert. The audience sees you as having knowledge and being open and caring about them. This format also helps clinicians who have a bit of stage fright because you no longer are "on stage." You are a therapist facilitating a group – and most of you have done that several times before.

The other reason this works so well is that the content is limited. Many therapy business owners (in their marketing role) are nervous that they do not have enough content for a 75 or 90-minute talk. So they over-prepare and stuff their talk with too many points. They end up rushing to get the content in and can appear stressed to the audience. This is another case where "less is more." Give them bite-sized tips and invite them to interact with you and they will love you.

When I was first speaking to groups, my tendency was to "leave it all on the court." With every talk, I would try to tell the audience absolutely everything I knew about the topic. This led to the audience being fire-hosed and they left glassy-eyed. Or they left late because I would always go over the time that I was allotted. None of this made me very attractive to the audience members. I began experimenting with less content and more interaction with very positive results. I highly recommend it. Just have a few points, a few sweet success stories that go with your points, and where possible, deliver it in the format listed above. They will love you.

Some therapists tell me that speaking does not work to attract clients. Sometimes it is due to the therapist being very stiff, perhaps due to fears, or alternatively, fire-hosing the audience. But I think that there is a nugget of truth here.

You see, there needs to be a bridge that helps someone shift from audience member to a client in your office. Most people coming to a community talk are not seeking a therapist. But they are self-identifying as having the problem you are speaking about. One of the goals (arguably the most important goal) is to invite them into your office. How do you do this? I suggest you do so with free consultations that you offer at the end of your speaking engagement.

Imagine attending a community presentation on "how to find a great partner when you're really busy." The speaker is engaging and invites your participation and the audience loves to talk. The speaker has given you a couple of things to think about that are new to you... things you hadn't considered before. Perhaps there was an exercise where you were to list your last five relationships and then list when you knew they would not be the right match for you. As you did the exercise, you realized that you usually knew pretty quickly and yet became involved in relationships that didn't go anywhere.

Now imagine that at the end of this community presentation, the speaker offers a free consultation in her office to help you "discover what might stop you from finding a great partner." You liked the speaker. You liked her points. You liked her energy and the way she listened to the audience as they shared their ideas, too. And now she's offering a simple way for you to understand more – and to continue learning about you. Some might consider this an irresistible offer.

After your community presentations, you can offer the audience members the opportunity to learn more about their individual situations with a free consultation in your office. I highly recommend that you do these free consultations with audience members in your office or wherever you usually do your treatment. I also recommend that you do them for the same length of time as your regular sessions. This is where and how you work best and you will imprint the time and the place into your clients. Many a therapy business owner has suggested to me that they will do these free consultations in 10 or 15 minutes over the phone. Rarely if ever do I find that these convert into clients who come regularly. Besides, by inviting them into your office, it pre-qualifies them as people who see you and your services as valuable enough for them to travel to your place of business. Some people might be very happy to pick your brain in 10 minutes over the phone, but never be willing to come into your office.

Sometimes, there's confusion when I discuss offering free consultations. I want to be clear. I am only talking about offering free consultations *after a speaking engagement* – not everywhere and to anyone, but simply to those people who have heard you speak. This is because those audience members have already joined with you. They feel like they know you and your personality. They have already warmed to you. If you offer free consultations other places, such as on your online locator listing, you may find more "tire kickers." This is a personal choice, but I just want to be clear on my recommendation. I am recommending that you offer free consultations at the end of your speaking engagements as a bridge to help audience members become clients.

The free consultation, however, is not an initial intake session. I highly recommend you do not take a full history. The purpose of this session is for them to get to know you a bit better and for you to decide if this person would make a great client for you.

Here is the structure I use for these consultations:

In the free consultation, you want to ask the person what is going on now with them (as related to your talk), and what the ideal situation would be for them. In this case, it might be that the audience member (now in your office for the consult) wants to find love and worries that he won't. He might be concerned that he gets involved too quickly with women who are not good for him. You can compassionately support him as he explains his problem. The next step is to ask the person about what he really wants – what is his dream? He might say he is tired of the single life and his ideal is an amazing partner who adores him. Encourage him to paint the picture of what he really wants.

During this consultation, the primary intervention I recommend you use is active listening. Channel Carl Rogers. Understand when the audience member (now in your office) talks about the difficulties of his current situation and be excited when he talks about what possibilities he wants for his future. People will sense your compassion and your understanding. Those two steps – identifying their current problem and identifying their life as they would like it to be – are two-thirds of your consultation. And, if the person never becomes your client, you still have provided him with some attention, care, and support. That is something most of us long for.

The next part of the consultation is to help the client see the implications if they choose to continue on the path they are on. What happens if nothing changes? Many people today complain about their circumstances and fantasize about the future they really want. But how many of us ever ask ourselves, "What happens if nothing changes?" It can be a startling question. It can prompt us to look at the implications of not changing our ways.

And it can help a free-consult person become your client.

In our example, the man might think about what happens if nothing changes and realizes he will end up alone. He touches the emotion of that and really is aware that he does not want that to happen. He looks up at you.

"I don't want you to end up alone either. I want you to find the love you are searching for. I'd like to help you find the areas where you may be attracting or staying with the wrong partners so you can find the love that you want. Would you be interested in knowing how we might work together?"

Then you can go into the last part of your intake call script.

"My sessions are held right here in my office. And the sessions are 45 minutes in length – just like this one. My fee for each session is $175. I have openings during the days or evenings – what would work better for you?"

Then, as with any counseling inquiry, you will be asked questions about your fee, insurance, etc. Just stay in your heart space and answer the questions as you have them in your Operations Manual scripts.

Can you see how speaking (with the bridge of a free consult) could be a great strategy to bring new clients into your practice? Well, just to encourage you a little more, let's look at the metrics.

If you speak in front of a group of 60, you could have 10% to 50% (or between six and 30) sign up for the free consult. You will likely have some no-shows. These are people who got excited about the free consult offer, but changed their minds later. You did nothing wrong – this happens. So say 30% don't show up or change their minds. This leaves between four to twenty audience members who might come in. Let's say you convert 50% of them into clients. This means you could have two to ten new clients from this one speaking engagement.

This can work with small groups, too. A clinician told me recently that she did a talk where there were seven people, two requested free consults and one became a client. That doesn't sound like a lot, but if that client spends $2,000 over the lifetime of treatment, then that speaking engagement was quite lucrative.

I suggest you offer the free consult on a feedback form in your handout. Explain at the end of the talk that you have a very special offer for them – a chance to connect with you one-on-one where you will hear their story and see if you can help them. Be excited and proud when you offer it. Some therapists get nervous about seeing it as a great offer for the audience member since they are not going to do any major interventions during this session. But, trust me, we would all love to sit with you and have you really hear and support us – and support our dreams and hold the vision of a positive future – even if we never meet you again. The session is THAT valuable.

I usually raffle off a gift card or something else that the audience members can sign up for on the feedback form as well. I then collect the feedback forms at the event and wait to read them until I get home.

The next step is critical. Get back to all the people who signed up for the free consultation within 12 to 24 hours. **This is critical**. The longer you wait, the more people will change their minds. Call them back and schedule them. When you speak to them (or if you leave a message), you can say, "I really enjoyed talking to your group and I am looking forward to knowing more about your situation and seeing if I have some input for you. I have these three times open. Please let me know if any of them work and if not, let me know some other times that might work."

Yes, it will take some phone tag on your part. If you have an online scheduler, that can help. If you cannot reach them live, you can leave a message directing them to your online scheduler and invite them to schedule an appointment. Try to get them in as soon as possible. If you leave a message and don't hear back, I would call again in two days. If you don't hear from them then, you can infer that they changed their minds. Some will do that. Again, expect that up to 30% might no-show or change their minds. But this process works incredibly well when done right.

What can you talk about in your community presentations? You can create unique and fresh topics about the specialty that you work with. Check out the books that experts have written on your specialty and play a bit with their titles. "How to find someone who IS into you," for example. Or for parents of teens: "What to do when your daughter says, I hate you!! I am never going to speak to you again! But first can you help me find my iPhone charger?"

How do you find speaking engagements? Take a moment and review your Empathy Map. Where does your ideal client hang out? Places of worship? Women's groups? PTAs? MeetUps? There are literally dozens of groups filled with your ideal clients. (I once spoke to a group of occupational nurses! They were ideal clients for me – smart, successful women trying to keep their relationships and families running smoothly.) Then contact the program director. You may need to do this several times before you connect, as the program director is often a volunteer position.

Many clinicians are very sensitive about being rejected when they ask program directors if they need a speaker for their meetings. Expect and accept that you will not be a match for every organization where you apply. You may only get 10% of the people you ask to invite you to be a speaker. Yes, this is a numbers game. Continue to reach out to the program directors. Build the relationship with them. They will love you for it.

Develop a system for speaking – for getting the booking, for prepping the talk, and for doing it.

If we go back into our operations role for a moment, consider how you might develop a system that you implement regularly for your speaking plan. You could document your call, letter, and email script – where you introduce yourself as a therapist in the area specializing in xxx and you are wondering if they might be looking for speakers. You could also document the process of how often you follow up. Then, there are all the tasks on the day of the talk that I love having documented in a checklist so I don't forget anything… such as bringing your bio for someone to introduce you. Can you see how helpful it would be to have this documented? It would increase your ease and save you time.

Community Networking

Since so many clinicians started marketing online, a vacuum has been created in the community. There are many people and professions who have clients who need therapy, but they do not know who to refer to. Think about that for a moment. They want to refer to someone, but don't know anyone.

There are many ways to meet and connect with other professionals who also see your ideal client. If you (once again) take a look at your Empathy Map, you can predict who else might be offering services to her. Does she go to a place of worship and confide in clergy? Does she talk about her problems with her physician?

A good referral partner is someone who offers non-competing services to your ideal client. What other professional services does your ideal client use? Does your ideal client use the services of acupuncturists, nutritionists, or aestheticians? Identify these people and build relationships with them. When they know you and enjoy you, they will want to refer to you.

Many therapists tell me that networking "does not work." Often this is because there is a misunderstanding about how to network effectively. My friend and colleague Elizabeth Marshall taught me the most important rule of networking: Relationship before request.

What does that mean? It means that asking people for referrals does not work if you do not have a relationship with them. It means we must take the time to connect one-to-one with people – to find out about them and their lives and businesses. To show that we care about whom they are and what they need. It means looking for areas we have in common and searching for ways to "be relevant" to them.

Tim Sanders, author of the books *Love is a Killer App* and *The Likeability Factor,* is my master teacher about how to be relevant. If you want to know more about how to improve your connections with those who might refer clients to you, please read either of these books. It will be well worth your while.

I learned from Tim that there are three ways to be helpful when building relationships. You can share:

- your knowledge (what you know about things your potential referral source is interested in)

- your compassion (your emotional connection and support for them in their highs and lows of life)

- your network (the people you know who might have things in common or be able to support this potential referral source)

He suggested making a list of people you'd like to get to know. And then you can reach out to at least one potential referral source a day.

You can reach out in a variety of ways: email, phone call, text, handwritten note or card, meeting in person, or a small gift. Here are some examples of how to do this:

1. Share your knowledge. Perhaps a potential referral source is a clergyperson. If you see an article online about the joys and stresses of today's clergy, you could send the clergyperson an email with the link and a short note: "Not sure if you saw this, but I thought about you when I read it. I admire what you do each day!"

2. Share your compassion. This will be easy for you. Pay attention to potential referral sources and you will learn about what is important to them; what is going on in their lives. Congratulate one on his new book. Share your condolences when another has suffered a loss. Speak from your heart and worry less about getting referrals and they will love you. (And *that* is what often leads to referrals!)

3. Share your network. Many people would love to be connected with others who share their interests. Introduce two people who may not know one another, but who have something in common. Perhaps one is a couples' counselor and the other treats children. Or maybe they both love golden retrievers. Even if it is not a love connection for your two colleagues, both will consider you helpful and kind.

The first step:

I recommend you start by making a list of people you already know or you would like to get to know. Then you can begin your plan of reaching out on a regular basis. Start first with people in your circle. One woman shared with me that she literally forgot that her best friend was a family court judge. Once she shared about her practice, the family court judge was able to connect her with many attorneys. Another clinician told me that her husband's partner worked with doctors who had had substance abuse problems. Since substance abuse was this clinician's field, she was able to chat with her friend and ask if she may be of service. So don't overlook those in your current circle of influence.

But I'm not suggesting that you start out asking for referrals. Remember: "relationship before request." So how do you build relationships? With exactly the steps listed above from Tim Sanders.

Make your list of 20 (or it could even be up to 90) and plan to reach out to at least one person (preferably three to five people) per day sharing your knowledge, sharing your compassion, or sharing your network.

Here's an example of how it might work. On Monday, you wake up and look at your list of 20. As you scan the list, you see your son's baseball coach. As you think about this man, your heart breaks because he recently lost his wife. You quickly grab a card that you have in your desk and write him a short note of condolence. You share with him how much he means to you and your family. You address and stamp it and it's ready for the mail. You look again at the list and you see a friend who works with bullies in the workplace. That sparks a memory of an article you saw this morning online. You write a quick email to your friend with the link and a note saying, "Not sure you saw this, but I thought of you. Hope all is well with you." You continue to look at your list with an eye towards how you could introduce two people to one another. You notice your aesthetician's name. You remember she said that she was looking for some search engine optimization help. You love your search engine optimization person and so you write a quick email to both of them introducing them to each other. In that email you write, "I have no idea if this is the right connection for either of you, but I wanted to introduce you to each other."

You could keep going. Is there someone on the list that you

would love to take out for coffee and get to know better? Is there a professional, such as a dentist, that you would like to meet with? Perhaps you could call the office manager and ask if you could have a tour of the office since you are looking for a good dentist to refer to.

If you just reach out to three people a day, five days a week that is over 700 contacts in a year. Even for the shyest among us, this is possible. Let me be clear. You're not going on 700 first dates, so let's talk about following up and continuing to build the relationships.

After your initial connection with someone, document for your records:

- The person's name and contact information
- The manner in which you connected (call, email, one-to-one meeting, handwritten letter or card, or small gift)
- The date you connected
- Things you discussed, both business and personal (especially personal)
- The next time you plan to contact them

Next, put your tentative next contact date on your calendar as a to-do item. For most of your contacts, this will be in a month to six weeks from when you last contacted them. If you've met with them one-on-one, it may be socially appropriate to send them a quick email: "I really enjoyed our lunch today. I'm looking forward to getting to know more about you and your business."

For those of you who are new to networking, connecting in this way may surprise you. You may have thought that networking was all about giving out as many business cards as possible, telling people about your practice, and asking them to refer to you. I want you to think for a moment how you would feel if someone did this to you. You would probably be unlikely to give them referrals.

I don't want to understate this point. With both my businesses, Be A Wealthy Therapist and the Orange County Relationship Center, I am contacted on a regular basis by people asking me either for referrals or to promote them in some way. I am personally offended that these people are asking me to do something for them without getting to know me at all.

Unlocking the Gate

I have spoken at length about how to get past the gatekeeper in other books I've written, so I won't belabor the point here. But, I will share the general strategy.

Let's talk about who the gatekeeper is. The gatekeeper is the church secretary, the office manager, the school secretary, etc. The gatekeeper's job is to make sure that only "qualified" people get past them to the boss. Otherwise, doctors would be talking to every drug rep that happened to catch them on a slow day. Clergy would be talking to every parishioner who had the slightest question that could be answered by someone else. The gatekeeper's job is to help the general public find the right resource. And only some people will get past the gatekeeper to the business owner or professional they wish to see. You want to be one of those people.

You can usually do this pretty easily by making the gatekeeper your new best friend. Share your compassion with the gatekeeper. Thank them for doing all the work that they do. Show them some respect.

When I call the church, my usual script is, "Hi. My name is Casey Truffo and I am a therapist in the area specializing in helping couples get along better. I know that the person who answers the phone is the person who really runs the place. So that is you! So now I know that you are the right person for me to talk to so I can figure out how to best serve over there. I'm sorry. I didn't ask you your name. What is your name?"

Once I have their name, we can then continue. "Thank you, Jennifer. As I was saying, I know who really runs the place *(with a smile on my voice)*. I am a therapist in the area and I'm feeling called to serve there and I am betting that you know exactly whom the right person for me to speak to is. Whom do you think would be the best person for me to speak to about how I might be able to help out with couples who are having trouble getting along?"

As I continue to build up that relationship in a brief phone call, it is likely that Jennifer will give me some names. In actuality, I have done this several times. Sometimes I get the name and contact information for the main pastor. Other times I get the name of a lay minister who is in charge of all things related to couples. I then contact that person with the opening "Jennifer told me you are the right person for me to speak to. I am a therapist in the area working with couples to help them get along better. I'm feeling called to help you and your parishioners in some way. Would you be open to meeting for 15 minutes to see how I might be able to help?" The fact that "Jennifer approved" goes a long way.

Facing Networking Rejection

The reason I personally feared networking was I was very concerned that I would be rejected. I had visions of meekly asking to meet with someone and being laughed at and told what a ridiculous idea that was. This vision was enough to keep me from picking up the phone, sending an email, or even dropping in to the office.

In reality, I don't think that my worst fear came true even once. However I have been rejected many, many times. For example, when I was first building my practice back in the 1990s, I reached out to every church in the Catholic Diocese of Orange County, California. There were only three that were willing to meet with me. (I've had much better luck since then due to figuring out the gatekeeper script.) The truth is that all three of those churches were instrumental in bringing my practice to a full caseload and keeping it there for many years. But I was rejected a lot of times before I found those three.

But what were they really rejecting? Were they rejecting me personally? Possibly, but I doubt it. I think that my needs and their needs were not a match at that time. The same will be true with any of your networking contacts. Some will be very interested in you. Some will be lukewarm or neutral. And some won't want anything to do with you. (And guess what? Some will be people or places that *you* choose to reject.)

A colleague of mine once gave me some sage advice. "Casey, in meeting new people, you will find that not all of them will want to build a personal or business relationship with you. On average, one third will really want to get to know you, one third won't put any effort into the relationship, and one third will outright reject you."

This advice was given to me right before I went into a roomful of potential referral sources. And her numbers turned out to be exactly right. I was so grateful. I was speaking to one man and asking him about his business. The entire time he looked over my head. While I am only 5'1" tall, I put him into the *outright rejecting me* category and I wasted no more time with him. I know it might be difficult, but please stop worrying about rejection and start finding people that you want to build relationships with.

But when do I get to ask for the referrals?

Years ago during a presentation on networking, someone asked me, "You said *relationship before request*. When do I get to make the request?" In the first place, you may not ever need to do so. Your networking purpose is to help people so they see you as kind and caring about them. Many people will then want to know how to support you in kind. Zig Ziglar said, "You can have everything you want in life if you help enough people get what they want." So focus on being of service. Remember, as we've said before, that is all marketing really is – being of service.

When people like you and like being around you, they will want to refer to you. Feel free to occasionally share success stories to help people understand even more about what you do. You could even ask, "I have some openings in my caseload these days. Might you know of anybody who would be a good connection for me to meet with?" This can help remind somebody that you're looking for referrals.

Networking Groups

There are three types of networking groups. There are groups organized around social activities or volunteer causes, for example, the Junior League or MOPS – Mothers of Preschoolers. Then there are general business networking groups such as the chambers of commerce. Business owners meet regularly to get to know one another.

The third type of networking group is business referral networking groups. With these groups, the goal is to specifically share referrals with one another. Each member acts as the sales force for the other members. Usually in business referral groups, there is one member per professional classification, such as one family law attorney, one chiropractor, one cake decorator, etc. The group members learn about each other's services and keep their eyes and ears open for places where they can make referrals to group members. My favorite group of this type is called BNI (Business Network International).

Clinicians tell me they have differing results in groups like this. Some have amazing results – ending up with referrals worth upwards of $8,000 to $10,000 per year. Others have difficulty with people referring to them. I have two suggestions for those who would like to have better results with these types of referral networking groups.

The first suggestion I have is that you meet one-to-one with at least two members outside of the group per week. These meetings are like intake sessions where you get to know one another. Spend time learning about the other person, their business, and how to refer to them. The more that you are interested in their life and their business, the more likely they are to refer to you. This is where my second recommendation comes in. Please make sure you educate group members on how to make a referral to a therapist. Many people are reluctant to do so because they simply don't know how. Give them a nonthreatening way that they can refer business to you and you are likely to have great positive outcomes.

When I was in BNI, I was often envious of a few members who seemed to get a lot of referrals each week: specifically the makeup sales rep and the cake decorator. That said, the financial advisor, family law attorney, mortgage loan broker, and I (the therapist) received far fewer referrals. Then I realized our referrals netted us much more revenue per client than the makeup sales rep or the cake lady. So don't be discouraged if you don't get lots of referrals immediately. Build the relationships with the members of the group – especially in one-on-one meetings outside the group.

In Summary:

The marketing role is one that some of us do not give enough time to. Expect to spend at least five more hours per week marketing your business if you want to build or maintain your current caseload. You can do this. This is just marketing. It's not rocket science. It's just putting one foot in front of the other, setting a plan, and doing something every single day. How much time should you spend marketing your business? As much as you can. If you want 20 client hours a week and you currently have five client hours, that means you have 15 hours a week to market your business. Remember, it takes two to seven years to build a full practice with focused consistent marketing. And if you are focused and consistent, you will be rewarded.

But what happens when your practice is full? When you have done so well in your marketing role and your clinician role that you cannot take on any more clients? Let's look at how we can continue to increase your income and impact – without burning out in our next section.

Next Steps:

1. Develop your list of referral sources that you know or would like to meet.
2. Create a contact system where you document the information about each contact you reach out to, and the next time you plan to do so.
3. Build those relationships by sharing your compassion, your knowledge, and your network.

CHAPTER EIGHTEEN

Beyond One-to-One Sessions

As you become a more confident CEO, amazing things happen. As your therapy business grows, one day you realize your caseload is full. Sometimes this happens without us being aware of it. One of the first signs of a full caseload is a reluctance to answer the phone. One clinician told me, "I see that I have messages and I just cringe. It's going to take time to call them and then I have to tell them that I don't have availability to see them. I worry about saying no to them. I also worry about what will happen to the referral source that sent the potential client my way if I'm turning down their clients. So I avoid the phone."

This problem of feeling discomforted when our caseload is full is a direct result of our current private practice business model. We deliver services primarily as "one fee for one unit of treatment for one time period." In other words, we see clients in our offices usually for a 50-minute session. I call this the "Butt in Chair" business model. And when we run out of butt in chair hours (aka availability to see clients), we aren't sure what to do. Taking on more clients can lead to burnout. Also with this model, you do not have money coming in when you are on vacation, caring for an elderly parent, on maternity leave, or gone for any other absence.

This Butt in Chair business model also means that there is a cap on our income. Yes, you may be able to raise your fees, but at some point there will be a ceiling on the rate the market will bear.

I've heard this business model described as "owning our jobs." And even though I adore my clients, on my bad days I'm not so sure it's a *good* job. My (private practice) job has limited benefits in that I have to pay for my own retirement, insurance, sick time, and advanced training. Unlike when I worked at a corporate job, I get no paid vacation time.

So how can we reach more people in the community and break through the income ceiling without taking on more clients than we can handle and burning out?

About a decade ago, I started researching modifications we could make to our business model to increase our impact and profit. I studied marketing gurus such as Jay Abraham and million-dollar consultant Alan Weiss. Here is what I learned:

If you want to make more money, you can do so in one of four ways:

1. Sell your services to more people
2. Raise fees
3. Create new services to sell to new and existing clients
4. Sell other people's time or services

I began a decade-long experiment of testing all of these options and I will share in this chapter what I have learned.

1. Sell your services to more people

If you do not currently have a full practice, then your way to more income is to increase your marketing. We know that people want psychotherapy – as evidenced by the over 1.5 million searches online a month. If you get the word out about your business and build referral relationships, I fully expect you will attract new clients.

2. Raise your fees

This can increase your income and profit over time. We discussed this quite a bit in the operations section of this book. Remember to use the business decision triangle whenever you consider raising your fees – especially if you consider doing it with existing clients. If this is not well thought out, you can actually lose money by raising fees. That said, if your schedule is two-thirds to three-quarters full, consider raising your fees for new people. See if you get pushback. Always make sure, though, that your fee is congruent with your self-image. If not, you will not be able to get people to pay it. In other words, if you are undercharging and not happy about it, get some support to help you see yourself as a therapist worthy of a higher fee.

3. Create new services to sell to new and existing clients

In 2009, I started talking about changing our business model from the Class Private Practice model (aka Butt in Chair model) to Private Practice Plus model. My intention was to invite therapists with semi-full practices who were, frankly, tired of doing therapy to consider adding new services to their current menu for fun and profit.

I discussed adding VIP or concierge services where clients pay a premium for longer sessions or after-hours contact. I talked about creating information products such as audio or digital products. I mentioned adding coaching services.

And you know what? I tried each of them. Every single one was fun and had moments of excitement. I had a ball playing with each of these income streams. Some did produce extra income. But what about boatloads of PROFIT? What about truly moving beyond the Butt in Chair model? Not really. My Private Practice Plus model was great for fun and as a creative outlet, but it was not a very good, full-time profit generator.

But then, I was reminded of the fourth way to create additional income.

4. Sell other people's time

Sounds odd, right? Sell other people's time? I thought that, too. I realized this meant to, in a way, clone the clinician role of the therapy business owner. If I hired additional clinicians to come into the counseling practice, the practice then would take a portion of the fee in exchange for space and administrative support such as scheduling and billing. In other words, selling other people's time meant creating a counseling center.

In my role as mentor/coach, center owners started asking me to help them become a better CEO. I would teach them about all the roles in their business. We would define the client journey and develop the policies and procedures necessary to smooth out the operations role. I taught them to know their numbers and about good HR policies.

As I saw their success, I realized that THIS model – adding clinicians to a practice – is a very solid way to more profit if the practice is full. Adding clinicians helps us reach more people than we ever could alone. With this model, we truly have moved beyond the Butt in Chair business model for ourselves. We really will have money coming in when we are on vacation! In fact, I feel so strongly about this model that I devote the entire next chapter to it!

How do you decide which revenue stream to pursue?

Before you decide to add an additional revenue stream beyond one-to-one sessions, I want you to think about what your business purpose is for adding the revenue stream. Are you trying to increase your profit? Do you want to reach more people in the community? Is the plan to create a legacy with something that will live on, perhaps a product, long after you've retired? Are you to share your hope for people, perhaps in written form like a book?

This is an important question, because you want to evaluate any potential new revenue stream by your goal for it.

This is where the business decision triangle comes in again. You can have a meeting with your operations director, the clinician, the finance director, and your visionary (even if you are all of those roles). Really think about how you want to spend your time, beyond one-to-one sessions.

Most of us would like to, in some way, clone ourselves. We would like to be able to do two things at once: spend time on a beach with our family and be paid for helping clients. If that is your goal, then the next chapter (Expand Your Reach with a Leveraged Business Model) will be for you!

Let's take a closer look at some new revenue stream options, just in case you aren't sold on adding clinicians yet. I want to mention this is not an exhaustive list, but it might get your creativity jump-started.

1. Become a coach

Daily, people tell me that they would like to become a coach so that they could make more money. In fact, many of us thought that coaching would be a new, ideal career path for many clinicians. We could treat high-functioning clients from home in our yoga pants – and be paid a lot of money for doing so.

This hasn't come true for most of us. I believe that it is actually easier to sell therapy than coaching services. This is due to the rich history and tradition of psychotherapy. For the most part, our culture understands what therapy is and many see it as a solution to a problem they have. Remember, there are 1.5 million searches for therapists online each month.

When I first began marketing my "life coaching" practice, I spent a lot of the time explaining what a coach is. Business coaching is a little bit easier to understand, but if you're doing life or relationship coaching, it's a concept that sometimes has to be explained. In my experience, if I have to explain a concept, I am further away from the sale.

The other problem with coaching is that the delivery model is similar to therapy in that many people do it as one-to-one sessions. While you may be able to coach over the phone or internet, you're still selling one hour to one unit of treatment for one fee. It doesn't give you the opportunity to leverage and to really increase your income.

What about the promise of riches for coaches? A recent study showed that coaches made on average between $66,000 and $115,000. Now, there are some exceptions, with some coaches making significantly more – especially when they "own" a niche. But I worry when I hear therapists thinking they will double their income by becoming a coach. That said, if you wanted to do executive coaching and get in with companies, that is a possibility. It does pay well. My question to you is do you want to spend the time and the effort to build another business and get into companies? This can take a lot of work. Are you up for that? Is that what you're looking for?

Some clinicians say that they want to do coaching so that they can practice across geographic lines that they may not be able to with their therapy license. I'm going to suggest that you speak with your personal, mental health attorney about this before doing so. You must identify how your coaching is different from your therapy so that your licensing board doesn't think that you're just trying to get around the geographic limitations.

2. Creating an information product, such as an audio or a video or eBook that people would buy online

This is the one income idea that people most often ask me about. They have a passion about a particular topic and want to share that with others. I ask them, "What is your business purpose for creating this additional stream of revenue?" If their answer is "Because I have something to say and I want to share it with the world," then I am fine with them creating an information product.

If the answer is, "I'm tired of butt-in-chair hours and I want to significantly increase my income," then I suggest we run some financial projections. This means identifying how much to charge and how many units you would need to sell in order to make the kind of income that you want. It means looking at the effort required to make that many sales. Let me share an example.

A therapist came to me and said that she wanted to create an eBook about relationships to sell as a Kindle book on Amazon. I asked her what her business purpose was and she said, "I want to make a LOT of money." We then ran the projections.

She planned to sell the eBook for $9 on Amazon. I then asked her what her average hourly counseling rate was, and she said it was $180. I said, "Okay, so you need to sell 20 of these eBooks to make what you make in one hour for doing therapy." She agreed.

I asked, "How many are you expecting to sell?" She thought about that for a minute. She said, "Well, I do a lot of speaking in my community. I could probably sell four or five a month to people in my community." If she sells five eBooks a month, she's now earned $45 a month (and that's before Amazon takes its cut).

She said, "But I really want to sell them online to people who don't know me."

This would necessitate creating an entirely new online business. She would need to build a following that would want her eBook. Let's say for every thousand people that follow her, one or two would buy her eBook. The amount of effort it would take to build that following is going to be substantial for what appears to be a limited return. In the end, she chose not to create the eBook.

Again, asking about the business purpose is key. If she had said that her purpose was to fulfill a dream of becoming an author, then the eBook would have been a great idea! If she said, "I want a free item to give away to help me build credibility," then a free eBook would have been a great idea. But it was probably not the right revenue stream if she wanted a big time profit-maker.

3. Be a seminar leader

Some clinicians have told me that they've seen people like Michael Yapko and Sue Johnson create seminars that they run around the world. Indeed, this can be done, but it's not an easy life. It's going to take time to do a lot of branding and marketing to find enough people who would want to come to see you speak. If you have a great message and you're willing to put the time into it, building with small audiences first, it's possible that you could become a seminar leader. You could also connect with one of the CEU companies who might be willing to hire you to do so.

There is some difficulty trying to do this along with seeing clients regularly in a practice, due to the travel involved. I know many of you reading this book might be certified in a particular type of therapy, such as Gottman, and you might have the opportunity to lead seminars under that branding. This can give you some additional revenue. Is it going to help you reach the number of people that you want to? Is it going to help you have the profit that you want? It might, but the point is to run your projections and figure out how many units you would need to sell, or how many people would need to come to a workshop in order for you to get paid a certain amount of money. Then compare that to the effort you would need to put into it in order to make that happen. Your decision will usually be obvious – one way or the other.

4. Writing books

Writing and publishing a book can be one of the great joys for anyone who has something to say. The man who helped me self-publish this book told me he knows of authors who screamed like a little kid the day that they opened the box and saw their finished product. It is quite an accomplishment.

Many, many people want to write books, and yet few do. If you have something to say, if you want to write a book, let's talk about your purpose in doing that. Is your purpose to use it to build visibility and credibility for your therapy business? By all means, it's a great way to do so. Are you using it to potentially lift your credibility so that you can get more speaking engagements? Absolutely.

If you are doing it to make money on the book sales, I'm going to ask you again to run your projections. What is your income goal? How many books do you need to sell? How much do you make per book? You might make anywhere from a dollar to $10 per book, depending on whether you have a traditional publisher or you're self-published. How many books would you need to sell in order to really make the kind of income that you want?

If you're writing a book because you have a story to tell or information you want to share, or you would like to have it as a credibility enhancer, then write that book! It's an additional resource in your tool belt. But if you're writing strictly to make money, my friends who have written anywhere from 15 to 30 books suggest that you choose another option.

Is it time for you to run some projections of a new revenue stream? Here is the list I use to evaluate my options.

1. Income Stream Idea:
2. Primary Business Purpose (pick only one as the primary purpose): *Increase income, create something for fun, become an author, create a legacy*
3. Additional Purpose(s):
4. Revenue Potential: *How many do I need to sell to make a certain amount of income? What is realistic?*
5. Cost to deliver the service: *What hard cost expenses are involved? What learning do I need to do and how much would that cost?*
6. Gross profit per week or month based on projected sales: *Income minus hard costs to produce or deliver the service.*
7. Additional expenses to produce or deliver the service: *Are there any additional costs such as marketing?*
8. Growth potential: *How quickly do I anticipate growth? As I grow, what additional income and expenses might be incurred?*
9. Ease of attracting people to purchase this revenue stream: *Easy, Moderate, or Difficult*
10. Amount of time required to implement and realize profit: *How long will I need to fund this project before making a profit?*
11. Reasons NOT to choose this model: *Management guru Peter Drucker said, you don't have an argument for something if you don't have an argument against it.*

In Summary:

The business model we have adopted (one fee for one unit of treatment for one period of time) is one we know and love. But when the caseload grows to full, this model has limitations. In this chapter, I have reviewed some myths of passive income and shared how to run projections to see what additional business models might work for you. The first question to ask is always, "What is the purpose of adding a new service or product?" That will guide you.

Next Steps:

1. Have you considered any additional income streams?
2. If so, run your projections and see which, if any, make the most sense for you.
3. If you'd like to consider the addition of clinicians as a business model, turn the page!

CHAPTER NINETEEN

Expand Your Reach with a Leveraged Business Model: Add Clinicians to Your Practice

In the last chapter, we reviewed different types of income streams that a clinician might add to her practice. I shared with you the process I use to run the projections to assess the value of adding an income stream. If your goal is to significantly increase your income, then as we saw, some of those ways will not prove to be good choices.

That is why I am very excited about this chapter. When your practice is full and you are receiving between three to four or five additional calls each week that you are either referring out or not answering, then it is time to consider expanding your practice by adding clinicians. I call this "creating a center" or group practice.

Let's take this business model – adding clinicians to our practice – and run the projections:

1. Income Stream Idea: Adding clinicians to my practice (creating a center)
2. Primary Business Purpose: Increase income

3. Additional Purposes: Serve more people in the community than I could alone. Mentor clinicians. Create a team atmosphere.

4. Revenue Potential: If the associate sees 10 clients a week at $150 = $1,500/week increase in revenue to the center

5. Cost to deliver the service: If the clinician were paid 55% of the fee, the clinician's pay would be $82.50 per session. If they served 10 clients a week, it would cost $825 per week.

6. Gross profit per week: If one associate clinician (as a contractor in your center) saw 10 clients a week at $150 per session, it would result in a net income to the center of $675 per week. Assuming a 44-week year, that is an additional $29,700 per year gross profit.

   Note: If you have an insurance-based practice, then the center will probably net around $40 per session after paying a contracted associate clinician. Ten sessions per week from your associate translates into $400 per week net additional income to your center. Assuming a 44-week year, that is an additional $17,600. Double that if you have two clinicians seeing 10 clients a week for $35,200 a year – all for taking your overflow!

   Also, if your associate clinician is an actual employee of your business, your compensation to the center will be reduced by roughly 9 to 10% based on the payroll taxes you need to pay the government when you have employees.

7. Additional expenses: There would be additional expenses for insurance, marketing (online therapy locator listings, business cards, and office name plates, etc.), and adding

another user to the practice management software. These could conservatively be estimated at $1,500 a year, still leaving a nice profit.

8. Growth potential: As the center grows, there will be more income and expenses for admin support and additional space. The decision to grow could be made after the first clinician is onboard and the business model tested.

9. Ease of Attracting People to Purchase this revenue stream: Easy. If the practice is already turning away clients, there are people ready to purchase this service. If the practice is not full or turning away business, this would be a hard model to implement. If you didn't have enough calls coming in, you would want to increase your marketing until you had enough clients to fill your schedule.

10. Amount of time required to implement and maintain profit: This model will take a fair amount of time initially. Then it should lessen as more systems are developed and implemented. If the center continues to have a good reputation in the community, the number of client inquiries should increase over time.

11. Reasons NOT to choose this model: It will take a fair amount of time to set up. It does require "being the boss." It also requires assuming some risk since the practice will no longer be a solo-practice.

12. Your thoughts?

I resisted this for quite a while, until I ran the numbers. Adding clinicians, by far, is one of the most profitable ways to build your therapy business. If you are already a known commodity for helping people in your community, then you can lean back on what you already have built in order to add more money to your practice.

Taking your therapy business beyond a solo practice by adding clinicians can be scary. There are so many things to think about – legally, operationally, and financially. And of course, there is the "being the boss" and managing people aspect that can feel a bit overwhelming at first.

Here is the truth: you have every right to be concerned. There is a sense of feeling in control when you are simply managing yourself and your own clients. There is more responsibility when adding additional people to your team. And there is responsibility to the end client – the client that you will not be treating. So, of course, you would be nervous at first. This anxiety or fear can manifest as resistance to the idea. You might have thoughts such as, "I don't want to worry about other people. I don't want to have to get them clients."

But there was a time when you were a brand new private practitioner, too. When you got your first office space and started attracting your first clients. You had no idea back then all the roles and functions involved in running a therapy business. You made it through that time. You asked questions of others who had done it before you. You reached out and got legal advice as needed. You are a smart cookie and you can do this, too. The bigger question is do you want to increase your impact and income by taking on the roles of center owner and manager of other practitioners?

If your interest is piqued, let's explore the myriad of options you have when building a center with additional clinicians. Then if you decide you want to explore this business model further, I'd advise you to connect with an attorney, an accountant, and a center owner who has done it or helped others do it.

Most of the work in opening a center will come when adding your first associate clinician. The CEO role will need to access all the other roles in order to make this model work for you. The visionary will be invited to make some decisions. Once those decisions are made, the operations role will work at developing policies and procedures for the center. If you have already created an Operations Manual for your solo practice, this is not too difficult, but you will need to make some changes. The finance role will be heavily involved in the compensation decisions. I coach many center owners who have come to me wondering why they are not making more money. Usually it is because of overpaying their associates. Once the decision is made, the marketing role will get involved since there will be some changes to the marketing you are doing currently. And the clinician role will be instrumental in setting the clinical policies for the center.

While there is a lot to do, it can be broken down into a series of decisions followed by an action plan. Let's take a look at the first decision you will face when you decide to add clinicians to your practice.

Your Business Model: Decisions for the Visionary

Your visionary role will be the first role to "get busy" because everything stems from your vision.

Think about your practice. (I am now calling it a center if you are adding an associate.) What image do you want to project to the community? This will likely be a continuation of your current mission, image, or brand.

1. Do you want to bring in pre-licensed people or people who have been licensed already?

    When you bring in pre-licensed people, you have the opportunity to shape and train them in your way of working with clients. Since most of the time they are under supervision, you'll know what is going on with their therapeutic interventions and help guide the treatment. Pre-licensed people are often very passionate about the work, hungry for real cases, and interested in learning and doing great jobs.

While you don't have to, you can choose to offer therapy with pre-licensed clinicians at a lower fee to the community. Pre-licensed people can be amazing therapists. I personally think that pre-licensed people are closer to their education and closer to their passion. In some ways, they may be better than licensed people who have "seen it all" and may be nearing burnout.

At the same time, pre-licensed therapists have less experience, and some center owners would feel more comfortable offering the pre-licensed services at a more affordable rate. This can help reach those who may not be able to afford more expensive therapy. If you decide to bring in less experienced therapists (especially students or those who have had little experience actually counseling people), you will need to spend more time supervising and mentoring them. For some center owners, this is a plus as they love teaching and mentoring. For others, it may feel like too much time for too little reward. Know yourself and choose wisely.

The other option is to bring in senior-level clinicians or at least clinicians with more experience post-licensure. Experienced, licensed clinicians can often give you a sense of ease in that you know these clinicians have handled difficult cases before and know the legal and ethical requirements. They are also less likely to require a lot of supervision. That said, if you bring in licensed associate clinicians from agency settings or government settings, expect that they might need some mentoring from you. A private practice setting is quite different from agency work.

2. Do you want your associates to be credentialed on insurance panels or will they be fee-for-service only?

    The decision also comes from your current way of doing business. In your visionary role, look ahead and see what makes sense for your business. If you choose the managed care or insurance route, consider what steps will be necessary to credential the associates. You may choose to have them credentialed under your practice or individually credentialed. Look at the pros and cons of both.

3. Do you want to bring in contractors or employees?

    Not only will the visionary role be making this decision, but you will also need input from your attorney and accountant. Different countries have different laws around this. In the United States, you can either bring associates into your business as employees where you will pay the payroll taxes for them or they can be 1099 contractors where you cut them a check and they pay their own payroll taxes. There are specific IRS rules related to contractors, so getting outside consultation from both an accountant and an employment attorney is a good idea.

4. What type of business structure will you have?

    This also is a legal and accounting question. When you are the only clinician in your practice, your choice of business structure may not be as important as it is when you decide to add additional clinicians. Get advice from the experts. I cannot tell you how many people I see on social media asking other people what type of business structure they should have. I see new center owners asking, "Should I be an LLC or S-Corp?" Please don't let people who don't know you, and who may not know the laws for your specific location and license type, give you legal advice. For example, the marriage and family therapist laws regarding corporations in California were written before LLC was a valid type of corporation. So the law shows what type of corporation marriage and family therapists can have in California. LLC is not on that list at all, so when I opened my practice, my attorney encouraged me to make it an S-corp. Oh, and there are very specific laws about naming a practice. In fact, my corporation paperwork was sent back because I didn't have the right words in my name the first time I submitted it.

5. How will you compensate your associates?

Most centers offer their associates administrative support and office space in exchange for a portion of the fee that the client pays. You can either pay them a flat rate per session or you can have them pay a percentage of the fee for each session back to you. You may choose to have the center do all the fee collection; this means that the credit card income, checks, and cash go into the center's bank account first. Then the associates are paid the total for the clients they saw minus the portion that is going back to the center. You can also choose how often you will pay your associates: weekly, biweekly, or monthly.

As you can see, the finance role needs to join the visionary role to decide how much to compensate the associates. Compensation is a very serious decision and, if not well thought out, can create big problems later.

I hear a lot of people talk about "industry standard pay" for associate clinicians. I have yet to read anything that really is an industry standard. What I do know is that many clinicians are making the decision to hire somebody without consulting the financial role of their business. They are not looking at the numbers to see what they can afford. This results in overpaying clinicians. I can't tell you the number of therapy center owners that I coach who are running at break-even or even running at a loss because they are paying their people too much. It costs money to run your business. You want to make sure that the people coming in really do add to your bottom line.

Discussing compensation can make some center owners a little nervous. They feel that the associate should get the lion's share of the fee since, after all, they saw the client. Please don't downplay or minimize the value of marketing, administration, and office space. If these associates didn't work for you and wanted to open their own office, they would need to sign their own lease, do their own billing and banking, manage their own facilities and technology, get their own practice management system, figure out how to answer their own phone and schedule sessions, develop their own Operations Manual, etc. You are offering them a lot – including a team atmosphere – so please do not undervalue your contribution to the associates.

Finally, as we have discussed, if your associates come in as employees, remember you will pay about 9% or 10% in payroll taxes depending on your area. (Each will be different so discuss this with your accountant.) This comes directly from your share of the fee. If you pay your employee-associates 60% of the fee, then you are really paying them about 70% when you add in payroll taxes. That doesn't leave a lot for all your expenses. And remember, the point of this business model is for you to increase the number of people you can serve *and* increase your profit.

Again, if you have any questions on the fee structure, please talk with your attorney and accounting professionals. Some clinicians worry that paying a percentage of the fee is considered fee splitting. My legal advisor explained that it's not fee splitting at all. The money that the associates pay me as part of that fee is for administration, marketing, space, facilities management, etc. As always, check with your legal and ethical advisors if you have any questions.

6. Will you perform the marketing role for your center (acquire clients for the associates) or will you ask them to do their own marketing?

This is one of those decisions that also has powerful consequences. If you have been performing the marketing role for your practice, and you now have more inquiries than you can handle, I would strongly advise you to continue in your marketing role. This way, you can hire good clinicians that want to stay in the clinician role. As we know, not all clinicians are good in the marketing role. Those clinicians who are good at the marketing role are often very entrepreneurial.

One of the problems with hiring an entrepreneurial person is they often have a dream of opening their own practice. If you require them to go out and do their marketing, they will ask themselves why they are working for you. Entrepreneurial people are more likely to leave your practice and sometimes take their entire caseload with them. My recommendation is that you assume the marketing role for your center and hire non-entrepreneurial people who are great in the clinical role. The better they are at treating clients and ethically keeping them in treatment as long as the client needs it, the more profitable your center will be.

Your Brand (Reputation)

If your therapy business brand has always been you and your name, it might be time for a change. This is so your referral sources and new clients are willing and happy to see the associates. One of my clients had a center that was named after her and when people called, they insisted on seeing the owner. You may consider, over time, moving your branding from Mary Jane's Counseling to Counseling in Topeka with a sub-line of "Mary Jane Counseling and Associates," and then eventually removing your name. If you want people to see your clinicians, then brand yourself as a group practice or center. I encourage therapy business owners to downplay their position in the center as well. For example at my center, I am the last listed on our "Meet the Therapists" page.

Consider whether you want to have a center or group practice full of disparate specialties or brand around a niche. (HINT: If possible, do the latter.) If you start a center comprised of a lot of therapists who all want to work with different specialties, it can be harder to fill each of them.

For example, one of my therapist clients owns a large counseling center. She built it by inviting clinicians she liked to work there. She asked them, "What would you like to have as a specialty?" They picked different specialties: geriatrics, OCD, sex therapy, children, eating disorders, and biofeedback. It became clear quickly that this myriad of specialties was hard to market. She would need, in her marketing role, to market each specialty individually. This meant connecting with different referral sources for each. She was struggling to find the time to market all the various specialties, so she asked the associates to market themselves. They did not and she had to work more hours just to pay for the expenses of her big center.

Contrast that with other center owners who developed a center around a niche or specialty. Several center owners I know have centers branded around relationship counseling. All the associates are trained couples counselors. Additionally, there might be a sex therapist for difficult sex issues (fetishes comes to mind) and an LGBT therapist. These centers are able to fill their therapists' schedules more easily than if they had one therapist who worked with OCD and one who worked with geriatrics. When clients call and you only have one therapist who can treat that client, it limits your reach and opportunity.

If you build your center for every population you could possibly see, the likelihood of you seeing any of them is none. (NOTE: The opposite is true in rural areas, however. If you are opening a center in a rural area, you can be more general in your niche. You can appeal to more populations.)

Central Front Office Support (phone answering and scheduling)

The first thing I do when I coach a center owner is to get clarity on the client journey. I want to know what happens from the first client inquiry through termination. Often we find that this activation of the operations role and improving policies and procedures can advance the center's performance and profit quickly.

My first question is, "How do new clients first contact your center?" More than one client has told me that each therapist has their own contact information on the center's website. Think about that for a moment. What happens if the client contacts one of the therapists on the site and that therapist, for some reason, can't get back to the client immediately? The client will move on to the next referral they have. And this may not be a therapist in your center.

If there is one central point for front office contact, you have more options and more opportunity to place that client with any of your therapists.

Some therapists make what I consider a mistake by having the associates schedule their own sessions with new clients. While I understand this, it can actually not be good for the business. For example, let's say I call your center to schedule a couple's session for my husband and me. Imagine that the person answering the phone directs me to hang up and call your therapist, Jamie, to schedule the appointment. It is very possible that I won't call Jamie. I might forget about it or move on to my next referral. Some center owners say, "We will have Jamie call you." But I might not want to wait for Jamie to call me and instead start calling other therapists.

The more stop points, the more points of interaction, between my call and the point at which I am scheduled, the less likely I am to schedule with that particular center. My recommendation is that you and the associates in your practice agree on the days and times that they are available to work in your center. Then either you or a front office person answers the phone and schedules accordingly.

As part of my marketing and finance roles, I pay for Psychology Today profiles for the clinicians in my center. The phone number on each listing (for each clinician) is our center's front office phone line. This means if anyone calls for any of the therapists in our center, they will get our front office person answering the call.

Recently I received a call from Psychology Today for one of the therapists in my center who was on vacation. I explained that all of our therapists are senior-level therapists specializing in couples counseling. I was able to place that client with another of our therapists. And the client was happy to go with the first available therapist. If we had phone numbers for each of the individual therapists on the Psychology Today profiles, the client would not have reached the vacationing therapist. She would probably have moved on to another therapist and the center would have lost the client.

Recruiting, Hiring, and On-boarding

Once you make the decision that you're going to bring in a new clinician, you will actually add a role under your CEO umbrella: Human Resources (HR). You will create new policies and systems regarding bringing in new people.

Here are some things to consider in your HR role:

1. What will the agreement or contract between you, the center owner, and the associate look like?

   Both you and your new hire will want to have a document that spells out your rights, responsibilities, and expectations. Make sure your mental health attorney has reviewed any contract you have prior to offering it to any new hires. This is step 1. Don't move forward and talk with any applicants without your expectations (and this contract) in place.

2. Where will you find applicants?

   You can find clinicians for your practice either through existing clinicians you know or you can visit agencies or hospitals where they have therapists and let them know you have openings. I have advertised on Craigslist, LinkedIn, and my association website's online classifieds. The latter has been the most beneficial to me. Before you do any advertising or interviewing, please make sure you are clear on the roles you want for your associate (clinician role alone or clinician and marketing roles) and on the compensation.

3. How will you interview/assess for appropriateness or a "good fit"?

   Assess their long-term goals. Do they match your CEO and visionary goals for your center? Assess their clinical skills. Develop a good list of interview questions and create a process that uses your time effectively. Consider a probationary period.

4. How will you train them on your policies, systems, and procedures?

This is where your Operations Manual comes in.
Review all of your policies with your associates.
Create a new hire process to make sure you show
them how to best work in your center.

Add Your New Associates to Your Tracking Metrics

After you bring in your first associate, you'll be giving them clients.
Track the number of new clients you give them and then watch
their clients' average length of stay. One of the most challenging
things for some center owners is helping non-entrepreneurial
therapists keep their clients coming into the office regularly. In your
clinical role, you can mentor any of your clinicians who are having
difficulty. You may wish to add the Feedback Informed Treatment
to your clinical procedures.

If your associate clinicians cannot keep their clients attending
regularly, your business is not going to be financially viable. So watch
the metrics. Review the Advanced Metrics in the CEO Dashboard
section earlier in this book. When you look at your profit and loss
statement, you want to be able to identify if your associates are
adding to your bottom line.

In Summary:

When private practitioners first decide to add associates into
their business, there is a lot to do. This is where you truly need to be
the CEO of your business. All of your roles (clinician, marketing,
finance, operations, and visionary) will have decisions to make and
action plans to implement. And now you are adding yet another
role, human resources, with more tasks and responsibilities.

That said, when you can, develop the systems as we've discussed for each part of your business: front office operations, back office operations, clinical policies, finance policies, and HR systems. In metrics tracking, you will find that over time, the amount of time it takes you to manage your center will be less. Then one day you will notice that you really do have passive income.

Again, if you are receiving phone calls for a minimum of five hours/clients a week that you are not able to take yourself, then you might want to consider adding a clinician. You can start with just one part-time clinician who is in your office five hours or eight hours a week. But as always, run this decision through the income stream decision tree including your financial projections in order to make the decision.

It is important to note that this is not a get-rich-quick scheme. There is quite a bit of work to get started. But it has significant possibilities – both for more profit for you and for helping more people in your community.

Finally, please reach out for help. You need expert legal and accounting advice. You also need a mentor who understands what is involved in opening a center and who can shave years off your learning curve – and in the end save you a lot of money.

Next Steps:

1. Run your projections. Does this feel like a good business model to you?
2. Review your tracking. Are you getting five calls a week that you are not taking? How many could you refer to an associate? (If you like this model but don't have enough to refer yet, increase your marketing efforts.)
3. If you decide this might be a good model for you, learn more about it. We offer programs to help new center owners learn how to add clinicians.

CHAPTER TWENTY

How You See the World
(and Why It Matters)

If you remember, in our first chapter, we talked about the five ingredients to a happy, healthy, and wealthy therapy business:

- Money Wisdom

- Business Strategy

- Creation Plans for Growth

- Action Steps/Plans

- Perspective

In this chapter, I want to talk about the last ingredient: Perspective. This is how you see the world and your place in it. It is how you view success and your personal ability to achieve success.

How is it that some people are so clear that they deserve abundance and good fortune and others decide they are unworthy of a good life and income? As therapists, I am sure we have a zillion clinical answers to that question. But we could probably agree that regardless of how we got them, many of us have beliefs that hold us back. You've probably heard them described as "limiting beliefs." These are thoughts or beliefs that come from our history, sometimes they come from our family of origin, and sometimes they come from previous experiences.

No matter where they come from, they can impact your thoughts, actions, and outcomes – and you might not even be aware of it.

Even though people often assume I'm confident and that I never feel afraid, the truth is different.

I actually put off writing this book for a long time because I was afraid of what people might say about my writing. My previous book had received a couple of negative reviews and that tapped into my insecurity as a writer. Even though I have a lot to say and a lot I want to share, I had a limiting belief about whether or not I was good enough to share this content about how to be a confident CEO in this form. That belief stopped me from writing another book for four years.

How I moved through that limiting belief is something I will share with you in just a bit, but let's stay with this idea of limiting beliefs a bit longer.

I think that most of us have some limiting beliefs. The key is to recognize them. It is the examined life that is well lived. Let's take a look at some common limiting beliefs and identify some ways that you might work your way through them.

Some common limiting beliefs:

- "No one will pay my full fee."

- "I am not good with money."

- "It is selfish (or I am greedy) if I want to make a lot of money."

- "I am greedy if I work toward making my business profitable."

- "I am not worth a fee of $xxx."

- "People won't like me if I make a lot of money. I will be judged, shamed, or criticized if I am successful."

- "I am a therapist. I am supposed to *help* people – not *charge* them. I am making money off of people's pain."

- "I am a good 'insurance' therapist but I don't know that I could really offer private pay services."

- "Who am I to want to be successful?"

- "I am afraid to put myself out there because I might be rejected." (I find these same people also have this belief: "If I put myself out there, too many people will want me and I will be too busy." Interesting juxtaposition, right?)

- "There is never enough (time, money, love)."

- "I can't do this."

- "No therapy clients will come during the day and I don't want to work nights."

- "I don't deserve to enjoy the finer things in life."

Wow. I bet these only scratch the surface of the wonky thinking that causes us to not have the success we want.

I am curious. Did any of those beliefs listed above feel familiar? And speaking of "feeling" – how did you "feel" when the familiar ones grabbed you?

Sad? Afraid? Angry? Envious? Anxious? Hopeless? These are common reactions to beliefs that are actually not true – but we feel bad because we are *afraid* they are true. I call this "wonky thinking." When I have wonky thinking, I feel instantly bad about myself – almost ashamed. And I feel it right away in my stomach.

But here is where I get excited. If I start to feel very angry or very scared, what that means is that I am simply *feeling* a *thought* such as "I could never be successful at doing this" or "that person always takes what I want. I'll never get what I want."

Those thoughts create the feeling of anger or fear or envy. When I recognize that I'm having a strong feeling, it usually means I'm *feeling my thinking*. The great part about this is that I know that my thinking is probably wonky. If somebody else has some success that I envy, it doesn't mean I can't have it, too. Perhaps I could study how they achieved that success and learn from them. Perhaps I can look at them as a mentor... a manifestation of what is possible.

This is one of the shifts I made that helped me write this book you're now reading.

When I am feeling my thinking, my go-to reaction now (on my better days) is to do nothing. I take no action when I get that scared feeling in the pit of my stomach after thinking a limiting belief. I know that the strong feeling means that I am feeling my thinking. And even though it *feels* true, it doesn't mean it *is* true. So now, if I have a really strong negative feeling, I know this is my cue to do nothing. I recognize that I am feeling the result of a wonky thought. This non-action tactic is what I call stop, drop, and roll.

I have discovered that if I take action when my thinking is wonky, the action will likely be ineffective or hurt me or someone else. I wait until I feel better. When the negative feeling passes, it means my wonky thinking has cleared and I can assess the reality of the situation. Then, I can take appropriate and much more effective action.

Here's an example of feeling my thinking and then what happened when I employed stop, drop, and roll.

A few months after we moved into our new office space, our Property Manager confronted me. The outside doors to our office building are locked on the weekends, so in order to allow entry for our clients, we would prop the outside door open.

My Property Manager explained to me that this was a violation of my lease. I immediately had a very strong emotional reaction. In less than 60 seconds, I was terrified. I started to worry. "How are we going to open the door for our clients? Our clients are not going to be able to get in and they're going to leave us. We're going to lose all of the money that we could have earned on the weekends. We're going to have to close our center or we're going to have to move, etc." My wonky thinking was off and running and I was starting to panic.

Luckily, we had our three-day private practice conference that week, and so right after I got the news about the door situation, I left for the conference and hosted three days with some amazing therapists.

The conference was incredibly fun and affirming. I got in touch with my love for this work and I ended the conference feeling fabulous and confident. I returned to the office and the situation was still the same. But I was not feeling my thinking; I was not in my catastrophic thinking. I was clearheaded. Since I had chosen not to act on my fears (instead, choosing to stop, drop, and roll), I was able to come up with some perfect action to solve the door dilemma. Our Associate Clinicians have apps on their phones where clients could text them if, for some reason, the door was locked. We are very prompt with our sessions, so there's always time between our sessions that we could go to the door and open it if the client was locked out. We were not going to need to close the center; we were not going to need to move.

All was well. I planned to try this new way for a few months and assess our impact. If there were a problem, I would return to the Property Manager and work out some possible solutions such as a keyed entry that would allow our clients to put in a key code and then come into the building.

When I was feeling my thinking, I became panicked. Had I opted to act on that panic, my business would have been impacted. If I had gone to the Property Manager and caused a scene, my relationship with her might have been impacted. If I had decided we needed to move, there would have been a big financial impact to that.

The best part for me is that when I now feel a very strong emotion, I can guess that my thinking is probably wonky. It means I am upset or worried about something that is probably unlikely to be true. This actually gives me great comfort. As I pause and take no action on the panic, the wonky thinking eventually subsides. That, my friend, is freedom. It's good for you, it's good for your health, and it's good for your business.

Other ways to deal with those old, pesky limiting beliefs

As a profession, we've come so far in the last decade regarding issues with money, and yet there are still some remnants of beliefs that don't serve us. Besides recognizing them as wonky thinking, what else can we do?

1. Evaluate the truth of the belief. Is it 100% true? Really?
2. If so, ask if it is true for *everyone* or just you. And if it is true for you alone, why is that? Dive deep.
3. If others have or do what you want, what would you need to do, believe, or allow to have it too?

Let me share a story. Yesterday I talked to a clinician in private practice, Marcie, about her income struggles. Her complaint was a common one. "Everyone in my area wants to use their insurance. No one wants to pay cash. And I don't take insurance." I could tell her mood was sad, almost hopeless. I recognized this as wonky thinking, but Marcie was pretty convinced it was true.

I asked her, "Is that 100% true? *Everyone* wants to use their insurance? Not one single person wants to pay cash?"

She thought for a minute and then reported, "Well, I do have a handful of fee-for-service clients... just not enough. And everyone who calls asks about it."

I agreed with her that a lot of people would ask about using insurance. I kept probing. "Is there anyone in your area that does not take insurance?"

She reported that three close colleagues had full, cash practices and she knew of others, too. I could see that the knot of this limiting belief was loosening. I gently asked her, "Are you are saying, then, that it is possible for others to have full, cash practices but it is not possible for you?"

Her voice became almost a whisper. "I think if I knew what to do to get clients, then I could have that success, too. But I thought it was true for me. Because what I am doing now isn't working. I don't have a full practice."

That was the opening I was looking for. Then we could address what she needed to do, believe, or allow. She instantly saw that she had unintentionally held herself back by judging herself as less successful than her peers. Her new belief (the bridge belief to more success) was, "I just need to learn what to do and do it. I can be successful, too. It is up to me."

Her mood brightened. She made a plan to learn solid marketing strategies and create action plans to implement them. She agreed to look at her CEO tracking metrics – specifically her conversion of inquiries to clients. She would work to improve that conversion.

She would do this by answering her phone more often, taking a leadership role on the intake call, and having a script ready for when people ask about insurance. This moved her from victim to victor. This wonky, limiting belief was gone.

While I agree that limiting beliefs can impact our success, it's important not to jump to the conclusion that a lack of success is all due to a poor money mindset. If you are not achieving the success that you want, why is that? Is it simply your limited thinking getting in your way? Or is your wonky thinking affecting your actions?

Recently, a client told me that he had not made any progress in marketing his business because he had a limiting belief about money. While I am sure he did, he also had not identified one marketing strategy or taken any steps to do any marketing. It's a lot like being angry you haven't won the lottery when you haven't bought a ticket.

If growing a business scares you a little, this is understandable. There are risks to expanding your business. It takes clear thinking and a review of the potential risks – and your ability to tolerate risk – to see if being a successful business owner is right for you. There's no right or wrong answer to this.

In the book *Psycho-Cybernetics,* author Maxwell Maltz tells us that it is very difficult to do anything that is not within our self-image. I believe that by taking small steps forward and working on our self-imaging, we can really do all that we're called to do.

For those of you who are willing to tolerate a short woo-woo moment... my personal belief is that we are spiritual beings having a human experience. I think it is important that when we are feeling nervous, insecure, or scared, we need to recognize that these are normal human experiences. As imperfect human beings, we make mistakes and have fears. It is to be expected. If we were to put on a constricting suit of armor, we would not expect to hit the bull's-eye when throwing our first dart. Yet, even in our human, clumsy suit of armor, we can continue to practice. We can continue to envision ourselves as amazing dart players. If we do that – if we tap into all of the wisdom seen and unseen around us – I bet we can throw bull's-eyes.

What is your target?

In Summary:

Your perspective about yourself and success can make your CEO tasks harder than they need to be. If you find yourself fearful or judge yourself negatively at times, try to be gentle with yourself. This is normal. Business *is* risky and even the most confident can feel insecure at times.

Pay attention to your feelings. If you have a quick, strong, hit of negative emotion, relax. You are probably feeling your wonky thinking. Stop, drop, and roll. Do nothing. It will pass. If you have beliefs that you feel truly hold you back, review them for truth. If you find they aren't 100% true for everyone, then figure out what you need to do, believe, or allow to have what you want.

Next Steps:

1. Notice when you feel a strong negative emotion. Check in: Am I thinking a thought that just created this feeling? Look for judgments that might be holding you back. Forgive yourself for making these judgments. After all, you are only human.

2. Try daily journaling. Look for self-judgments or limiting beliefs that you worked through during the day. Look for any places you need to forgive yourself or others. High five to you!

CHAPTER TWENTY-ONE

Thinking Like A CEO

In the last chapter, we talked about perspective. This is how you see yourself and what you think about your ability to succeed in the world. In this chapter, I want to share with you some of the best advice I've been given as I've grown into the CEO role of my business. This is an ongoing journey for all of us – from clinician to confident CEO. And my goal with this book is to shave years off your learning curve as my mentors have done for me.

Here are nine wisdom nuggets that have helped me on my CEO journey.

1. Make decisions for the good of all concerned

Therapists have the biggest hearts in the world. We are often willing to sacrifice our own needs and our own desires to make sure that other people are happy. But as we begin to make decisions using the business decision triangle, and consider the points of the business, the clinician, and the client, we need to make sure that the decisions we make are the best for all. This means there will be times when you make decisions and one of those parts isn't going to be as happy as the others. It means that at times someone might be angry with you or dislike you because of your decision.

We've discussed this before that one-third of the people you meet will like you, one-third will be neutral, and one-third won't care for you. There will be times when you need to make decisions that are in the best interest of the business and the client, but the clinician may be unhappy. For example, in my center recently, one of the therapists wanted to market a different type of therapy intervention that did not go with our current specialty. I considered her request from the business decision triangle. Would clients benefit from adding a new specialty to our center? Probably, but we would have to do a whole lot of extra marketing to get those clients in. Other clients might find it odd because our brand was now bifurcated and it didn't really make sense.

Ultimately, I made the decision not to market her new specialty and I explained why. To her credit, she totally understood and agreed. Had I tried to please her and gone ahead and marketed the other specialty, the clients might have been confused and the business might have suffered in the long run. And neither she nor I wanted that.

As a CEO, there are going to be times when people will be upset with you. For example, if you enforce your cancellation policy, there may be times that people are upset. As we've mentioned in earlier chapters, I don't recommend that you immediately enforce it, but that you consider not charging for their first missed session and then have them recommit to the policy. Even then, the client may still be unhappy.

The goal is to try to make the best decisions for the good of all concerned. And at the same time, understand that sometimes someone may be unhappy with your decision.

2. Understand that as a CEO of a therapy business, you are the captain of a large vessel

Large vessels don't stop on a dime and they can't make fast, sharp turns. Think of your business as a ship moving at a steady pace. Any changes to its heading are going to take a conscious decision and a bit of time.

If you want to change your fees or other policies, usually it is best to do so with new clients rather than your existing clients. For example, if you decide to stop working evenings, the first step would be not accepting new clients in your evening slots. Then as your evening clients terminate, you will eventually have your evenings free. This is much less disruptive to the business and the client as compared to trying to move client sessions around to immediately free up your evenings!

So understand that you are the captain of a big ship. If you want to make a shift, consider doing so slowly and with new people.

3. But where possible, be nimble

At the same time, if you are clear on a direction that your business needs to take, try to implement it as soon as possible while impacting the least number of people. For example, if you decide to add an online scheduler to your business, test it yourself for a couple of weeks to make sure that you like it. Then offer access to it to your existing clients so that they can reschedule their own appointments, eliminating some telephone tag. Then, after you see that your current clients can use it with ease, make it available to new clients.

This is a really quick way of implementing a new procedure and you have phased it in, impacting the least number of people. It gives you a chance to really decide if you like the software and can use it before putting people who don't know you through it. Some people might put a new calendar up right away without testing it. Then, if they don't like it, they have to explain that to all their clients. This phased implementation can be done quickly and very nimbly.

4. Pay attention to the CEO role that you don't have time for

Many of us enjoy being the clinician seated across from the client. We enjoy helping them grow and find peace and happiness again. Some of us are even willing to do the marketing. But pay attention to the role that you are avoiding because that role could be the one role that gives you the most income or profit and extra time. If you are avoiding doing your billing, then know that there's probably a lot of money that's yours right there in your accounts receivable. Sometimes people are preoccupied with increasing income by getting new clients when, in reality, they have lots of money waiting for them if they would just ask for it in terms of their billing.

It may be that the role you are avoiding is the financial role. Maybe you're not looking at your profit and loss reports. But if you did, you might be able to make significantly better decisions on how you spend your money. Of the five roles – clinician, marketing, operations, finance, and visionary – look for the one that you're avoiding, that you don't have time for, and I bet right there is the pot of gold at the end of that rainbow.

5. Ask why

So many times we develop habits from former employment situations. In some places that I have worked, it has been a requirement that the notes be so detailed that they literally could not be done on the same day I saw the client. This resulted in notes that were delayed. I went into the office many weekends to catch up with those notes. The quality of the notes weren't any better when I waited to create them. I was further away from the actual session and the content of the note was from memory. If you've taken habits like this into your private practice, ask yourself why you are doing it this way. Then decide if you wish to continue or to modify the procedure in your business.

If someone else has suggested a piece of software for you to use, ask why. If somebody has said that you can't get clients to come in during the day, ask yourself if you think this is true. Then test your assumptions. We have so many preconceived ideas that are simply limiting beliefs in disguise. I know several clinicians who have full daytime practices with couples. Think about that for a moment. Both people in the couple come for a therapy session during the day. It is possible. If you believe that it is *not* possible, then your belief will indeed be true for you.

If you invite other people for recommendations or opinions, be curious as to how they came to their conclusions. This is the secret to really knowing your business. Beware of abdicating decisions just because you feel overworked. This can cost a lot later in terms of both time and money.

6. Nothing is ever wrong; it is simply a missing or broken system

That statement is actually one of our ruling values at Be A Wealthy Therapist. We believe that if there's a problem, either with a client or with a team member, it is simply because somehow we have miscommunicated. We need to improve the communication and improve the system for that communication. This view helps us get past hurt feelings and blaming. When mistakes are made, we simply ask what system could have helped us avoid the mistake. We figure it out, we fix it, and we move on. Time is saved and we all get along better. There are no negative judgments with this view.

7. With every task you do, ask if this is the best way to do it

Shortly after I was licensed, I was a group therapist in an outpatient program. The program ran five to fifteen groups a day. At the end of the day, five therapists were in a conference room charting their groups. Since many of the groups consisted of the same clients, we were fighting over the charts. The simple mechanics of getting Suzy's chart from Ted Therapist at the other end of the table made us look like a bumper car rally.

One day I had had it and called a quick meeting. "How can we share these charts more easily?" We all pondered it. The next day, someone brought in a large Lazy Susan. We put all the charts on it. When a therapist needed a chart, they could, from their seat, simply spin the Lazy Susan and get the chart.

We instantly got along better. It was an amazing system and we were able to actually do chart notes for each of our groups in an hour. This ease came from us asking, "What is the best way we could all share these charts in a very short period of time?"

Here is another example. For a brief period of time, I was on managed care panels. In the morning before my first client, I would prepare what I could for billing my clients that I would see that day. I would do all the prep before they came in. Then after I saw the client, and before the next client, I just had to either hit a button on the computer to enter it or put that form in the mail depending on whether I was doing electronic billing or not.

My point is to continually ask yourself, "Is this the best way to do this task?" My motto: Wherever possible, make things lighter and easier.

8. Own your own value

I believe that you have incredible value. You save lives, you save relationships, and you heal broken hearts. That is amazing work. Own that. It breaks my heart when therapists question their value or worth. It can happen when we get triggered with wonky thinking. It can happen when we envy a colleague's success. It can happen when a client fires us. Stop, drop, and roll until your thinking clears.

There will be people who question you in all kinds of ways. Never let anybody make you question your value. When you are clear on your value, you don't ever have to prove you are good enough. You don't have to try to sell therapy. You don't have to try to convince people to come in. You own your value. Clients and colleagues will feel it. It's a beautiful thing. I think if there was one wish I had for all therapists, it would be to own your value. (And if you find this is hard for you, please get some help with this. I want YOU to know in your heart what a wonderful person and therapist you are.)

9. Note your mistakes but don't judge yourself so harshly

In the book *Psycho-Cybernetics*, Maxwell Maltz mentions that moving toward a goal is like a self-correcting missile moving toward an intended target. We're going forward in a direction and we get off course. We then make adjustments (course-corrections) and continue moving closer to the goal. But often, we overcorrect in the opposite direction so we need to course-correct again. We are moving toward our goals with a series of moves, a series of successive *approximations* towards the goal.

You will make mistakes. Things will go wrong and every single bad thing that happens is an opportunity for you to learn something. These are your gifts in dirty paper.

One of the biggest problems that therapists have is that we expect too much of ourselves. We judge ourselves so harshly. I don't want that for you. If you'd like to implant me in your brain, go ahead because I want to be your cheerleader. I am jumping up and down with a sign that says, "I love you. You can do this. I believe in you!"

Another idea is to create a success journal. Take time once a day and note all of the efforts that you have made in your life and business. These could be personal growth efforts. These could be any efforts towards and steps forward in any of your roles: clinician, marketing, operations, finance, or visionary. Perhaps today you let your runaway visionary take a break and actually wrote some action plans down for your marketing. Or perhaps today you worked with your accountant to better understand your profit and loss statement.

Any success that you experience and any effort that you expended can be documented daily in your success journal. During those days when you start to forget how valuable you are or you start to judge yourself too harshly, pull out your success journal. Mistakes happen. Things go wrong. But if you start to get down or judge yourself, go back and thumb through your success journal. Keeping a daily journal like this breeds confidence. That is what I want for you – to be a spectacular and wonderful and confident CEO who runs her business with ease.

In Summary:

Remember that the ultimate goal of your business is to financially support a wonderful lifestyle for you and your family. Not only is your business here to serve the community, but it must serve your needs as well. As you make decisions with the business decision triangle and all of the metrics and data that we discussed earlier, don't forget your ultimate goal is to make money so that you can have the lifestyle that you want.

You will also disappoint people at times. Expect and accept this. This is part of being a good CEO. Make sure that you stay on your own side. Business is tough enough without us having to fight our own inner critic.

Be curious about how and why you do certain tasks in certain ways. Look for ways to make your life and business lighter and easier.

Finally, in case you forget or are having a bad day, remember you are an extraordinary person with incredible value. Own that. Review your success journal to remind you of your effort and successes.

Next Steps:

1. Review these tips and strategies. Are there ones that you feel might be of help to you?
2. Consider taking one or two of them and exploring them in personal reflection or with colleagues.

CHAPTER TWENTY-TWO

How to Find More Time in Your Day

Each night before bed, I do a ritual of evaluating and journaling about the day. I reflect on the actions I took during the day. As I review the day, I identify the three best things that happened and savor them. At the end of that process, I set my intentions for the next day. Most nights, my intentions for the next day are:

1. Be completely present with all my clients, in my classes, and with my husband.
2. Have "peaceful productivity" throughout the day.

How do we achieve peaceful productivity? This is really a challenge for many of us. You have your calendar filled with client appointments. You have responsibilities outside of your work, including family and community obligations. We are just so darn busy! I am not sure when "being incredibly busy" became a sign of success. You know what I mean, right? People start one-upping each other on how busy or tired they are, as if this is a good thing.

Before we get into the specific strategies to help you have more peaceful productivity, let's think about time. Everybody has the same 24/7. Nobody can really manage time or get more hours in the day. We can choose how to use it. We can choose prioritizing our options. We can choose how much time we give any one task.

A main principle of this book is that there are certain CEO tasks you need to schedule and do. One of the biggest mistakes I see clinicians make is not making time for roles beside clinician. The operations tasks of billing or notes or returning phone calls aren't done. The finance tasks of reviewing profitability and cash projections aren't done. The visionary role is put away until "there is time to think." As we have seen so far in this book, if you don't take the time for all your roles, you will miss out on the ease and profit that is possible. You'll find yourself too busy, unfulfilled, and eventually burned out. I do not want that to happen to you.

Let's look at some of my favorite ways to invite more peaceful productivity into your life.

1. Manage your energy, not your time

You have a lot to get done. You need more time, right? But time is a finite resource. You only get 24 hours each day. But what if you had more *energy*? You may be able to get a lot more done in the same 24 hours if you could renew your energy. In *The Power of Full Engagement*, authors Tony Schwartz and Jim Loehr discuss ways to increase your energy throughout the day across four different continua: physical, emotional, spiritual, and mental. Paying attention to each of these dimensions results in greater engagement and happiness. Your actions don't have to be huge; perhaps it is as simple as making sure you hydrate and move around between sessions. The authors pointed to pro golfers and tennis stars who took very short breaks between shots and, as a result, did very well.

This is due to the renewed energy they received during those fleeting moments between shots.

The authors also shared that living your values, and taking time to really rest can make huge differences in your energy level. As I write this book, I work in 25-minute sprints and then take five minutes to stretch (or do pushups), drink tea, and check in with my husband Bob. After a few 25-minute writing sprints, I take a longer break (25 minutes) and watch a reality TV show, go for a walk, or have a snack. Then I feel renewed and energized. In some ways, it reminds me of what game designer Jane McGonigal would call a "power up." I feel refreshed and renewed! When you have more energy, you can accomplish more, which in turn feels like you really have magically manifested more time.

Take a couple of minutes between clients. Do your breathing exercises. Do a short meditation. Eat. Make sure that you have some type of food and drink every couple of hours. Make sure that during the week, there's time spent in spiritual pursuits, with family, or simply having fun. Let's stop using how busy we are as a badge of how well we are doing. Let's remember that the reason you have this therapy business is so you can make the money to have the lifestyle that you want and you need. Let's make sure there is time and energy left for the life you want.

2. Beware of your self-talk

Negative self-talk can make everything take longer. How many of us wait until the last minute to complete tasks with the excuse, "I work better under pressure?" I believe that we may accomplish more under pressure because we have turned down the volume on the inner critic. I have found that giving myself permission to create a "first draft" on any task helps me get it done quickly. Usually once I get started, I shift into a flow and things start to go faster. So watch your inner critic.

3. Manage your caseload. Work with clients who energize you

Take out your existing calendar and look at your schedule for the next week. Look at each of your clients and ask yourself, "Am I more energized after seeing this client or less energized?" If you find that you are less energized, then ask yourself why that is. Maybe this is a difficult client that you really enjoy, but you have him either at the first session of the day or the last session of the day when perhaps your energy is not the best. If your lower energy is coming from a scheduling problem, consider changing your schedule. After all, you want each client to have the best of you, so make sure you're putting them in a spot where they can get that.

Are you feeling drained because this client is really done with his work and it's time for him to go? Is it because this is not a client that you can do your best work with and he really needs to be referred to a different therapist?

If you find you have clients in your caseload that you don't really care for, I invite you to consider how you might lovingly, gently, legally, and ethically remove them from your caseload. You may wish to talk to an attorney about this. If this client is not one with whom you feel you do your very best work, there's another therapist out there who will. Let's help him find that therapist.

4. Choose your schedule rather than letting your clients choose your schedule

Here comes the fun part. We are going to create your ideal week.

Think of a time of day you really want to be doing therapy. Are you more of a morning person, afternoon person, or do you prefer evenings? Now, I know that you will think, "Well Casey, my type of clients will only come in the _____(fill in the time frame here)."

That's possibly true if you're working with adolescents or children. They are probably not going to come into your office from nine to noon weekly as a rule. However, a lot of people told me that couples won't come in the daytime... but they do. Would they prefer evenings? Many of them would, but when there are no more evening appointments available, they will take the daytime appointments.

I schedule my individual coaching clients in the mornings. That's when I'm the freshest. That's when I'm the most on fire. If I coach people later in the day, I'm a bit more sluggish and I don't think I'm as good. I choose the times that I'm willing to work and then I invite people to coach with me during those times.

Don't let someone else tell you when you should work. Decide what works for you and then do the marketing to get the clients who are willing to come during those times. You may have to work more in the marketing role to make that happen. When I stopped my evening practice, I only lost two clients, but I had to increase my marketing to make sure that I could fill those daytime slots. When you choose times when you are at your best, everybody wins, including the clients.

5. Batch your tasks. Consider blocks of time for each role

Are there certain days that are better for you than other days? How can you batch your tasks and your clients so that you can make the best of your time? In my therapy practice, I see clients two days a week – Wednesdays and Sundays. In my coaching business, I do coaching primarily one day a week – Thursdays. Mondays are my class teaching days and my mentorship coaching days. We also have our Be A Wealthy Therapist team meetings on Mondays. Tuesday is my project day. This is the day that I will work on marketing or creating operational procedures.

Fridays are my finance and visionary days. This is the day that I review how both the counseling center and Be A Wealthy Therapist are doing financially. I spend time forecasting my finances and reviewing our tracking. I'll also think about things such as "Where do I want my companies to go?" and "Is it time to hire a new clinician?" I can then make those visionary decisions from an informed place because I have the CEO Dashboard and financial data to do so. Friday afternoons and Saturdays are my leisure days. Then Sunday mornings for a few hours, I see therapy clients at my center.

Another trick that Amber Miller, our Operations Director, taught me was to batch specific tasks together in a block to make it go faster. When I write blog posts, I try to write four at a time. I pay bills twice a month. Once a week, after I review my income, I make my transfers to my profit and tax bank accounts for both companies. By doing these tasks together, I save the "ramp up time." I get in the flow and things just seem to go a lot faster.

6. Leave "white space" on your calendar (aka "Swiss cheese" calendar)

I actually printed my online calendar and colored in blocks of time for personal appointments, teaching time, doing therapy, managing the center, coaching, and running Be A Wealthy Therapist. I used a different color for each type of time. The first time I did it, there was no white space after everything was colored in. I thought it looked quite pretty. The problem was that I was scheduled every minute. You really need to have space where you can choose what it is you want to do during that time. Otherwise, we're simply back to our busy schedule leading to exhaustion.

There are times now on my calendar where I have the option to work with the task of one of my CEO roles or I can choose leisure time. This gives me some sense of ease and freedom. Years ago, I heard this described as the "Swiss cheese calendar."

Face it. Unexpected things happen every day. If you schedule things too tightly, as soon as something happens that is outside of that day, your whole schedule is going to go wonky. As long as you have enough white space, you can adjust for any unexpected events without feeling frantic. I read a blog post from a coach years ago who said, "There was not even enough space in my day to say hello to the UPS man. That was when I realized that I needed to create some space and have a Swiss cheese calendar."

When you set up your calendar for the year, put your vacations in from the beginning of the year. This doesn't mean you can't take spontaneous vacations. But I want to make sure that you always have some time away from your work to refresh and renew your body, heart, and mind.

I also want you to be realistic about the amount of time that you have. I read a study that reported that CEOs of big companies had 28 minutes of productive time a day. Twenty-eight minutes a day. Let's be realistic about what is actually possible.

7. A task will fill the size of the time you allocate for it

Amber and I call this "tidying up before company arrives." Imagine it's Saturday morning and you wake up planning to spend the entire day cleaning your house from top to bottom. Fifteen minute later, your mother-in-law calls, telling you she is on her way over with bagels. You look around your house. You have 30 minutes to make it mother-in-law worthy. You whip into focused action and your place looks quite respectable when she arrives!

A narrow window of time helps us focus on the most critical tasks to do; we are able to do them rapidly. In those few moments, we don't worry about anything else. We just tidy up. (We also don't worry about the piled up clothes in the laundry room because that is not a priority since you don't expect her to go there!)

If you give yourself three weeks to write your website copy, my guess is that you will take the entire three weeks. In our marketing boot camp course, the website homework assignment is to do your entire website text in two to four hours. And our students do it. They tiptoe past all those beliefs that say it's impossible and just do it. Give yourself a time frame. Hold yourself to that time frame. You will be amazed at how much you can accomplish.

8. Three daily actions mean 60 actions a month!

If it is true that busy CEOs only have 28 minutes of productive (non-client) time, then how they use that time is critical. Look at your roles. What tasks need to be completed to help you become a more confident CEO? To move your business forward?

Break each task down into what you think you could complete in 20 minutes. Instead of a huge task, such as "do my billing," break it down into manageable tasks. The first might be "gather the client records for clients that need to be billed." The next task might be "bill the first five clients." Pick three tasks that would each take roughly 20 minutes. Commit to three tasks each day. This is one hour of work on projects or necessary tasks in other roles besides clinician.

If you do three things a day, five days a week, at the end of a month, you've done sixty things to move your business forward! Sixty tasks toward more ease, more profit, and more time off. In a year, that is 720 tasks to improve your business! That's phenomenal.

Again, my recommendation is to chunk down your to-dos into 20-minute segments. Instead of "Get speaking engagement" break it down into smaller chunks:

1. Develop two talk titles. (20 minutes)
2. Write three to four sentence abstracts (perhaps three things people will learn from this talk) for each talk title. (20 minutes)
3. Research groups that might be filled with the ideal clients. (You can get started on that in 20 minutes.)

If you do those three things, in just one hour you've made a lot of headway toward getting speaking engagements.

Perhaps the next day, your three things might be:

1. Identify places of worship that might want a speaker. (20 minutes)
2. Get the contact information for ten places of worship in your general area. (20 minutes)
3. Develop an inquiry letter and "call script" to ask if you could be of service as a speaker for them. (20 minutes)

On the third day:

1. Make the speaking inquiry calls for the people you discovered on day 1. (20 minutes)
2. Do the same for the places of worship you identified on day 2. (20 minutes)
3. Write and mail your inquiry letters to the people you discovered on day 1. (20 minutes)

You see how much you have accomplished in three days in just one hour a day? You have your talk titles created with descriptions. You've identified some possible speaking opportunities, acquired contact information, created a verbal and written script to ask how you might be of service, and contacted them! There's a lot you can accomplish if you don't tell yourself that you don't have the time.

You can use this process of "three 20-minute things a day" to stay current on your notes, finances, and the creation of your Operations Manual. In other words, this is where you can find (or make) the time to move your business forward in one of the roles besides the clinician role.

9. Use your breaks wisely

Earlier, I shared what some experts teach about how to renew your energy throughout the day. The time between your sessions is a crucial time. Take those 10 to 15 minutes and be intentional about how you want to use them.

Between clients, make sure you move your body, eat, and hydrate. You do not do your clients any favors if you are dehydrated or famished. Don't forget to use the restroom. (That sounds funny, but I bet I am not the only one who has started a session with a full bladder.)

As you create your ideal day and week, make sure you leave time between every couple of sessions so you can call and reach out to those people who have called you for an appointment. If you think of every call that you get as worth anywhere from $500 - $2,000, think of all the money that your business is losing if you're not answering the phone. Remember the first one who talks to the client gets the client. Make sure that in your scheduling, that operations role, i.e., the front office role, is taking care of it – even if you're the one answering the phone.

10. Create new CEO habits (notes, billing, end sessions on time)

My best tip is to set up some **non-negotiable habits**. These are things you commit to doing every day no matter what. Research shows us that when we do any task or behavior daily for 32 days, it is likely to become habit. Once you create a habit, it is hard to **not** do the task or behavior.

I first learned this as a young woman in my twenties. I was working a corporate job with many 12 and 14-hour days. When I came home, I would often take off my clothes and fall into bed. My aesthetician asked me if I was under a particular amount of stress because my skin did not look very healthy. She asked about my skincare regime. When I admitted that I often "forgot" to wash my face before bed, she sighed. "Please, Casey, before you go to bed, remove your makeup and wash your face. Do that every night for at least 32 days. Let's see what your skin looks like then." At first it was hard to remember and when I'd miss a night, she'd suggest I restart the 32-day mission. Now, years later, I cannot go to sleep if I haven't washed my face.

What are some tasks you could turn into habits so that you couldn't end your day before completing them? I would love for you to have your billing done every single day. Your notes should also be done every single day.

Now, if you're like many therapists, you're rolling your eyes right now. You cannot imagine doing billing and notes every day. But if you don't make time for these very important tasks each day, when will you do them?

At our center, our session length is 45 minutes. At the end of those 45 minutes, the therapists will go on to our practice management system and fill out a templated note form. It is a very brief form and they fill it out, especially identifying any risk factors or anything unusual that happened. The clinicians can do their notes in five to seven minutes. Then they can use the restroom, hydrate, and if they need to, still have a few moments to return a call. This is all done before the next client comes in at the top of the hour. On the rare occasion that they need more time to finish or augment a note, they do so at the end of their shift. In our online practice management system, the associate clinicians report the clients they saw during that shift, and the monies collected or owed. Our billing person then takes care of any remaining billing needed within twelve hours.

There's a feeling of confidence, competency, and relief that comes when we take care of business. Doing your notes on a daily basis is one example. Billing is another example. This is one of the secrets to feeling more in control over your time and your business.

When you take care of your business – when you pay attention to all your roles – you are going to feel like a real CEO. You're going to find more ease in your life, I promise you.

11. Commit to punctuality

Being punctual is a matter of respect. If you are late, you are in essence saying that whatever you were doing is more important than the other person. I strongly encourage you to create a habit of punctuality.

How to end your sessions on time:

Many therapists struggle with ending their sessions on time. Not only does this mean they have no time for the personal and business tasks needed, it can lead to harried therapists and frustrated clients.

A lot of times, therapists believe it's a gift to give our clients more time. While I understand that, let's look at the decision to go over the session time from the business decision triangle. How does a lax policy on session length affect the clinician, the client, and the business?

The clinician does not get a decent break if the sessions are back to back and the sessions go over time. This can mean reduced energy when working with the next client. Clients who routinely have sessions that go over time may feel upset when the clinician wants to stop at the originally agreed upon time. In fact, I once had a client ask me if he did something wrong when I suggested we stop our sessions on time. I had been "giving him the gift" of extra time so often that he had imprinted the new, longer session length as the expected session length.

Let's look at why it is easy for sessions to go over the expected session length. As the session is nearing the last 15 minutes, clients are often processing what you have worked on in that session. They will share some final thoughts. We therapists sometimes like to have the last word in the session. Our "last words" often get the client thinking and processing again. Here's the way it goes. We'll say something we think is profound or helpful in an attempt to end the session. The client will process it for a minute and say something back. If we think they don't have it quite right or we want to add something, we share our thoughts. This invites a response from the client. This back-and-forth exchange with each wanting to put the period on the session is often how sessions go over time.

One of my mentors early on gave me some sage advice. This may not work for you, but it has served me well. He said to me, "Don't do any interventions other than active listening in the last third of the session." Again, that may not work for you. If you do decide to try this, you may want to start it with new people. Remember if you have been going over your time with current clients, they have come to expect it. It may cause a therapeutic break if you try to "take back your gift of extra time." Going over time is not a gift to your clients if you're feeling stressed about the next session and if you're not able to use the restroom, hydrate, or stretch.

If you find that you cannot do your best work in 45 or 50 minutes, consider setting your own session length. I know clinicians who regularly work in 75 or 90-minute sessions.

Finally, what is the impact of the lax session length policy on the business? If you are not punctual for your next client or if you are stressed, your next client may be negatively impacted. If your sessions go over time and you don't have time to return phone calls, the business income may be impacted. So, as we evaluate the decision to have a lax session length policy from all three points of the business decision triangle, you can see it probably needs reshaping. If you'd like to feel more in control of your session length, start your tighter session length policy fresh with new people and consider some of the tips offered here.

In Summary:

Remember that time is not a renewable resource, but energy is. Exhale. Use your breaks wisely. Choose your clients and make sure that you have people who energize you. Stop using busy as a badge of something good. Create your ideal week with lots of white space, making sure that you leave time for your other roles besides being a clinician. Set up non-negotiable habits with yourself about what you're going to do daily. Try them for 32 days and then they will become a habit that you don't feel you can break. End your sessions on time by empathically connecting with your client as they process during the last 15 minutes or so.

Again, if you're changing anything, make sure that you change it with new clients only. It's very hard to change things with the existing clients that you have.

Next Steps:

1. Which of these tips spoke to you?
2. Develop a 32-day plan for one or two new habits. Don't try to do more than one or two. You can add more in the next 32 days.
3. Watch for any negative self-judgment. The area of productivity is an area that many therapists struggle with – especially when they become aware of all the roles they really do have. Be gentle with yourself.

CHAPTER TWENTY-THREE

Putting It All Together

M ost therapy business owners ask me, "Where do I start?" Let's review the topics and steps discussed in this book. This can help you create a roadmap to awaken all the roles in your business. From there, you can create, build, and manage the financially sustainable business you deserve.

Recognize the roles and functions needed to run a successful therapy business

Your business – even a solo practice – needs a CEO. In a large business, several departments report to the CEO. Even if you don't have a lot of other people working for you in those roles, the functions still need to be done. These roles are:

- Clinician
- Marketing
- Operations
- Finance
- Visionary
- For those with staff or centers, Human Resources

If you are worn out or if your business is struggling, it is likely that all of these functions are not being performed. The first step is to recognize this and begin to assess what roles and functions are missing or not performing well. For example, some clinicians will tell me that their caseload is low; they assumed that more clinical training would help them make more money. But often the answer lies within a sleeping role. Maybe the phone is not being answered in a timely manner and the caseload is down. Perhaps a lack of good policies and procedures has caused the business to lose money or clients not to return. As you come to this new understanding, you can begin to comprehensively assess what you need to do to improve your business stability.

Assess what is working and what is not working

Using the appreciative inquiry assessment, ask yourself:

What is working? Why is it working? What would be ideal? What is not quite ideal yet? What are the next steps to move toward my ideal vision?

Now that you have learned about your business roles, this should be a much easier task. You can look at what roles have been asleep and begin to triage where you might want to start making changes.

Expect and accept that in order to have more ease, more time off and more profit, the roles besides clinician need time and attention

As soon as a therapy business owner understands that she has multiple roles and functions to perform, her next question is usually, "Where am I going to find time for this?" This really is the defining moment. It is up to her to decide whether she is going to stay overworked and not enjoy the success she might have or grow into the CEO her business needs.

I won't kid you. This will take some reorganization of your time to develop corrective action plans. My goal is not to have you add more tasks to the already overworked schedule you have, but to invite you to immediately see where you can make small improvements for more time and more ease.

Start quickly

There are some changes you can make right away (or at least with new clients) that should immediately give you more confidence and usually more income. Figure out how to answer your phone more quickly. Shore up your fee policies and your cancellation policies. Take more of a leadership role on the intake call and in your initial sessions. A few tweaks here can give you the jumpstart you need.

In the beginning, you can also start tracking the data for the initial development of your CEO Dashboard. Note how many inquiries you have each day and how many turn into clients. This data can help you assess your action steps later. The business decision triangle can help as you begin to look at different decisions.

Also, consider what experience you want for your clients. Once you know what you want for them – not only clinically but also in every interaction with you and in your space, you will begin to develop the systems to create that experience for them.

Make peace with your finances

The first step is to understand what you need to earn in order to cover your personal expenses, your business expenses, profit, and taxes. The best way to start is by looking at what you have spent to live the way you are living now. Gather your last three months to a year of bank and credit card statements. (I prefer a year.) Separate your expenses into business and personal categories. Put the expenses in subcategories so you can really see where you have spent your money. Remember – this is a judgment free zone, so don't change your spending while you are gathering your data.

After you have your data, prioritize your categories. Create a joyful spending plan that helps you to spend your money in ways that bring you the most happiness. After all, you are working hard to earn this money. Let's make sure you spend it in ways that bring you joy.

Once you know how much you need to earn to support the business and lifestyle you want, you can create the plans to do that. You can calculate how many sessions you need to do in order to meet your income goal.

The next step is to stay on track with your budget and income goals by regular reviews of your profit and loss financial statements. Once you know what the P&L report is telling you (such as under-earning or overspending), you can take corrective action. You can also compare your P&L report data to similar time periods in other years. If you are freaking out because the summer is slow, it can bring reassurance if you look back and realize you are actually doing better than you did last summer.

Define the client journey and create policies, procedures, and systems to make the journey smooth for the client, easy for you, and profitable for the business

The client journey starts with the way the client is first acknowledged when they reach out to you. It usually ends with their graduation.

In between, you can create policies for your clinical interactions, as well as operational policies (front office and back office), finance policies (billing and who pays you and when), facilities, technology, and quality assurance. By creating systems to easily implement your policies, you will turn your business into a fine running machine. Your clients will be happy, as will you, the clinician. And if you are watching your finances and implementing your policies, your business will make more profit. This is why you went into business.

Creating your policies and the systems to implement them doesn't happen overnight. Start with the front office and finance policies. Then continue with any changes to your cancellation policies. Remember, if you are changing policies, you may want to do it for new clients only.

Develop your marketing action plans

While you are developing your policies and systems, you can also start on your marketing tasks. Start with the Empathy Map. Time spent here will help you really understand the head and the heart of your client. Once you are clear on the way the client describes his or her problem, it is time to quickly create your client attractive website copy. You can use that same copy in your online therapy directories.

Consider who else might service your ideal client. Develop a list of 20 to 90 people with whom you could explore building relationships. Remember, networking is about building relationships: relationship before request. Ask how you can support others and be interested in their lives and businesses. Only then might they be interested in giving you referrals. You can reach out to at least one referral source a day. As Tim Sanders suggests, share your knowledge, your compassion, or your network. You can reach out via phone, email, handwritten note or card, a one-to-one meeting, or a small gift. Relationships (as you know) take time to build. Be patient. Be attentive. Keep track of when you last saw people and what you spoke about. Calendar the next time you wish to reach out.

Would your ideal client attend a public lecture? If so, consider groups that are filled with your ideal client. Create a couple of talk titles with descriptions and reach out to the program directors of those groups. Ask if they ever have outside speakers and volunteer your services. When you do get a speaking engagement, beware of fire-hosing the audience with too much content. Consider the time with them as facilitating a group discussion. Interact with them instead of lecturing. Let them see you as the approachable expert. And most importantly, offer them a free consultation on the subject matter of the talk. Conduct that in your office in the format described in this book. Keep track of how many take you up on the free consult offer and of those, how many become clients.

Note: I am not recommending free consults in all your marketing – just after speaking engagements. The audience members have already experienced you and the free consult is an invitation to them into your practice.

Beware of shiny new marketing ideas. Do your research and make sure they will truly give you the return you want. The methods described here work for therapists in many countries. I am concerned when people rush to the quick-fix-shiny-idea and avoid the tried and true because it doesn't look at all cool or fun.

Awaken the visionary. What happens when your caseload fills?

If you do the steps listed above consistently, there will come a day when your practice is full. For most therapy business owners, this takes between two and seven years. So hang in there and keep doing the steps.

When your practice is full, you can simply refer your overflow out or you can refer the overflow to people who work in your practice. These could be employees or independent contractor clinicians. You would be the CEO of the group practice or counseling center and perform the roles of marketing, operations, finance, visionary and HR, as well as clinician if you are still seeing clients.

You could develop a central phone answering and scheduling process to convert the maximum amount of callers into clients. The clients make their payments to the center and you pay the clinicians. Get some legal and accounting expertise to set it up correctly in the beginning. My recommendation is that you first look at your tracking metrics to make sure you have at least five new inquiry calls a week. If so, you start with one associate clinician. From there you can clarify and improve your procedures. When you are close to filling that person's schedule, it will be time to bring on a new one.

Some center owners require their associate clinicians to do their own marketing. My concern with hiring entrepreneurial people is that they may not see a reason to pay you anything. They may take their entire caseload and leave your practice.

Adding clinicians is by far the most profitable way to leverage your time and it comes the closest to making "passive income." You are still managing the center, but you do make money when you are on vacation and your associates are seeing clients.

Some clinicians are attracted to the idea of "passive income" from products or eBooks. If you are considering that, run the numbers. Will you really make the profit you want from an eBook or product? There are so many free resources online that it is really a tough way to earn money. You would need to build a large following and keep in touch with them regularly in order to make eBook sales.

It is not an easy business model. That said, if you want to create a product or write an eBook as a creative venture, then enjoy!

Watch your perspective

As you follow and repeat these steps, you will gain confidence in your abilities as a CEO. Watch where negative self-talk, harsh judgments, or people-pleasing behaviors come up. This is normal and you don't need to beat yourself up for beating yourself up!

Take time to examine your thinking and actions. Note where you might want to course-correct. When you are hit with a strong negative emotion – a judgment of you or someone else – start with the assumption that it is simply wonky thinking. Do nothing for a bit and see if it clears. I trust you will know what to do then. And of course, if not, ask someone who knows you and can see clearly for support.

Be curious about all things in your business. Ask questions when you don't understand. Ask yourself how you can make your business a better experience for you and the clients you serve. This journey is ongoing.

Celebrate

Don't forget to celebrate the victories – both big and small. I set benchmarks as mini-goals. When our center had its first 100-session month, we celebrated. Enjoy this journey.

Get support when you forget

I started teaching these principles more than a decade ago. And I have ended every presentation with this:

"You are a precious and special, wonderful and unique, unrepeatable miracle. Live your life with that knowledge and get support when you forget it. And I love you."

The final word until we meet again

I do love you. I love this profession. And on behalf of all the clients who never thank you, I say, "Thank you." Thanks for making the world a better place. Each time you help someone, those in their world are impacted for the better. Your gifts and efforts make ripples of happiness. Thanks for sharing your gifts with the world.

And thanks for giving me the gift of letting me share this with you.

Enjoy your journey from clinician to confident CEO.

Love and blessings,
Casey

BONUS CHAPTER

Frequently Asked Questions about Managed Care/Insurance

How to get paid is in the forefront of all therapy business owners' minds.

Every time I speak to a group of private practitioners, I'm asked my opinion about being on managed care and insurance panels. "Is it a good idea?" "Should I do it?" I decided to collect the questions I am asked most often and put them into this chapter.

One point of clarification: Throughout this chapter, I will use the words *managed care panels* and *insurance companies* interchangeably. In actuality, it is a little bit more complicated. But for the sake of this discussion, I am referring to being a contracted or preferred provider on either managed care panels or insurance companies as "being on insurance panels."

Here are the questions I'm most frequently asked:

1. Is it better to be on insurance panels or have a fee-for-service practice only?

This choice is a values decision. I cannot tell you which is best for you. As I've said many times, it's a lot like asking if it's better to be single or married. There is no right or wrong way to accept payment or attract clients. There are only choices and you want to pick the right one for you. The best thing you can do is educate yourself on the pros and cons of each type of practice and decide which one fits best for your lifestyle and goals.

2. Will I make more money if I accept fee-for-service clients only?

If you accept fee-for-service clients only, you set the rates you want to be paid for treating those clients. You can set a rate that is higher, sometimes much higher, than the amount you might be reimbursed if you are on the panels.

But here's where the misunderstanding comes in. You will not be working fewer hours for more money in the fee-for-service practice. Yes, you may be paid more per session-hour with a fee-for-service client, but you will need to spend more time in your marketing role to attract those fee-for-service clients. So you might be working the same number of hours – or even more hours – but your paid clinical hours could be at a higher rate.

3. What are the advantages and disadvantages to being a provider on these panels?

In an earlier chapter, I shared with you that the conversion percentage from caller to clients is 70% to 90% for those who have insurance practices as compared to the 30% to 60% conversion for cash practices. From those numbers, you can see that having an insurance client means that more of your callers will become clients. Having your name and number on the insurance company provider lists can be a great way to get clients into your practice.

Many therapists I know are called to offer affordable counseling options to those in their community. By being a provider on insurance panels, these therapists are able to do just that and still bring in a fair amount of money for their practice. For the most part, electronic billing has made the claims process easier than ever before. Providers often see their claims paid quite quickly as compared to the way it was years ago. This keeps cash flowing into the business.

There is one misunderstanding that I would like to correct. Some therapists believe that getting on insurance panels means that they will not have to market their practice. This may be true if you were an early adopter and have been on panels for many years. This may also be true if you have an extraordinarily unique specialty that no one else has in your area.

For the rest of you, I think you're going to need to market your practice for the rest of the time that your business is open. Even though the insurance company websites list your name and practice information, they are also listing the names of all of your colleague-competitors. The public has dozens of therapists, if not hundreds of therapists, to choose from that are on their panel in your area. Any marketing that you do for your practice will help you build your credibility and visibility in the local community. This will help you stand out among the sea of other therapists on those managed care and insurance panels.

There are some disadvantages (from my point of view) to being on insurance panels. They, not you, are in charge of your revenue.

What if, for some reason, they decide to drop you as a provider? What if they decide to change their reimbursement rates? A few years ago, I heard that one insurance company lowered their reimbursement rates to their providers by 30%. Think about that. Therapists who were solely dependent on that company lost almost a third of their revenue overnight. How could they make up the shortfall? Many of them already had full caseloads and adding an additional third to their caseload was not possible. And what about therapists who accept Medicare as reimbursement? A recent article on Forbes.com by Merrill Matthews reports, "Doctors who still accept Medicare patients could see an average reduction of 21.2 percent in Medicare reimbursement rates, according the Department of Health and Human Services." Who knows what will happen in the future of course? My advice is to simply beware of dependence on any one insurance or managed care company.

While the original intent of managed care was to be helpful to clients, my personal concern is that someone (a case manager) who is not in the room with you determines your length of treatment. One time I was turned down for reimbursement by an insurance company who claimed that my client was being noncompliant with appropriate treatment by her psychiatrist.

The insurance company saw that the psychiatrist had given her a diagnosis of major depression. The case manager felt that an antidepressant was in order. The psychiatrist had recommended it to my client, but both the psychiatrist and the client were concerned because the client was pregnant. The client did not want to take an antidepressant while pregnant. The insurance company told me that they would not authorize my treatment with the client as a result. This, of course, may be an isolated incident and perhaps I don't have all the facts. Regardless, that was the day that I chose to leave the managed care panels.

Some clinicians don't buy into the medical model of psychotherapy. But in order to get paid by insurance companies, clients need a DSM diagnosis. Others worry about patient records and confidentiality with treatment reports available online to many insurance company employees. Many clinicians have chosen not to get on managed care panels for these reasons.

Another thing to consider if you choose to be on insurance panels is that there is a fair amount of additional administrative work. You will either have to do the billing yourself or incur the cost of a biller. There will be treatment that is denied that you will need to appeal and hope you get paid. There will be claims that accidentally slip through the cracks and they'll have to be followed up on. So expect there to be some additional administrative work or expense.

4. What about EAPs?

EAPs are employee assistance programs. EAP companies contract with employers to provide behavioral or mental health care to their employees as a company benefit. Usually employees will get one to three (or one to six) sessions of free counseling per year for work, relationships, life struggles, addiction, etc. The idea is to help the employee when they need some short-term interventions.

When I was a provider on EAP panels, I was told that the goal was to "cure or refer" within the allotted number of sessions. Some clients, of course, needed longer care and I would get them to the right resource. My personal goal was to be a bit of an assessment person. If I felt we could meet their treatment goals in three sessions, we did so. If I felt that longer treatment was needed, I helped them get to the right resource quickly and not just use up all their free EAP sessions.

Some EAPs will allow you to self-refer. For example, if you believe the client needs more than their three sessions, you can offer to see that client using their insurance if you are a provider. Other EAPS will not allow self-referrals. Make sure you understand the rules for any EAP panels you are on prior to treating EAP clients.

Just as with any insurance contract, make sure you understand your EAP contract. The contract will clearly spell out how you handle missed or late-cancelled sessions. Many will say you cannot charge your client or the company if a session is missed. Please make sure you abide by the agreement you made or risk losing that contract.

5. How does one get *on* the panels?

I have a friend and colleague, Barbara Griswold, who is passionate about offering affordable counseling to people who want to use their insurance. To learn more about all things insurance – including how to write a managed care resume to increase your chances of getting on the panels, visit her at http://navigatingtheinsurancemaze.com. She's also written a book, *Navigating the Insurance Maze.* I love her passion and respect her knowledge. I highly recommend her if this is the path you wish to pursue.

6. How does one get *off* the panels?

Getting off a managed care panel is like getting a divorce. It is not a decision to be made lightly. Make sure you engage all your CEO roles – especially the marketing and finance roles as you collect the data to make this decision. The bottom line is that you want to make sure that you have enough money coming in from fee-for-service clients before you exit from any of the panels. Before you start the process, be very clear on how much each managed care panel or insurance company is paying you.

Here's your plan to remove yourself from panels while ensuring that your business is financially stable in the transition. This plan will take anywhere from two years to five years depending on your marketing efforts, and your current dependence on managed care.

The first step is to spend the next year with at least five hours a week (or more if possible) marketing your practice. Go through the steps discussed earlier in this book: create your Empathy Map and build your marketing plan. Spend as much time as you can per week marketing your practice with good, solid marketing strategies. Please try to avoid the shiny strategies that have not yet been proven.

Make sure that your phone is being answered regularly and as soon as possible. As the CEO in your business, you know that front office support is really important. Track your calls and conversions. How many people are calling or inquiring with calls, text, or emails? How many of those are turning into clients? Remember, your insurance conversion rate should be about seven to nine becoming new clients for every 10 inquiries. Make sure you take a leadership role on the intake call.

If your conversion is lower than this, review your intake script and process.

As you consistently market your practice and track your inquiries and new clients, you will now have new and accurate data. From that data, you can assess if your marketing efforts are increasing calls to your practice. If your marketing is *not* increasing the number of inquiries (if you're getting the same amount as you did before you started marketing), then your marketing is not working and you might need some marketing support.

If your efforts are paying off, you should see an increase in calls and people wanting to become clients.

Right about this point, someone will challenge me. "But I only want new clients that are fee-for-service. Is there a way to market for only fee-for-service clients? I don't want new *insurance* clients."

Here are the facts. Fee-for-service clients do not hang out in some special, secret place where we can market only to them. They are among the general population along with your insurance clients. You cannot increase your marketing efforts and only get calls from fee-for-service people.

But if you want to get off the insurance panels, you need to develop marketing strategies that attract people into your practice. You do not have to take every caller as a client. But we do want your marketing to be effective and the way you know it's effective is with more people in your community calling you. And some of those people will be willing to pay cash (become fee-for-service clients).

Beware of trying to talk any callers out of using their insurance if you are still on panels. This is most likely against your contract and might cause you difficulties with the insurance companies. You don't want them to fire you before you are ready to fire them.

The next step is to be patient and consistent in your marketing and tracking. Remember that I said this was a two- to five-year plan to get off the panels. As you begin to notice more calls, you can project the income you would receive if you only took fee-for-service clients. Now that you have data, you can make these projections more accurately – rather than guessing.

When you believe that you have enough calls coming in and can afford the risk, select one of the insurance or managed care companies to work with first. Contact provider relations at that company and ask to be put on hold for three months. How do you select which one? You can either select the one that annoys you the most or you can select the one that is the least impactful. If you are risk averse, I would encourage you to start with the one that is the least impactful.

Continue to see your current clients on that panel for the next three months as you normally would. When new prospective clients on that panel call you, you can apologize and explain that you are not accepting new clients right now. Also, consider tracking how many new inquiries you get from each insurance company while on hold. This might help you with your decision after the three-month hold period.

At the end of three months, activate your finance role and review your numbers. (Income and call tracking data.) Assess the financial impact of not taking on any new referrals from that particular insurance company. See if you can live with the impact. If so, then you resign from that panel and you start the process again with the next panel.

If your marketing starts to slow, you might hold off on resigning from a panel and you can ask Provider Relations to take you "off hold." A note of caution here: some companies will not allow you to be put on hold; they either want you active or not on the panel. If that is the case, you can still follow the plan of building your marketing and watching your numbers while still active on the panels. At some point, you will have the data to say that you can leave one panel and open up for more fee-for-service clients.

Some people tell me they are done with managed care and they don't want to wait two to five years; they want off now. (They want a quickie divorce.) This is hard to do if you are dependent on the managed care or insurance income.

If you do have other sources of income, there is another way to get off the panels. Look at how many clients you have from each panel, how much each panel pays you, and what the client copayments are. Calculate what would happen if you saw those insurance clients at their co-payment only. For example, the client may have a $40 copayment. Could you live on that? If you have other income coming in, you might be able to do so while you are implementing your marketing plan.

If you could live on their co-pays, then you could resign from that panel and then work out the treatment, meaning see those clients until they're terminating at their co-payment only. Then you're done with the panel. Again, you don't make these decisions from an emotional place; make these decisions by looking at your numbers.

That is the process to get off the managed care or insurance provider panels with the least amount of impact to your business. Again, I'm not recommending that you do get off panels. There are advantages to being on managed care panels, and there are advantages to having a hybrid practice –meaning a practice that has both insurance clients and managed care clients.

A note of caution: You don't want to drop off a panel and then say to a client you've been seeing for six months, "Hey, I'm sorry, but I'm not taking your insurance as of tomorrow, so by the way you're now going to pay me $xxx per session." Make sure you get legal counsel and create the least impact for your clients. After all, you are the one leaving their insurance company – not the other way around.

7. What are the pros and cons of accepting both insurance and fee-for-service clients in a practice?

I call this a hybrid practice. The advantage is that you have less dependency on any one source of income. In some ways, it's the best of both worlds. On the other hand, you do need to market your practice. (Although in the section above I said you need to do this regardless of whether or not you are on panels are not.)

When you have a hybrid practice, you still have to be careful not to try to talk people out of using their insurance. If you have questions about this, please talk to your mental health attorney. I personally recommend that you have your own mental health attorney and not rely 100% on your association's attorney. While the association attorneys are wonderful, you want somebody who is concerned first and foremost with your needs.

8. What if I am not a provider on a client's insurance panel but they have out-of-network benefits. Should I offer receipts or statements of services for clients to submit their own billing to their insurance company?

This is certainly an option. If you choose to do so, you can do so in one of two ways. You can call the insurance company yourself to do the insurance verification of benefits for the client to help them understand what is covered and what is not covered. Or you can simply give them the statement of services receipt for them to turn into their insurance company.

Some clinicians will ask the client to call to verify benefits. As a client, I see that as a "barrier" to seeing you and may move on to the next therapist. When my husband needed an MRI, if I had been asked to call to verify benefits I would not have known what to ask for.

Be very careful to explain to the client that you are not a party to their agreement with their insurance company. Unless you have verified their benefits, tell them that you have no idea if your services will be covered or if their deductible has been met. Watch for any transference that might arise if for some reason the treatment is denied. At least three times in my career, I have had clients very angry with me when their insurance company would not pay for their services with me. I promise you, I was very clear with these clients from the beginning that I was not a party to the contract with their insurance company. It even said so on my statement of services. But when clients first come to see a therapist, they are in pain. They often don't hear everything that is said. They just assumed it was covered and weeks later found out they weren't going to be reimbursed by their insurance. I was the target of their frustration.

If you are going to put a DSM diagnosis on that statement of services, make sure to discuss that with the client and the potential impact of that diagnosis.

You can also offer as a service to clients to directly bill the insurance company on your client's behalf as an out-of-network provider. Let's say you are on a few insurance panels, but not this client's panel. Instead of just offering a statement of services, you can actually do the billing yourself. This does mean a bit more bookkeeping for you, but can be perceived as a huge benefit by clients. Be sure the client has out-of-network benefits before indicating that the company might pay. Some managed care panels offer no out-of-network benefits.

The truth is that no one is ever 100% certain of the reimbursement until the check is in the hand of you or the client. There are too many variables. But billing as an out-of-network provider can be another way to see insurance clients even if you are not on their panel. You may get questions from the company and treatment review requests. This is normal. They want to make sure – even if you are not on their network – that the client is getting good and appropriate care.

If you notice, I use the words receipt or statement of services rather than superbill. I am on a one-woman mission to eradicate the word superbill from our vocabulary. After all, what client ever wants to hear they are getting a SUPER bill? A receipt, statement of services, or even invoice sounds more client-friendly and more accurate. Okay, off my soapbox.

9. What additional tips do you have for those of us who do accept insurance?

As I mentioned before a couple of times, don't try to talk people out of using their insurance if you are a provider on their panels. Don't try to sell services to them that you know their insurance won't cover simply to get extra cash. This can put you and your client in a difficult situation and potentially cause you a lot of problems.

Make sure you understand your contracts when you create your cancellation and no-show policy and especially before you bill the client or the insurance company for no-show or late cancellation appointments. Many contracts have this specifically addressed and you want to make sure you follow the agreement that you signed.

And one more point… this may sound odd and I am surprised I even have to mention it. But every once in a while, I hear from a frustrated and overworked therapist who is annoyed that her contract doesn't allow her to bill for no-shows. So she goes ahead and bills as if the client showed up. "I just bill the company and the client as if it were a regular appointment. It would have been if the client showed up!"

I am not an attorney so please get advice from one if you are considering doing this, because I think that billing an insurance company for a session that you did not perform might be insurance fraud. And that could mean fines, loss of your license, and a whole lot of problems worse than an unpaid, missed session. Again, get legal counsel as needed.

In my experience (and this may not be true for everyone), clients who use their insurance tend on average to have a longer length of stay with me. Fee-for-service clients, on the other hand, sometimes come for symptom relief as opposed to long-term work. (I know that is a sweeping generalization and there will be lots of exceptions.) I still would encourage those on managed care or insurance panels to take a leadership role on the intake call and in the first session. We want the clients to stay in treatment as long as is ethically appropriate. We want them to really meet their treatment goals. Consider using the feedback informed treatment measures as taught by Scott D. Miller to avoid therapeutic breaks and premature terminations.

Expect and accept that you will need to do treatment reviews with case managers on occasion. This is true even for those of you who are not contracted providers, but provide a statement of services for your clients to submit to their insurance company. This is simply a cost of doing business, so understand that it is part of the service you are providing your client. It is also a way to help you get paid.

Finally, please resolve to never complain about working with managed care companies or insurance companies again. You hired them to help you get the word out about your practice. You contracted with them to do so at a specific rate. As part of that agreement, you committed to providing whatever treatment reports and reviews the company requested. If you are now unhappy with the agreement you made, then work toward extricating yourself from that agreement. Blaming them serves no one and just creates negative energy. You can always look at this as your gift in dirty paper. It helped you get started and it will help you gain clarity on what you want for your business now. Quite honestly, since it takes a while to build a fee-for-service business anyway, it's probably nice that you have their income coming in in the meantime.

10. Do you offer help or coaching around getting off of insurance panels?

Yes. I have a skilled team of trained coaches who can help you decide if this is the right decision for you, and can assist you in creating a plan and implementing that plan. Our coaching application page is http://BeAWealthyTherapist.net/help

In Summary:

There is no better or worse type of business model in terms of fee-for-service or managed care/insurance. It's a choice. There are advantages and disadvantages to both. Many clinicians choose to accept both fee-for-service clients and managed care/insurance clients. This can hedge against too much dependency on any one payer. You will need to market your practice even if you want managed care or insurance clients. Creating a marketing plan and implementing it consistently will help you rise above the other dozens of therapists in your area.

Contrary to what many people think, there is no way to build a marketing plan for fee-for-service clients only. You cannot increase your marketing efforts and only get calls from fee-for-service people.

If you wish to work your way off of the panels, do so thoughtfully and one at a time. The details are in the body of this chapter. Remember to get legal and ethical counsel if you choose to do so.

Next Steps:

1. Review the advantages and disadvantages of being a managed care or insurance company provider. Is there a clear choice for you? Fee-for-service or managed care insurance?

2. Create a plan to increase your marketing before making any final decisions about removing yourself from any panels.

3. If you wish to start removing yourself from the panels, review your numbers. When you see that you are getting a significant enough increase in calls in fee-for-service clients, decide which panel you will approach first. Don't forget to get legal and ethical advice before implementing anything described in this chapter.

Book Resource Section

You can view or download some additional resources to help you at http://beawealthytherapist.net/resources. There you can find downloadable copies of:

- The Empathy Map
- The intake call script for solo and group practices (including the "Do you take insurance?" answer script)
- Sample Inquiry Tracking Sheet
- Sample response to reply to emails requesting information, re: your fees, etc.
- Sample policy for first session (intake) (from OC Relationship Center)
- Sample cancellation policy (from OC Relationship Center)
- Sample introduction letter to program directors for speaking
- Sample CEO Dashboard
- Process: how to find the right online locators for you
- A few videos to help you set, collect, and negotiate your fees.

One of the things about publishing a book is that there is always more to share. If you'd like to get my latest thoughts and updates, as well as additional free videos and other resources, sign up for our newsletter and advanced notice list at http://beawealthytherapist.net

I look forward to our paths crossing again soon.

Love and blessings,

Casey Truffo

P.S. On the next few pages are the resources referenced here in case you want to view them while reading this book.

Your Empathy Map

WRITE DOWN WHAT YOUR
IDEAL CLIENTS...

SAY	THINK BUT DON'T SAY

WANT/ DON'T WANT	DO AND DO NOT DO

FEEL	FEAR

Intake Call Script for a Solo (One Clinician) Practice:

Remember, the first therapist to speak to the client usually gets the client. This is what I would say when answering the phone for a solo practice.

"Hi, this is Casey Truffo of the Orange County Relationship Center. How can I help?"

When a prospect calls requesting an appointment, they often start out with questions such as "Are you taking new clients?" or "How much do you charge?" I suggest you don't answer those questions right away and that you say the following:

"We don't even know if I am the right therapist for you yet. So why don't we start at the beginning? Why don't you tell me what is happening now? Let's see if I can help."

I listen to their story for about 90 seconds to two minutes. During that time, I am listening for what I don't want – for me that would be eating disorders, domestic violence, or people abusing substances.

If I decide I don't want this client, I say, "I can see you have a lot going on and I think it would be good for you to be seen soon. Unfortunately, I am not able to do that. May I offer you some referrals of some people who might be able to see you pretty soon?"

(TIP: Always ask if people want referrals – don't just start offering them without the person saying "yes" to that question.)

If I decide I do want the client, I validate and join with them and say, "Wow. I can see you have a lot going on. I think it makes sense to come in. May I tell you how I work?"

(Tip: Always wait for an affirmative response to this question. Don't launch into your script until they say, "Yes." Once they say yes, I say the following four items.)

"My office is located near (a landmark).

"My sessions are 45 minutes in length.

"My fee for each session is $xxx. (Make sure you say 'dollars' or whatever your currency.)

"I have openings Wednesday at noon or Friday at 5:00 p.m. Do either of those times work for you?"

Then your job is to be silent and let them process all this info. They will next do one of three things.

They will ask if you have a different time, as they can't make the time you offered. This is great news! They are onboard. Look at your schedule and see what you can do.

They might say "I can't afford that" or "I didn't think it would cost that much." Create your answers to those questions beforehand so that you are not flustered in the moment. If you have clarity on your fees before answering the phone, you will be more likely to respond in ways that support you, your business, and the client.

They will ask if you take insurance. If you do not take insurance, consider your reasons why not and create a script for the answer to that question. (See mine in this section.) If you DO take insurance, please do NOT use this script. It will most likely cause you problems with your insurance or managed care contracts.

Here is the script I use when asked, "Do you take insurance?" (since I do not take insurance at this time)

As noted, please do NOT use this if you DO take insurance.

I start by validating the question: "You know, a while back, my husband had surgery and he needed an MRI beforehand. I was so grateful to have insurance to cover those expenses. But there are risks to using your insurance to pay for therapy. Are you interested in knowing what those are?"

313

The people who call you are (usually) adults and can make their own decisions. That said, I do not think that most people understand the potential risks to using insurance. Most people understand the benefits, but do they know the risks?

The reason I ask if they want to know about the risks is so we don't waste time if the potential client really wants to use insurance. So first I validate their desire to use insurance and ask if they want to hear about the risks. About 80% of people do want to hear about the risks. For those I continue...

"There are several reasons I am concerned about using insurance companies to pay for therapy. First, in order to have your insurance pay for your therapy, I have to give you a mental disorder diagnosis. I really don't want to give anyone a mental disorder diagnosis. That's just not the way we like to work; we just focus on helping your relationship.

"Then, depending on the insurance company, the therapist has to write a report every five to ten sessions to show that you're still sick with that mental disorder. For the insurance company to continue paying for therapy, the report needs to show that you're still sick and getting better, but that you aren't cured yet. I really don't want to write a report like that – sharing the details of your mental disorder.

"Then someone from the insurance company who doesn't know either of us is going to read that report and assess how well our work is going and decide if they will continue to pay for the therapy. It's like they are sitting in the room judging us and how we are doing. Of course, no one from the insurance company really is in the room with us, but it can feel like they are. I don't know about you, but I think how well the therapy is going should be something that you and I decide – not someone who doesn't know either of us.

"Recently I have heard that thousands of employees at the

insurance companies may have access to your records. I am not sure if that is true or not, but I just don't feel comfortable with that possibility.

"And I don't know exactly how it works now, but four years ago, I had a vitamin deficiency that was first diagnosed as *rule-out depression*. That means that I was not diagnosed with depression, but they wanted to rule it out. It WAS ruled out (meaning I was not depressed) when they discovered it was the vitamin deficiency. A few years later when I applied for long term-term care insurance, the premium quote was a whopping $40,000 extra over the course of my lifetime due to that *rule-out depression* diagnosis. They wanted me to pay an additional $40,000 in premiums!! And that was when I did *not* have depression. Can you imagine if I *had been* diagnosed with depression? That may not be true now (due to changes in health-care policy), but I am not comfortable with the risk.

"Further, most insurance companies will not pay for relationship enhancement at all. They might cover family therapy as long as one of you is diagnosed with a mental disorder. And I have found that diagnosing one person in the relationship can create an imbalance in the relationship and make our work together more challenging.

"So those are the risks as I see them. That is why we have chosen not to work with any insurance companies. However, as I said, I totally understand your desire to use it. So, here are a couple of options: Either you can go back to your insurance carrier and get another referral or, I have openings Wednesday at noon or Thursday at four. What do you think you'd like to do?"

Then I am quiet, giving them time to process all that information.

Forty to fifty percent of the people hearing that script choose not to use their insurance.

The benefits of using insurance are clear. The risks usually aren't. By sharing these reasons, we have told the truth. The client can then make an informed decision.

Intake Call Script for a Group Practice

The intake call script/procedure is similar for a group practice, except that you want to both match the client to the best therapist for them and get them in as soon as possible. You can adjust the middle of the script (after you've joined with them) as follows:

"Our office is located near (a landmark).

"Our sessions are 45 minutes in length.

"Our fees for each session are between $xxx and $yyy as the therapists set their own fees." *(If they do, of course.)* (Make sure you say "dollars" or whatever your currency.)

Then you have several options… choose one or make up your own:

a. "We have male and female therapists available. Do you have a preference?" or

b. "We have daytime, evening, or weekend appointments available – when would you like to come in?" or

c. You can select a therapist and offer the client the times that therapist has available (beware of over-selling a therapist in the event that the times don't work out) or

d. You can offer a choice of the next couple of available sessions so they get in quickly.

Sample Inquiry Tracking Sheet

Date/Time	Type (call/email)	Name	Phone	Problem	Referral Source?	Scheduled?	If yes, Appt date/time	If not, why not?	Intake Paperwork sent?

This is the type of inquiry tracking sheet I use for our cash practice. If they book the appointment, we put the rest of the client and appointment information into our practice management system.

Sample Response to Emails Requesting General Information and/or Fees

Hi (name),

I appreciate you reaching out to us at the Orange County Relationship Center. My name is Casey Truffo and I am the Director.

At our center, our goal is to help people be happier in their lives and relationships. And we want you to have a happy relationship!

We have day and evening appointments. And we'd be happy to discuss fees with you, as they vary by which therapist you wish to see – basically they are between $160 and $195 per 45-minute session based on the therapist you choose. (They set their own fees.)

If you give us a quick call at 949-220-3211, we'd be happy to give you any additional information you might need. You can also schedule an appointment online at http://OCRelationshipCenter. com.

Warmly,
Casey Truffo, Director and Licensed Marriage and Family Therapist
OC Relationship Center
Newport Beach, CA 92660
949-220-3211

Sample Policy for First Session (Intake)

This is what I have documented as suggestions for the first session in my center. We are always improving our policies, so I invite the clinicians to share their thoughts with me. Yours may be different of course. This is just a sample for you.

OCRC First Session Recommendations

To our OCRC Clinicians – please note: If you disagree with any part of this policy – or have suggestions for improving the policy – please let the Clinical Director know. We are always striving for quality improvement and value your suggestions. Also, there may be occasions where you choose to not implement this policy. Please let the Clinical Director know when there has been an exception and help us to understand why.

Providing a consistent experience for clients helps them feel safe and can increase their confidence in their choice of therapists. It also can help to avoid (or handle) future problems. We want them to feel like they have made a good choice in choosing you and OCRC. We also want to normalize what is ahead and get some commitment to the process.

At OCRC, the first session is really to get to know the client; to give them the experience of feeling heard and respected. We listen to their story and make the decision if we can help. If we can, we let them know that we want to and believe we can help them to feel better and get along better.

Further, as therapists, we are keenly aware that many clients are nervous about therapy and are looking for confidence from the therapist, so we are willing to take a leadership role.

Below are some suggestions on how to take that role and make sure you and the client are on the same page regarding treatment. Please use your own words – and please discuss with the Clinical Director if you have any thoughts/concerns/questions.

One of the main things we wish to do is discuss the expectations of therapy. The clients are leaning on us to provide that for them. We are the experts on the therapy process and they are paying us for our professional opinion. If a client wants to come irregularly (from the beginning), I advise you to consider if this is really in the best interests of the client and of you. If the client cannot afford regular treatment, it may be in everyone's best interests to have them find a therapist (such as an OCRC intern) who can help them in a more cost-effective manner ... and where they can still come weekly.

Again, please let the Clinical Director know if you have thoughts, comments, or questions about this. We are always looking for ways to improve and would appreciate your input.

1. Set expectations and gain commitment (the Leadership Role)

So, in an intake session at OCRC, it is considered good practice to:

- Listen to the story from each partner with respect – helping them to feel understood.

- Decide if we want to continue with these clients – if not, gently explain and refer appropriately.

- If so, explain in an overview how treatment works and normalize what happens next. Certainly you want to use your own words, but the point is to help them commit to therapy with you.

For example, you might say something like:

"I would really like to work with you. I am very committed to relationships and I want yours to be what you'd like it to be. I want to help you *(insert their goals)* and I think if you and I are both committed to the process, we can help you get there. So let me share with you how my therapy works and how we might help you to *(insert their goals)*.

"Most people who come to us have been in a rut for some time. My goal is to help you out of that rut and learn new ways to interact so that you can be happier, get along better, and learn how to talk about and solve difficult problems *(or however they describe their goals)*.

"So here is how it is going to work. You might find that today when you leave you have two reactions – you may feel relief since you are finally opening up and getting some help... or you may have an argument. This is totally normal. Neither is indicative of whether or not therapy is working. It just means we have started poking around a little.

"As you come back regularly, we will be working together to help you get more relief and as mentioned, learn how to talk about things so that there are fewer arguments *(or their goals)*. So as you start learning new ways of connecting, you may find yourself feeling better for a few sessions and then you may, out of habit, fall back into that old rut. My goal is to help you get out and stay out of that rut. Most people fall into the rut a few times before they really trust that the new ways of connecting work well.

"So while we start looking for progress right away, most people come to therapy at least 10 times on a weekly basis in order to have the experience and practice the skills necessary to stay out of that rut. So when people come to us, we expect they will come at least 10 times on a weekly basis so we can get some traction.

"Now, that doesn't mean we are done at 10 sessions, but

we have a lot of traction there and a better ability to stay out of the rut. And that is when things can get much better and better faster. And just to make sure, I will always be checking in with you – each week – to make sure you are getting what you need from me and from our work together. If you aren't getting what you need, then I will modify what I am doing to help you get better results.

"How does that sound? What do you think? I am all in if you are!"

2. Discussion of Informed Consent

If you and the clients agree to treatment, we then discuss (and document in the intake notes that we discussed) key points from the informed consent paperwork including but not limited to:

- confidentiality
- cancellation policy
- how we will evaluate the relationship (either asking them each session or using the ORS/SRS)
- Secrets (or "no-secrets") policy

Please remember to document that you discussed these policies. As the lawyers say, "If it isn't documented, it didn't happen."

3. Schedule the next several sessions

Invite them to have a standing (set) weekly appointment time. We have seen that people who have regular sessions tend to be more compliant with treatment AND it will help you manage your schedule better.

Should they not wish to do that, see if they are willing to schedule the next two or three sessions. This way if they cancel or do not show for an appointment, the appointment after they missed is, at least, already scheduled.

Note: See the section on Scheduling Sessions in the Practice Management system for details as to how to add the future sessions to our practice management system calendar.

Additional Note: Some OCRC clients may benefit and be open to "double sessions" – 90-minute weekly sessions. We have found that some couples appreciate these as 45 minutes (our regular session length) goes by so quickly and neither partner feels completely "heard." If you want to offer the 90-minute sessions, you can explain the value and also let them know that the fee is then double the regular 45-minute session fee.

Also, please make sure you adjust the calendar to show it is a 90-minute appointment.

4. Obtain Payment Arrangements

Clients have the option of paying for their sessions three ways at OCRC:

- Cash
- Credit Cards and Debit cards with a logo (AmEx, MC, Visa, Discover)
- Check (not encouraged, but if taken, please have them made out to OC Relationship Center or Relationship Center)

If the client wishes to pay by credit card, please have them fill out a credit card authorization form *(blank ones are located in the hall cabinet)* and indicate if they wish to be charged once or on an ongoing basis. <u>Please make sure the card is in the name of the client and not a third party.</u> If a client indicates that a relative will pay, please explain that we cannot accept payment from someone who is not our client. We ask the client to pay for the session and then work it out however they wish with the third party.

Please also make sure the number on the credit card matches the number the client puts on the form and that everything is legible and all fields are filled in. (If you fill out the form yourself, you can then make sure the printing is legible and no fields are missed.) The client just needs to sign the form then.

Payment is expected at the time of service. However, if the client wishes to always pay via credit card, we will keep it on file for the client so the client only has to complete the authorization form once.

If a client pays cash and gives you more than the session fee, please indicate that on the invoice that you submit in the practice management system and on your daily tracking sheet. The client will get a credit in our system so they can pay less the next time. We don't have a system for "giving change." Please let the bookkeeper know if the client won't be returning and they have a credit balance. We will send them a check.

Please put the payment for this session (and all sessions for the day) in an envelope with your name on it and include in the envelope, the daily payment sheet for all the clients you saw that day. Please place the envelope in the kitchen area designated for that function.

NOTE: See the Practice Management section to see how to enter everything into the online system.

Please feel free to contact our bookkeeper, Bob Truffo, at xxx.xxx.xxxx if you have questions regarding client invoices or payments.

Sample Cancellation Policy: OC Relationship Center Cancellation and No-Show Procedure

We expect clients to miss sessions on occasion. We want to show compassion for them while at the same time providing consistent expectations regarding attending sessions.

Desired Result of Implementing this Policy: Clarity and consistency in handling missed appointments helps everyone. And when we implement with all our clients, it provides a consistent experience for each client and clear expectations for the client, clinician, and center.

Please note: If you disagree with any part of this policy – or have suggestions for improving the policy, please let the Clinical Director know. We are always striving for quality improvement and value your suggestions. Also, there may be occasions where you choose to not implement this policy. Please let the Clinical Director know when there has been an exception and help us to understand why.

1. Familiarize yourself with the cancellation and no-show policy.

At OCRC, we ask for 48-hours notice in order to cancel an appointment without a charge for the missed session. And while we have asked the client for 48-hours notice, internally we say that at least 43 hours notice is needed to waive the fee for the missed session. This gives them a few hours leeway – but we don't publicize that.

Each client gets one no-show or late cancel as a "free miss" – meaning that we do not charge them for that first missed session. Then we use some time at the beginning of the next session to remind them of the 48-hours notice policy, tell them we are waiving the fee this one time, and get a recommitment to the policy from the client.

Exceptions to the policy: The policy is that we *do* charge the full session fee (after the first missed session) for any subsequent missed sessions regardless of the reason for missing the session, except in any of the following cases:

- the client or the client's dependent is in the hospital

- the client was in an accident on the way to session

- the client calls in sick (with less than 48 hours notice) and the therapist would rather not do a session in a room with a sick client. (This is an unpublished exception and is available for the therapist to choose.)

Clinician Illness/Emergency: We respect our client's time as much as our own. So if an emergency or illness comes up for an OCRC clinician and the clinician is unable to give 48-hours notice to a client, the clinician gives the client their next session at no-charge.

Discussion of the Fee or Fee Waiver after a late-cancel or no-show: At OCRC, we strongly believe that money (and the fee) is a clinical issue and as such we discuss it in session – just like other clinical issues – rather than over the phone or via email or text. See steps below for the process to discuss the fee for missed sessions.

If you have questions or concerns, please discuss them with the Clinical Director.

2. Notify the client about the cancellation and no-show policy in the Informed Consent Paperwork

Client fills out the Informed Consent and Intake paperwork electronically prior to their first session. In the Informed Consent Paperwork, the 48-hour notice policy is clearly stated as:

Cancellation Policy: Your appointment time reserves my time for you. Should you need to cancel, please do so at least 48 hours in advance of your appointment time or you will be charged your full fee for the missed session. Cancellation can be done online or can be left on our voice mail at 949-220-3211. Our Client Ambassador is also available to help you reschedule your appointment. She can be reached from 8:00 am to 5:00 pm at 949-220-3211. Please initial below to note that you have read this cancellation policy and agree to comply.

3. Discuss the cancellation policy in the intake session.

When discussing the informed consent issues such as confidentiality, and your "Secrets or No-Secrets Policy," explain the cancellation policy and ask the client if they have any questions about it. You might say something like this:

"Your appointment time reserves my time for you. Should you need to cancel, please do so at least 48 hours in advance of your appointment time or you will be charged your full fee for the missed session. If you need to cancel, please call the office and the Client Ambassador will cancel the appointment and help you to reschedule. Do you have any questions about that?"

4. Contact the client at the first missed session – check in and confirm next appointment.

- We will waive the fee the first time the client late-cancels or no-shows.

  If it is 20 minutes after the session time and the client has not shown up, call the client and express concern that they haven't shown up, invite them to call you, and – if they already have a future session on the calendar – confirm it.

Use your own words, but the gist would be: "Hi, Dana. I had us down for 5:00 p.m. tonight and it is now 5:20 and I haven't heard from you. I hope all is okay. I have us down for next Thursday at 5:00 p.m. as well so I wanted to confirm that. If you want to check in before that, I'd love to hear from you. Please give us a call at 949.220.3211 (or your Google voice number). Take care and, again, I hope everything is okay."

- If the client calls and leaves a voice mail or texts you and cancels with less than 48-hours notice, contact the client to see that they are okay and confirm the next session.

Again, use your own words, but the gist would be: "Hi, Dana! Thanks for calling and letting me know you won't be at our 5:00 p.m. appointment this evening. I appreciate the call. I hope everything is okay. I will see you next week at the same time, unless you want to come in earlier. Just give me a call at (number) and let me know. I look forward to seeing you soon."

Note: At OCRC, we believe that discussing money on the phone or via email or text is not a good idea, as money is a clinical issue. So, we recommend that the discussion of the cancellation policy and resulting fee or forgiveness of the fee be done in person and not in any other way.

5. Note the missed session in the practice management system.

- If they did not show for the appointment, please mark them as "not arrived" on the Practice Management calendar and create a treatment note if you reached out to them.

- If they cancelled the appointment, please indicate that by clicking on the appointment, and then indicate that they cancelled the session (with or without notice in the note area) and a reason if they gave one. Please create a treatment note if you reached out to them.

6. Reiterate the policy at the next session and explain our one-time forgiveness policy.

At the beginning of the session, as the client is sitting down, you could say something similar to this: "Dana, it is good to see you. I missed seeing you last week. I am glad everything is okay." (*Or something related to the issue as "I am sorry you were sick."*)

"Dana, I am not sure if you remember, but when we first started together, I mentioned to you that I requested 48-hours notice if you are unable to make an appointment."

(You will get the deer-in-the-headlights look.)

"Well, I believe that everyone gets one free 'do-over' *(missed session, or get out jail free card, choose your metaphor)* so I will not be charging you for that session." *(They will be relieved.)*

7. Get an agreement regarding the fee for next cancellation/ no-show.

The client will most likely be happy that you are not charging for that missed session. Now it is time to get a renewed commitment to the policy:

Sample: "So yes, I am happy to give you one get-out-of-jail free card. *(Smile.)* That said, Dana, I just want to make sure you and I are on the same page. You see, your session time reserves my time for you. If it happens again that you need to miss and I don't get 48-hours notice prior to the session time, unfortunately I am going to need to charge you for the missed session. Are we on the same page here?"

(Nod – you want commitment.) *"Great! Okay!"*

NOTE: We do this at the beginning of the session in case there are any potential therapeutic breaks or if they need to process anything. You have lovingly set a boundary and that can trigger some people. That is why the recommendation is to do it at the beginning of the session. Again – money is a clinical issue.

8. Document in your notes that this client was waived the fee for the missed session.

- After you and the client have discussed the cancellation policy and they have recommitted to the policy, please make a note of it in your treatment notes.

- Also, making a note of the use of their "free one-time miss" on the client's demographic page under "General" in the notes section can help you remember if you have given this client one free session. If they miss again in a few weeks, it is easy to look for it there rather than go through all of your clinical notes or trying to remember.

Introduction Letter to Program Directors for Speaking

Date
Address
Address
Address

Dear xxxnamexxx,

I am Casey Truffo, a couples counselor and motivational speaker. I'd like to present the opportunity to speak to *group name* about how to create even better relationships.

My specialty is working with couples that once found the relationship easy, but over time it has been more difficult – due to children, work, illness or other pressures. My goal is to teach research-based (and fun!) methods to getting the love they want from their partner.

I would love to speak before your group. I absolutely promise you that your group will leave my presentation:

- Inspired to take action

- Empowered from learning three proven techniques to change the way they relate to their partner, and

- With more belief and confidence in themselves and their ability to get more of what they want (and less of what they don't want) from their partner.

Two of my most popular talks are:

1. "WHY DO YOU DO THAT?" How to get your mate to do what you want

(And stop doing what you don't want) and

2. HOW TO LIVE HAPPILY EVER AFTER: A guide to navigating the 5 stages of marriage.

I am also totally open to creating something brand new if you have special needs.

I will reach out next week to follow up to see if I might be able to support you and your group in some way. I look forward to connecting!

Warm regards,

Casey

Casey Truffo, LMFT and Director
Orange County Relationship Center
Newport Beach, CA 92660
949.220.3211

Sample CEO Dashboard

CEO DASHBOARD			
MM/YYYY	#	Comparison to last year	Notes
1. Income			
2. Expenses			
3. Saved for Profit			
4. Saved for Taxes			
5. Inquiries Rec'd.			
6. New Clients			
7. Conversion %			

How to Find the Best Online Therapist Locators (Directories) for You

There are over a dozen online therapist directories. I suggest being on two to four of them. How do you know which are the best ones for you?

Free Directories

Some professional associations offer their members the opportunity to put a listing on the site at no charge. If it is free, I'd strongly recommend taking advantage of this member benefit.

Niche-Specific Directories (Some are free and some charge a fee.)

Some specialties (AASECT sex therapists, for example) have specific therapist directories. Check to see if there is one for your specialty. I have seen them for relationships (marriagefriendlytherapists.com) and eating disorders (edreferral.com), as well as ADHD (chadd.org). There are others specific to treatment modalities such as gottmanreferralnetwork.com. Explore potential options that are specific to your niche.

Subscription Directories

To find the best online therapist locators (directories) for you, search online using the search terms you think a potential client would use. For example, *couples counseling Albany NY*. Then see which listings come up. You will probably see some or all of these: Psychology Today, Theravive, Good Therapy, Network Therapy, Find-A-Therapist and more, including some local to your region.

Look for the two or three services that come closest to the top of the search results. These are most likely your best bet. Then look within those to discover how many therapists are in your target area. If there are literally thousands of therapists, it may not be the best choice. Write a client-attractive listing and try the services for at least six months. Track your results. Measure your results. If an online locator cost you $300 and you received even one client that spent $600 with you, that is a good investment.

Videos to Help You Set, Collect and Negotiate Your Fees

To view short and practical videos to support your practice, visit: http://beawealthytherapist.net/bookvideos

Special Appreciation

This book is a culmination of years of study, experiments, failures, and successes. I am incredibly grateful to those who have helped me along this journey. Most authors say that to thank all the people who have helped this book be born would fill another book. That is certainly true here. I adore and thank all of the teachers and clients who have helped me learn the lessons I write about in this book. Thank you for your wisdom, your patience, and your support.

Without a few special people, my mission would still be a dream and this book would still be in my head.

To Barbara Grassey, thanks for helping me make this manuscript better. You helped me through my fear of writing. I am grateful for your support, humor, and skill.

To Jose Ramirez, my heartfelt thanks. In your hands, I knew the manuscript would be published and available worldwide. Thanks for your care for this project and me. And thanks for working within my crazy time frame.

To my practice-building coach colleagues: Lynn Grodzki, Joe Bavonese, Juliet Austin, Tamara Suttle, Miranda Palmer, and Kelly Higdon, your lights have paved the way for future generations of therapy business owners. Thanks for your support and encouragement – and for what you do for therapists worldwide.

To Steve Frankel, my attorney and colleague, I am a much better therapist and business owner as a result of your counsel. I am proud to call you my friend.

To my business coach, Julie Steelman, thanks for hanging in with me when I avoided looking at my therapy business finances for two full years. And thanks for helping me continue to grow into the CEO I want to be. You are incredibly special to me.

To the colleagues and teachers who taught me a lot about being a good business owner and a good therapist, specifically Michael Yapko, Diane Yapko, Bill O'Hanlon, Mike Michalowicz, Michael Port, Amy Mead, Scott D. Miller, Bill Doherty, Elizabeth Thomas, Ofer Zur, and all those I haven't mentioned. You all have very special places in my heart and I wouldn't be here without your support, guidance, and inspiration.

To my amazing Orange County Relationship clinicians, Larry Valentine, Marni Reinhardt, and Rebecca Pistilli, thanks for being such powerful examples of what is possible when you *love people into and through our practice*. Each day I pinch myself to see if our center is a dream or if this is reality. You've made my dream come true. I appreciate you and adore you all.

To our Be A Wealthy Therapist coaching team: Arie Schwartzman, Helen Odessky, Stacy Perkins, Jeremie Miller, Jenny Glick, and Jyl Scott-Reagan, thanks for helping me realize my vision by championing the mission and helping so many therapy business owners to build successful businesses. I appreciate your dedication, your skill, and your commitment. Thank you. You guys are amazing.

To our Be A Wealthy Therapist community, and especially our Individual, Ruby, and Emerald mentorship clients, thanks for sharing your trust and sharing your experiences and successes with me. You inspire me every day with your courage and love. I look forward to continuing on the path to confident CEO with you.

To Rachna Jain, our Be A Wealthy Therapist Strategy and Marketing Director, you have taken my vision as your own and I could not be more grateful. You model a rare combination of enormous creativity, productivity, wisdom, vision, and passion. I am honored to know you and incredibly grateful to have your talents helping us to grow. You keep me grounded on bad days and celebrate with me on the good ones. I adore you.

To Amber Miller, my right hand and the Operations Director of Be A Wealthy Therapist: What can I say? Thanks for taking a chance on me so many years ago. You have helped me from day one and we continue to run seamlessly with your skill, love, and grace. Bless you and thank you. And to the rest of the Millers, whom I call family, Chris, Alyssa, Derek, Tanner, Renee, and Lori, I love you all.

To my family: Tiffany and Brad, Pam and Billy, and Barbara and Dad, thanks for your support, love, and thoughtfulness. I am grateful for the gift of our family. I love the time we spend together and breaking bread with you is one of my greatest joys. I look forward to seeing each of you soon.

And to my husband, Bob, who was with me when both businesses were just an idea. Thanks for taking care of our finances, our home, and me. And most importantly, thanks for being my date for life. I love you more than words (even these words) can say.

About the Author

I have always loved solving problems and puzzles. My first career was as a computer programmer. This was back when computers filled entire buildings and didn't have the power that is now in your smartphone. After moving up the corporate ladder to vice president, I changed careers to become a marriage and family therapist. I now had the opportunity to help people solve their problems and I loved the work!

But I had a new problem. I didn't know how to build a business that was financially sustainable. Learning how to do that for myself – and ultimately helping therapists on five continents to do it, has been the joyful mission of the last two decades.

I retired from my counseling practice in the early 2000s to run the Therapist Leadership Institute and BeAWealthyTherapist. net full time. We are a coaching and training company for private practitioners. A few years ago, I began coaching therapists who had built very successful counseling centers with multiple associate clinicians, but were struggling as CEOs in their businesses. They were burning out. This was a new problem to solve: how to help these center owners find more ease and more profit in their businesses. I am grateful for their patience as we worked to help them find some relief.

Along the way, I saw the financial opportunities of adding clinicians and the counseling center business model. It really was the answer to the "I want to make money while I am on vacation" lament we hear so often.

In 2013, I opened the Orange County Relationship Center (OCRC) in Fullerton, CA. I am grateful to my friend, Maria Xanthos, for letting us use her office space part time when we started. The center grew rapidly and we moved to Newport Beach in January of 2014. My goal for OCRC is to provide an upscale experience for clients who want to improve their relationships. We have a team of amazing clinicians and continue to grow as a result of their dedication and skill. Our mission is simple: Peace of Mind and Heart.

The more I grow (personally and professionally), the more I want for all of us. I have always loved the counseling profession and the tender-hearted people who choose it. I want to help private practitioners to become educated and skilled CEOs of their own financially-sustainable businesses. I am humbled to write that last sentence as I am also on the same path as you. We are both headed in the same direction – toward more confidence, time, knowledge, ease, and profit. I am delighted we are on this journey together.

My husband, Bob, is the CFO at both Be A Wealthy Therapist and the OC Relationship Center, and we live in Tustin, CA. Bob is a model train enthusiast and collects all things Lionel. Christmastime is our hobby and we start designing the Christmas train layout in June.

As I write this, I've recently celebrated my 62nd birthday and I wonder what is next for me. Of course I have no idea; I just know that I am grateful to have this amazing life with Bob, my family, and friends – and these really fun businesses to keep me solving problems and puzzles.

Thanks for reading this book and if you have comments, suggestions, corrections, etc., I'd be honored if you would share them with me. My team and I can be reached at Casey@ TherapistLeadershipInstitute.com

If you'd like to connect further or get great free goodies, please visit us at http://BeAWealthyTherapist.net.

Made in the USA
San Bernardino, CA
08 March 2017